THE U.S. CONSTITUTION
AND THE SUPREME COURT

edited by STEVEN ANZOVIN and
JANET PODELL

THE REFERENCE SHELF

Volume 60 Number 1

THE H. W. WILSON COMPANY

New York   1988

THE REFERENCE SHELF

The books in this series contain reprints of articles, excerpts from books, and addresses on current issues and social trends in the United States and other countries. There are six separately bound numbers in each volume, all of which are generally published in the same calendar year. One number is a collection of recent speeches; each of the others is devoted to a single subject and gives background information and discussion from various points of view, concluding with a comprehensive bibliography. Books in the series may be purchased individually or on subscription.

Library of Congress Cataloging-in-Publication Data

The U.S. Constitution and the Supreme Court / edited by Steven Anzovin
   and Janet Podell.
      p.   cm. — (The Reference shelf ; v. 60, no. 1)
   Bibliography: p.
   Summary: A compilation of seventeen previously published articles on the topic of the Constitution and its relationship with the Supreme Court.
   ISBN 0-8242-0765-3
   1. United States—Constitutional law. 2. United States-
-Constitutional law—Interpretation and construction. 3. United States. Supreme Court. [1. United States—Constitutional law. 2. United States—Constitutional law—Interpretation and construction. 3. United States. Supreme Court.]   I. Anzovin, Steven. II. Podell, Janet. III. Series.
KF4550.Z9U53 1988
342.73'024—dc19
[347.30224]   87-34912
                                                                  CIP
                                                                   AC

Printed in the United States of America

CONTENTS

III. THE CONSTITUTION AND THE COURT

PREFACE

The year 1987 marked the two-hundredth anniversary of the signing of the U.S. Constitution. Like all American national festivals, the Constitution's birthday was celebrated with plenty of fanfare and self-congratulatory hoopla. Amid all the noise, however, there was a general acknowledgment that the Constitution is by far the most important American contribution to world civilization—so important that the vast majority of the world's nations have used it as the basis for their own national charters. Even the Soviet Union's constitution owes much to the American model, although its provisions are honored mainly in the breach.

What makes the Constitution so influential? It is, of course, the foundation of the U.S. political system, and the spread of American culture throughout the world has earned it a great deal of attention. But this interest would be merely transient if it were not that the freedoms guaranteed in the Constitution and the Bill of Rights, revolutionary when they were first conceived, are still sought after by millions of the world's peoples, for whom the ideal of a free society remains a goal for the distant future. (Indeed, the Constitution remains revolutionary in the United States as well, where the balance among competing rights must be adjusted anew for each generation, and sometimes from year to year.) The Constitution's provisions that give individuals rights against their government, and that limit government's power over individuals, speak to the nearly universal desire for liberty; the carefully symmetrical, deliberately cumbersome system of government it details, while precisely copied nowhere else, offers a combination of political stability and flexibility that many nations envy.

The relevance of the Constitution to current problems has been convincingly demonstrated in two events in the past years: the Iran-Contra scandal and the successfully contested nomination of Judge Robert H. Bork to the U.S. Supreme Court. In the Iran-Contra affair, one crucial issue was whether President Reagan had knowingly approved arms sales to the Nicaraguan insurgents despite a federal law that specifically forbade such sales. (Article II, Section 3 of the Constitution requires that the President "take Care that the Laws be faithfully executed.") Even more

5

disturbing to many people was evidence that some Reagan Administration officials had sought to set up a domestic "shadow government" to carry out covert actions, a government that would be beyond the control of the Constitution. The investigation by the Congress into the conduct of the executive constituted a living example of the "checks and balances" arrangement built into the Constitution to prevent excessive malfeasance by any one branch of government.

In the case of the Bork confirmation hearings, the issue was a matter of constitutional interpretation: did the people want a jurist with such a narrow conception of the Constitution's domain that he might vote to end many previously established rights, or would the Supreme Court be allowed to continue expanding constitutional guarantees into new areas? In both cases, Americans were treated to valuable examples of how we must understand and wrestle with the Constitution to make it work.

The history, application, and interpretation of the Constitution have been debated in an immense body of literature. This compilation of articles and essays treats several important aspects of the subject. Section I delves into the document itself, its creation, and its dominance as the "sacred covenant" of the American faith. The second section shows how the Constitution, though flawed, is a living force, responsive to fundamental changes in American society yet highly resistant to change for change's sake. Section III covers a topic of intense current interest—the debate over how the Supreme Court should interpret the Constitution. Some theorists insist that the Justices must abide strictly by the intent of the Framers of the Constitution; others argue that the Court must be free to find in the Constitution rights and principles that are implied as well as stated.

The editors wish to thank the authors and publishers who kindly gave permission to reprint the material in this collection. Special thanks are due to Diane Podell of the B. Davis Schwartz Memorial Library, C. W. Post Center, Long Island University, for research assistance.

STEVEN ANZOVIN

JANET PODELL

January 1988

I. TO FORM A MORE PERFECT UNION

EDITOR'S INTRODUCTION

"If men were angels," wrote James Madison, "no government would be necessary." It was clear to most observant persons in 1787 that the United States was in desperate need of government. Six years earlier the states had ratified the Articles of Confederation, which created a national congress and states the general conditions for union. But the Articles of Confederation did not create a central government, and gave Congress little control over the state legislatures. As economic conditions worsened in the 1780s state began to feud with state, while Congress could do little more than watch. The social order seemed threatened as well. Revolutionary War veterans, farmers, and laborers, all ruined by heavy debts, rebelled in Massachusetts; many feared that the spirit of rebellion would spread to other states as well. With no body of laws to knit together the parts and make them work as a whole, to assure social justice and individual liberties, the new nation appeared to be in danger of dissolution. In the summer of that year a group of citizens met in Philadelphia to hammer out the form of a new government. The Framers, as they have come to be known, took a novel approach to their business, one that had never been tried before: they believed it possible to define a republic in a legal document that would be approved by the citizens of that republic. That document, the Constitution of the United States, became the foundation of the American political structure. It is reprinted here with all twenty-six amendments as the first selection in this section.

What kind of people were the Framers? It goes without saying—given the kind of society that then existed in the former British colonies—that they were all educated, affluent, white males. Historian James MacGregor Burns described them as the elite of their time, all among "the well-bred, the well-fed, the well-read, and the well-wed." They were schooled in the democratic, free-thinking principles of the Enlightenment; they saw themselves—especially James Madison, the chief author of the Constitution—as engaged in a "grand experiment" to fashion a free and stable society. But, as Ezra Bowen shows in his short history of the Convention from *Smithsonian* magazine, the second selection in this section, the Framers were also seasoned politicians, jockeying for regional advantage even as they sought to craft a document that could be accepted by the disparate states. Given the rivalries and intense passions that flared during the hot summer days of the Convention, it is not surprising that the delegates were satisfied to produce a compromise Constitution mainly concerned with the balanced structuring of national government—the issue that concerned them most deeply—and to append guarantees of personal liberties in a Bill of Rights that was passed after the Constitution was safely ratified.

The Constitution has often been called America's "covenant," the sacred text of a civil religion that allows a heterogeneous group of citizens to view itself as a unity. The principles established in the Constitution pervade most aspects of our daily lives—a point made in the third selection, an article by Lance Morrow reprinted from *Time* magazine. The Constitution by its nature adapts to the untidy course of history—it is "endlessly unfinished business," as Lance Morrow writes in the *Time* article, a covenant that we all are in the process of shaping. Only by reading and grappling with the Constitution, as novelist E. L. Doctorow does in an article from *The Nation* reprinted as the last selection, can we take responsibility for its evolution.

THE CONSTITUTION OF THE UNITED STATES[1]

WE the People of the United States, in Order to form a more perfect Union, establish Justice, insure domestic Tranquility, provide for the common defence, promote the general Welfare, and secure the Blessings of Liberty to ourselves and our Posterity, do ordain and establish this Constitution for the United States of America.

---

[1]This selection presents the Constitution and all amendments in their original form. Items which have since been amended or superseded, as identified in the footnotes, are bracketed.

Article I.

SECTION 1. All legislative Powers herein granted shall be vested in a Congress of the United States, which shall consist of a Senate and House of Representatives.

SECTION 2. The House of Representatives shall be composed of Members chosen every second Year by the People of the several States, and the Electors in each State shall have the Qualifications requisite for Electors of the most numerous Branch of the State Legislature.

No Person shall be a Representative who shall not have attained to the Age of Twenty-five Years, and been seven Years a Citizen of the United States, and who shall not, when elected, be an Inhabitant of that State in which he shall be chosen.

[Representatives and direct Taxes shall be apportioned among the several States which may be included within this Union, according to their respective Numbers, which shall be determined by adding to the whole Number of free Persons, including those bound to Service for a Term of Years, and excluding Indians not taxed, three fifths of all other Persons.]* The actual Enumeration shall be made within three Years after the first Meeting of the Congress of the United States, and within every subsequent Term of ten Years, in such Manner as they shall by Law direct. The Number of Representatives shall not exceed one for every thirty Thousand,** but each State shall have at Least one Representative; and until such enumeration shall be made, the State of New Hampshire shall be entitled to chuse three, Massachusetts eight, Rhode-Island and Providence Plantations one, Connecticut five, New York six, New Jersey four, Pennsylvania eight, Delaware one, Maryland six, Virginia ten, North Carolina, five, South Carolina five, and Georgia three.

When vacancies happen in the Representation from any State, the Executive Authority thereof shall issue Writs of Election to fill such Vacancies.

The House of Representatives shall chuse their speaker and other Officers; and shall have the sole Power of Impeachment.

*Changed by section 2 of the fourteenth amendment.
**Ratio in 1965 was one to over 410,000.

SECTION 3. The Senate of the United States shall be composed of two Senators from each State, [chosen by the Legislature thereof,]* for six Years; and each Senator shall have one Vote.

Immediately after they shall be assembled in Consequence of the first Election, they shall be divided as equally as may be into three Classes. The Seats of the Senators of the first Class shall be vacated at the Expiration of the second Year, of the second Class at the Expiration of the fourth Year, and of the third Class at the expiration of the sixth Year, so that one-third may be chosen every second Year; [and if Vacancies happen by Resignation, or otherwise, during the Recess of the Legislature of any State, the Executive thereof may make temporary Appointments until the next Meeting of the Legislature, which shall then fill such Vacancies.]**

No Person shall be a Senator who shall not have attained to the Age of thirty Years, and been nine Years a Citizen of the United States, and who shall not, when elected, be an Inhabitant of that State for which he shall be chosen.

The Vice President of the United States shall be President of the Senate, but shall have no Vote, unless they be equally divided.

The Senate shall chuse their other Officers, and also a President pro tempore, in the absence of the Vice President, or when he shall exercise the Office of President of the United States.

The Senate shall have the sole Power to try all Impeachments. When sitting for that Purpose, they shall be on Oath or Affirmation. When the President of the United States is tried, the Chief Justice shall preside: And no Person shall be convicted without the Concurrence of two thirds of the Members present.

Judgment in Cases of Impeachment shall not extend further than to removal from Office, and disqualification to hold and enjoy any Office of honor, Trust or Profit under the United States: but the Party convicted shall nevertheless be liable and subject to Indictment, Trial, Judgment and Punishment, according to Law.

SECTION 4. The Times, Places and Manner of holding Elections for Senators and Representatives, shall be prescribed in each State by the Legislature thereof; but the Congress may at any time by Law make or alter such Regulations, except as to the Place of Chusing Senators.

*Changed by section 1 of the seventeenth amendment.
**Changed by clause 2 of the seventeenth amendment.

The Congress shall assemble at least once in every Year, and such Meeting shall [be on the first Monday in December.]* unless they shall by Law appoint a different Day.

SECTION 5. Each House shall be the Judge of the Elections, Returns and Qualifications of its own Members, and a Majority of each shall constitute a Quorum to do Business; but a smaller number may adjourn from day to day, and may be authorized to compel the Attendance of absent Members, in such Manner, and under such Penalties as each House may provide.

Each House may determine the Rules of its Proceedings, punish its Members for disorderly Behavior, and, with the Concurrence of two thirds, expel a Member.

Each House shall keep a Journal of its Proceedings, and from time to time publish the same, excepting such Parts as may in their Judgment require Secrecy; and the Yeas and Nays of the Members of either House on any question shall, at the Desire of one fifth of those Present, be entered on the Journal.

Neither House, during the Session of Congress, shall, without the Consent of the other, adjourn for more than three days, nor to any other Place than that in which the two Houses shall be sitting.

SECTION 6. The Senators and Representatives shall receive a Compensation for their Services, to be ascertained by Law, and paid out of the Treasury of the United States. They shall in all Cases, except Treason, Felony and Breach of the Peace, be privileged from Arrest during their Attendance at the Session of their respective Houses, and in going to and returning from the same; and for any Speech or Debate in either House, they shall not be questioned in any other Place.

No Senator or Representative shall, during the Time for which he was elected, be appointed to any civil Office under the Authority of the United States, which shall have been created, or the Emoluments whereof shall have been encreased during such time; and no Person holding any Office under the United States, shall be a Member of either House during his Continuance in Office.

*Changed by section 2 of the twentieth amendment.

SECTION 7. All Bills for raising Revenue shall originate in the House of Representatives; but the Senate may propose or concur with Amendments as on other Bills.

Every Bill which shall have passed the House of Representatives and the Senate, shall, before it become a Law, be presented to the President of the United States; If he approve he shall sign it, but if not he shall return it, with his Objections to that House in which it shall have originated, who shall enter the Objections at large on their Journal, and proceed to reconsider it. If after such Reconsideration two thirds of that House shall agree to pass the Bill, it shall be sent, together with the Objections, to the other House, by which it shall likewise be reconsidered, and if approved by two thirds of that House, it shall become a Law. But in all such Cases the Votes of both Houses shall be determined by Yeas and Nays, and the Names of the Persons voting for and against the Bill shall be entered on the Journal of each House respectively. If any Bill shall not be returned by the President within ten Days (Sundays excepted) after it shall have been presented to him, the Same shall be a Law, in like Manner as if he had signed it, unless the Congress by their Adjournment prevent its Return, in which Case it shall not be a Law.

Every Order, Resolution, or Vote to which the Concurrence of the Senate and House of Representatives may be necessary (except on a question of Adjournment) shall be presented to the President of the United States; and before the Same shall take Effect, shall be approved by him, or being disapproved by him, shall be repassed by two thirds of the Senate and House of Representatives, according to the Rules and Limitations prescribed in the Case of a Bill.

SECTION 8. The Congress shall have Power To lay and collect Taxes, Duties, Imposts and Excises, to pay the Debts and provide for the common Defence and general Welfare of the United States; but all Duties, Imposts and Excises shall be uniform throughout the United States;

To borrow money on the credit of the United States;

To regulate Commerce with foreign Nations, and among the several States, and with the Indian Tribes;

To establish an uniform Rule of Naturalization, and uniform Laws on the subject of Bankruptcies throughout the United States;

To coin Money, regulate the Value thereof, and of foreign Coin, and fix the Standard of Weights and Measures;

To provide for the Punishment of counterfeiting the Securities and current Coin of the United States;

To establish Post Offices and post Roads;

To promote the Progress of Science and useful Arts, by securing for limited Times to Authors and Inventors the exclusive Right to their respective Writings and Discoveries;

To constitute Tribunals inferior to the supreme Court;

To define and punish Piracies and Felonies committed on the high Seas, and Offenses against the Law of Nations;

To declare War, grant Letters of Marque and Reprisal, and make Rules concerning Captures on Land and Water;

To raise and support Armies, but no Appropriation of Money to that Use shall be for a longer Term than two Years;

To provide and maintain a Navy;

To make Rules for the Government and Regulation of the land and naval Forces;

To provide for calling forth the Militia to execute the Laws of the Union, suppress Insurrections and repel Invasions;

To provide for organizing, arming, and disciplining the Militia, and for governing such Part of them as may be employed in the Service of the United States, reserving to the States respectively, the Appointment of the Officers, and the Authority of training the Militia according to the discipline prescribed by Congress;

To exercise exclusive Legislation in all Cases whatsoever, over such District (not exceeding ten Miles square) as may, by Cession of particular States, and the acceptance of Congress, become the Seat of the Government of the United States, and to exercise like Authority over all Places purchased by the Consent of the Legislature of the State in which the Same shall be, for the Erection of Forts, Magazines, Arsenals, dock-Yards, and other needful Buildings;—And

To make all Laws which shall be necessary and proper for carrying into Execution the foregoing Powers, and all other Powers vested by this Constitution in the Government of the United States, or in any Department or Officer thereof.

SECTION 9. The Migration or Importation of such Persons as any of the States now existing shall think proper to admit, shall not be prohibited by the Congress prior to the Year one thousand eight hundred and eight, but a tax or duty may be imposed on such Importation, not exceeding ten dollars for each Person.

The privilege of the Writ of Habeas Corpus shall not be suspended, unless when in Cases of Rebellion or Invasion the public Safety may require it.

No Bill of Attainder or ex post facto Law shall be passed.

No capitation, or other direct, Tax shall be laid, unless in Proportion to the Census or Enumeration herein before directed to be taken.*

No Tax and Duty shall be laid on Articles exported from any State.

No Preference shall be given by any Regulation of Commerce or Revenue to the Ports of one State over those of another: nor shall Vessels bound to, or from, one State, be obliged to enter, clear, or pay Duties in another.

No Money shall be drawn from the Treasury, but in Consequence of Appropriations made by Law; and a regular Statement and Account of the Receipts and Expenditures of all public Money shall be published from time to time.

No Title of Nobility shall be granted by the United States: And no Person holding any Office of Profit or Trust under them, shall, without the Consent of the Congress, accept of any present, Emolument, Office, or Title, of any kind whatever, from any King, Prince, or foreign State.

SECTION 10. No State shall enter into any Treaty, Alliance, or Confederation; grant Letters of Marque and Reprisal; coin Money; emit Bills of Credit; make any Thing but gold and silver Coin a Tender in Payment of Debts; pass any Bill of Attainder, ex post facto Law, or Law impairing the Obligation of Contracts, or grant any Title of Nobility.

No State shall, without the Consent of the Congress, lay any Imposts or Duties on Imports or Exports, except what may be absolutely necessary for executing its inspection Laws: and the net Produce of all Duties and Imposts, laid by any State on Imports or Exports, shall be for the Use of the Treasury of the United States; and all such Laws shall be subject to the Revision and Controul of the Congress.

No State shall, without the Consent of Congress, lay any duty of Tonnage, keep Troops, or Ships of War in time of Peace, enter into any Agreement or Compact with another State, or with a foreign Power, or engage in War, unless actually invaded, or in such imminent Danger as will not admit of delay.

*But see the sixteenth amendment.

Article II.

SECTION 1. The executive Power shall be vested in a President of the United States of America. He shall hold his Office during the Term of four Years, and, together with the Vice-President, chosen for the same Term, be elected, as follows.

Each State shall appoint, in such Manner as the Legislature thereof may direct, a Number of Electors, equal to the whole Number of Senators and Representatives to which the State may be entitled in the Congress: but no Senator or Representative, or Person holding an Office of Trust or Profit under the United States, shall be appointed an Elector.

[The Electors shall meet in their respective States, and vote by Ballot for two persons, of whom one at least shall not be an Inhabitant of the same State with themselves. And they shall make a List of all the Persons voted for, and of the Number of Votes for each; which List they shall sign and certify, and transmit sealed to the Seat of the Government of the United States, directed to the President of the Senate. The President of the Senate shall, in the Presence of the Senate and House of Representatives, open all the Certificates, and the Votes shall then be counted. The Person having the greatest Number of Votes shall be the President, if such Number be a Majority of the whole Number of Electors appointed; and if there be more than one who have such Majority, and have an equal Number of Votes, then the House of Representatives shall immediately chuse by Ballot one of them for President; and if no Person have a Majority, then from the five highest on the List the said House shall in Like Manner chuse the President. But in chusing the President, the Votes shall be taken by States, the Representation from each State having one vote; a quorum for this Purpose shall consist of a Member or Members from two thirds of the States, and a Majority of all the States shall be necessary to a Choice. In every Case, after the Choice of the President, the Person having the greatest Number of Votes of the Electors shall be the Vice President. But if there should remain two or more who have equal Votes, the Senate shall chuse from them by Ballot the Vice-President.]*

The Congress may determine the Time of chusing the Electors, and the Day on which they shall give their Votes; which Day shall be the same throughout the United States.

*Superseded by the twelfth amendment.

No person except a natural born Citizen, or a Citizen of the United States, at the time of the Adoption of this Constitution, shall be eligible to the Office of President; neither shall any Person be eligible to that Office who shall not have attained to the Age of thirty-five Years, and been fourteen Years a Resident within the United States.

*[In Case of the Removal of the President from Office, or of his Death, Resignation, or Inability to discharge the Powers and Duties of the said Office, the same shall devolve on the Vice President, and the Congress may by Law, provide for the Case of Removal, Death, Resignation or Inability, both of the President and Vice President, declaring what Officer shall then act as President, and such Officer shall act accordingly, until the Disability be removed, or a President shall be elected.]

The President shall, at stated Times, receive for his Services a Compensation, which shall neither be encreased nor diminished during the Period for which he shall have been elected, and he shall not receive within that Period any other Emolument from the United States, or any of them.

Before he enter on the Execution of his Office, he shall take the following Oath or Affirmation—"I do solemnly swear (or affirm) that I will faithfully execute the Office of President of the United States, and will to the best of my Ability, preserve, protect and defend the Constitution of the United States."

SECTION 2. The President shall be Commander in Chief of the Army and Navy of the United States, and of the Militia of the several States, when called into the actual Service of the United States; he may require the Opinion in writing, of the principal Officer in each of the executive Departments, upon any subject relating to the Duties of their respective Offices, and he shall have Power to Grant Reprieves and Pardons for Offenses against the United States, except in Cases of Impeachment.

He shall have Power, by and with the Advice and Consent of the Senate, to make Treaties, provided two-thirds of the Senators present concur; and he shall nominate, and by and with the Advice and Consent of the Senate, shall appoint Ambassadors, other public Ministers and Consuls, Judges of the supreme Court, and

*This clause has been affected by the twenty-fifth amendment.

all other Officers of the United States, whose Appointments are not herein otherwise provided for, and which shall be established by Law: but the Congress may by Law vest the Appointment of such inferior Officers, as they think proper, in the President alone, in the Courts of Law, or in the Heads of Departments.

The President shall have Power to fill up all Vacancies that may happen during the Recess of the Senate, by granting Commissions which shall expire at the End of their next Session.

SECTION 3. He shall from time to time give to the Congress Information of the State of the Union, and recommend to their Consideration such Measures as he shall judge necessary and expedient; he may, on extraordinary Occasions, convene both Houses, or either of them, and in Case of Disagreement between them, with Respect to the Time of Adjournment, he may adjourn them to such Time as he shall think proper; he shall receive Ambassadors and other public Ministers; he shall take Care that the Laws be faithfully executed, and shall Commission all the Officers of the United States.

SECTION 4. The President, Vice President and all civil Officers of the United States, shall be removed from Office on Impeachment for, and Conviction of, Treason, Bribery, or other high Crimes and Misdemeanors.

Article III.

SECTION 1. The judicial Power of the United States, shall be vested in one supreme Court, and in such inferior Courts as the Congress may from time to time ordain and establish. The Judges, both of the supreme and inferior Courts, shall hold their Offices during good Behaviour, and shall, at stated Times, receive for their Services, a Compensation, which shall not be diminished during their Continuance in Office.

SECTION 2. The judicial Power shall extend to all Cases, in Law and Equity, arising under this Constitution, the Laws of the United States, and Treaties made, or which shall be made, under their Authority;—to all Cases affecting Ambassadors, other public Ministers and Consuls;—to all Cases of admiralty and maritime Jurisdiction;—to Controversies to which the United States shall be a Party;—to Controversies between two or more States;—between a State and Citizens of another State;—between Citizens of different States;—between Citizens of the same State claiming

Lands under Grants of different States, and between a State, or the Citizens thereof, and foreign States, Citizens or Subjects.

In all Cases affecting Ambassadors, other public Ministers and Consuls, and those in which a State shall be Party, the supreme Court shall have original Jurisdiction. In all the other Cases before mentioned, the supreme Court shall have appellate Jurisdiction, both as to Law and Fact, with such Exceptions, and under such Regulations as the Congress shall make.

The trial of all Crimes, except in Cases of Impeachment, shall be by Jury; and such Trial shall be held in the State where the said Crimes shall have been committed; but when not committed within any State, the Trial shall be at such Place or Places as the Congress may by Law have directed.

SECTION 3. Treason against the United States, shall consist only in levying War against them, or in adhering to their Enemies, giving them Aid and Comfort. No Person shall be convicted of Treason unless on the Testimony of two Witnesses to the same overt Act, or on Confession in open Court.

The Congress shall have Power to declare the Punishment of Treason, but no Attainder of Treason shall work Corruption of Blood, or Forfeiture except during the Life of the Person attainted.

Article IV.

SECTION 1. Full Faith and Credit shall be given in each State to the public Acts, Records, and judicial Proceedings of every other State. And the Congress may by general Laws prescribe the Manner in which such Acts, Records and Proceedings shall be proved, and the Effect thereof.

SECTION 2. The Citizens of each State shall be entitled to all Privileges and Immunities of Citizens in the several States.

A Person charged in any State with Treason, Felony, or other Crime, who shall flee from Justice, and be found in another State, shall on demand of the executive Authority of the State from which he fled, be delivered up, to be removed to the State having Jurisdiction of the Crime.

[No Person held to Service or labour in one State, under the Laws thereof, escaping into another, shall, in Consequence of any Law or Regulation therein, be discharged from such Service or Labour, but shall be delivered up on Claim of the Party to whom such Service or Labour may be due.]*

SECTION 3. New States may be admitted by the Congress into this Union; but no new State shall be formed or erected within the Jurisdiction of any other State; nor any State be formed by the Junction of two or more States, or parts of States, without the Consent of the Legislatures of the States concerned as well as of the Congress.

The Congress shall have Power to dispose of and make all needful Rules and Regulations respecting the Territory or other Property belonging to the United States; and nothing in this Constitution shall be so construed as to Prejudice any Claims of the United States, or of any particular State.

SECTION 4. The United States shall guarantee to every State in this Union a Republican Form of Government, and shall protect each of them against Invasion; and on Application of the Legislature, or of the Executive (when the Legislature cannot be convened) against domestic Violence.

Article V.

The Congress, whenever two-thirds of both Houses shall deem it necessary, shall propose Amendments to this Constitution, or, on the Application of the Legislatures of two-thirds of the several States, shall call a Convention for proposing Amendments, which, in either Case, shall be valid to all Intents and Purposes, as part of this Constitution, when ratified by the Legislatures of three-fourths of the several States, or by Conventions in three-fourths thereof, as the one or the other Mode of Ratification may be proposed by the Congress: Provided that no Amendment which may be made prior to the Year One thousand eight hundred and eight shall in any Manner affect the first and fourth Clauses in the Ninth Section of the first Article; and that no State, without its Consent, shall be deprived of its equal Suffrage in the Senate.

Article VI.

All Debts contracted and Engagements entered into, before the Adoption of this Constitution, shall be as valid against the

*Superseded by the thirteenth amendment.

United States under this Constitution, as under the Confederation.

This Constitution, and the Laws of the United States which shall be made in Pursuance thereof; and all Treaties made, or which shall be made, under the Authority of the United States, shall be the supreme Law of the Land; and the Judges in every State shall be bound thereby, any Thing in the Constitution or Laws of any State to the Contrary notwithstanding.

The Senators and Representatives before mentioned, and the Members of the several State Legislatures, and all executive and judicial Officers, both of the United States and of the several States, shall be bound by Oath or Affirmation, to support this Constitution; but no religious Test shall ever be required as a Qualification to any Office or public Trust under the United States.

Article VII.

The Ratification of the Conventions of nine States shall be sufficient for the Establishment of this Constitution between the States so ratifying the Same.

DONE in Convention by the Unanimous Consent of the States present the Seventeenth Day of September in the Year of our Lord one thousand seven hundred and Eighty seven and of the Independence of the United States of America the Twelfth.

In Witness whereof We have hereunto subscribed our Names.
Go WASHINGTON
Presidt and deputy from Virginia

New Hampshire.
JOHN LANGDON
NICHOLAS GILMAN

Massachusetts.
NATHANIEL GORHAM
RUFUS KING

New Jersey.
WIL: LIVINGSTON
DAVID BREARLEY.
WM PATERSON.
JONA: DAYTON

Pennsylvania.
B FRANKLIN
ROBT. MORRIS
THOMS. FITZSIMONS
JAMES WILSON
THOMAS MIFFLIN
GEO. CLYMER
JARED INGERSOLL
GOUV MORRIS

Delaware.
GEO: READ
JOHN DICKINSON
JACO: BROOM
GUNNING BEDFORD JUN
RICHARD BASSETT

Connecticut.
WM SAML JOHNSON
ROGER SHERMAN

New York.
ALEXANDER HAMILTON

Maryland.
JAMES MCHENRY
DANL CARROL
DAN: OF ST THOS JENIFER

Virginia.
JOHN BLAIR
JAMES MADISON JR.

North Carolina.
WM BLOUNT
HU WILLIAMSON
RICHD DOBBS SPAIGHT.

South Carolina.
J. RUTLEDGE
CHARLES PINCKNEY
CHARLES COTESWORTH PINCKNEY
PIERCE BUTLER

Georgia.
WILLIAM FEW
ABR BALDWIN

Attest:

WILLIAM JACKSON, *Secretary.*

Articles in Addition To, and Amendment Of, the Constitution of the United States of America, Proposed by Congress, and Ratified by the Legislatures of the Several States, Pursuant to the Fifth Article of the Original Constitution.*

(The first 10 Amendments were ratified December 15, 1791, and form what is known as the "Bill of Rights.")

Amendment I

Congress shall make no law respecting an establishment of religion, or prohibiting the free exercise thereof; or abridging the freedom of speech, or of the press; or the right of the people peaceably to assemble, and to petition the Government for a redress of grievances.

Amendment II

A well regulated Militia, being necessary to the security of a free State, the right of the people to keep and bear Arms, shall not be infringed.

*Amendment XXI was not ratified by state legislatures, but by state conventions summoned by Congress.

Amendment III

No Soldier shall, in time of peace be quartered in any house, without the consent of the Owner, nor in time of war, but in a manner to be prescribed by law.

Amendment IV

The right of the people to be secure in their persons, houses, papers, and effects, against unreasonable searches and seizures, shall not be violated, and no Warrants shall issue, but upon probable cause, supported by Oath or affirmation, and particularly describing the place to be searched, and the persons or things to be seized.

Amendment V

No person shall be held to answer for a capital, or otherwise infamous crime, unless on a presentment or indictment of a Grand Jury, except in cases arising in the land or naval forces, or in the Militia, when in actual service in time of War or public danger; nor shall any person be subject for the same offence to be twice put in jeopardy of life or limb; nor shall be compelled in any criminal case to be a witness against himself, nor be deprived of life, liberty, or property, without due process of law; nor shall private property be taken for public use, without just compensation.

Amendment VI

In all criminal prosecutions, the accused shall enjoy the right to a speedy and public trial, by an impartial jury of the State and district wherein the crime shall have been committed, which district shall have been previously ascertained by law, and to be informed of the nature and cause of the accusation; to be confronted with the witnesses against him; to have compulsory process for obtaining witness in his favor, and to have the Assistance of Counsel for his defense.

Amendment VII

In suits at common law, where the value in controversy shall exceed twenty dollars, the right of trial by jury shall be preserved, and no fact tried by a jury, shall be otherwise reexamined in any Court of the United States, than according to the rules of the common law.

Amendment VIII

Excessive bail shall not be required, nor excessive fines imposed, nor cruel and unusual punishments inflicted.

Amendment IX

The enumeration in the Constitution, of certain rights, shall not be construed to deny or disparage others retained by the people.

Amendment X

The powers not delegated to the United States by the Constitution, nor prohibited by it to the States, are reserved to the States respectively, or to the people.

Amendment XI
(Ratified February 7, 1795)

The Judicial power of the United States shall not be construed to extend to any suit in law or equity, commenced or prosecuted against one of the United States by Citizens of another State, or by Citizens or Subjects of any Foreign State.

Amendment XII
(Ratified June 15, 1804)

The Electors shall meet in their respective states and vote by ballot for President and Vice-President, one of whom, at least, shall not be an inhabitant of the same state with themselves; they shall name in their ballots the person voted for as President, and in district ballots the person voted for as Vice-President, and they shall make distinct lists of all persons voted for as President, and of all persons voted for as Vice-President, and of the number of votes for each, which lists they shall sign and certify, and transmit sealed to the seat of the government of the United States, directed to the President of the Senate;—The President of the Senate shall, in presence of the Senate and House of Representatives, open all the certificates and the votes shall then be counted;— The person having the greatest number of votes for President, shall be the President, if such number be a majority of the whole number of Electors appointed; and if no person have such majority, then from the persons having the highest numbers not exceeding three on the list of those voted for as President, the House of Representatives shall choose immediately, by ballot, the President. But in choosing the President, the votes shall be taken by states, the representation from each state having one vote; a quorum for this purpose shall consist of a member or members from two-thirds of the states, and a majority of all the states shall be necessary to a choice. [And if the House of Representatives shall not choose a President whenever the right of choice shall devolve upon them, before the fourth day of March next following, then the Vice-President shall act as President, as in the case of the death or other constitutional disability of the President.—]* The person having the greatest number of votes as Vice-President, shall be the Vice-President, if such number be a majority of the whole number of Electors appointed, and if no person have a majority, then from the two highest numbers on the list, the Senate shall choose the Vice-President; a quorum for the purpose shall consist of two-thirds of the whole number of Senators, and a majority of the whole number shall be necessary to a choice. But no person constitutionally ineligible to the office of President shall be eligible to that of Vice-President of the United States.

Amendment XIII
(Ratified December 6, 1865)

Section 1. Neither slavery nor involuntary servitude, except as a punishment for crime whereof the party shall have been duly convicted, shall exist within the United States, or any place subject to their jurisdiction.

*Superseded by section 3 of the twentieth amendment.

SECTION 2. Congress shall have power to enforce this article by appropriate legislation.

Amendment XIV
(Ratified July 9, 1868)

SECTION 1. All persons born or naturalized in the United States, and subject to the jurisdiction thereof, are citizens of the United States and of the State wherein they reside. No State shall make or enforce any law which shall abridge the privileges or immunities of citizens of the United States; nor shall any State deprive any person of life, liberty, or property, without due process of law; nor deny to any person within its jurisdiction the equal protection of the laws.

SECTION 2. Representatives shall be apportioned among the several States according to their respective numbers, counting the whole number of persons in each State, excluding Indians not taxed. But when the right to vote at any election for the choice of electors for President and Vice-President of the United States, Representatives in Congress, the Executive and Judicial officers of a State, or the members of the Legislature thereof, is denied to any of the male inhabitants of such State, being twenty-one years of age,* and citizens of the United States, or in any way abridged, except for participation in rebellion, or other crime, the basis of representation therein shall be reduced in the proportion which the number of such male citizens shall bear to the whole number of male citizens twenty-one years of age in such State.

SECTION 3. No person shall be a Senator or Representative in Congress, or elector of President and Vice-President, or hold any office, civil or military, under the United States, or under any State, who, having previously taken an oath, as a member of Congress, or as an officer of the United States, or as a member of any State legislature, or as an executive or judicial officer of any State, to support the Constitution of the United States, shall have engaged in insurrection or rebellion against the same, or given aid or comfort to the enemies thereof. But Congress may by a vote of two-thirds of each House, remove such disability.

---

*Changed by section 1 of the twenty-sixth amendment.

SECTION 4. The validity of the public debt of the United States, authorized by law, including debts incurred for payment of pensions and bounties for services in suppressing insurrection or rebellion, shall not be questioned. But neither the United States nor any State shall assume or pay any debt or obligation incurred in aid of insurrection or rebellion against the United States, or any claim for the loss or emancipation of any slave; but all such debts, obligations and claims shall be held illegal and void.

SECTION 5. The Congress shall have power to enforce, by appropriate legislation, the provisions of this article.

Amendment XV
(Ratified February 3, 1870)

SECTION 1. The right of citizens of the United States to vote shall not be denied or abridged by the United States or by any State on account of race, color, or previous condition of servitude—

SECTION 2. The Congress shall have power to enforce this article by appropriate legislation.

Amendment XVI
(Ratified February 3, 1913)

The Congress shall have power to lay and collect taxes on incomes, from whatever source derived, without apportionment among the several States, and without regard to any census or enumeration.

Amendment XVII
(Ratified April 8, 1913)

The Senate of the United States shall be composed of two Senators from each State, elected by the people thereof, for six years; and each Senator shall have one vote. The electors in each State shall have the qualifications requisite for electors of the most numerous branch of the State legislatures.

When vacancies happen in the representation of any State in the Senate, the executive authority of such State shall issue writs of election to fill such vacancies: *Provided*, That the legislature of any State may empower the executive thereof to make temporary appointments until the people fill the vacancies by election as the legislature may direct.

This amendment shall not be so construed as to affect the election or term of any Senator chosen before it becomes valid as part of the Constitution.

Amendment XVIII
(Ratified January 16, 1919)

[SECTION 1. After one year from the ratification of this article the manufacture, sale, or transportation of intoxicating liquors within, the importation thereof into, or the exportation thereof from the United States and all territory subject to the jurisdiction thereof for beverage purposes is hereby prohibited.

[SECTION 2. The Congress and the several States shall have concurrent power to enforce this article by appropriate legislation.

[SECTION 3. This article shall be inoperative unless it shall have been ratified as an amendment to the Constitution by the legislatures of the several States as provided in the Constitution, within seven years from the date of the submission hereof to the States by the Congress.]*

Amendment XIX
(Ratified August 18, 1920)

The right of citizens of the United States to vote shall not be denied or abridged by the United States or by any State on account of sex.

Congress shall have power to enforce this article by appropriate legislation.

Amendment XX
(Ratified January 23, 1933)

SECTION 1. The terms of the President and Vice President shall end at noon on the 20th day of January, and the terms of Senators and Representatives at noon on the 3rd day of January,

*Repealed by section 1 of the twenty-first amendment.

of the years in which such terms would have ended if this article had not been ratified; and the terms of their successors shall then begin.

Section 2. The Congress shall assemble at least once in every year, and such meeting shall begin at noon on the 3rd day of January, unless they shall by law appoint a different day.

Section 3. If, at the time fixed for the beginning of the term of the President, the President elect shall have died, the Vice President elect shall become President. If a President shall not have been chosen before the time fixed for the beginning of his term, or if the President elect shall have failed to qualify, then the Vice President elect shall act as President until a President shall have qualified; and the Congress may by law provide for the case wherein neither a President elect nor a Vice President elect shall have qualified, declaring who shall then act as President, or the manner in which one who is to act shall be selected, and such person shall act accordingly until a President or Vice President shall have qualified.

Section 4. The Congress may by law provide for the case of the death of any of the persons from whom the House of Representatives may choose a President whenever the right of choice shall have devolved upon them, and for the case of the death of any of the persons from whom the Senate may choose a Vice President whenever the right of choice shall have devolved upon them.

Section 5. Sections 1 and 2 shall take effect on the 15th day of October following the ratification of this article.

Section 6. This article shall be inoperative unless it shall have been ratified as an amendment to the Constitution by the legislatures of three-fourths of the several States within seven years from the date of its submission.

Amendment XXI
(Ratified December 5, 1933)

Section 1. The eighteenth article of amendment to the Constitution of the United States is hereby repealed.

Section 2. The transportation or importation into any State, Territory, or possession of the United States for delivery or use therein of intoxicating liquors, in violation of the laws thereof, is hereby prohibited.

SECTION 3. This article shall be inoperative unless it shall have been ratified as an amendment to the Constitution by conventions in the several States, as provided in the Constitution, within seven years from the date of the submission hereof to the States by the Congress.

Amendment XXII
(Ratified February 27, 1951)

SECTION 1. No person shall be elected to the office of the President more than twice, and no person who has held the office of President, or acted as President, for more than two years of a term to which some other person was elected President shall be elected to the office of the President more than once. But this Article shall not apply to any person holding the office of President when this Article was proposed by the Congress, and shall not prevent any person who may be holding the office of President, or acting as President, during the term within which this Article becomes operative from holding the office of President or acting as President during the remainder of such term.

SECTION 2. This article shall be inoperative unless it shall have been ratified as an amendment to the Constitution by the legislatures of three-fourths of the several States within seven years from the date of its submission to the States by the Congress.

Amendment XXIII
(Ratified March 29, 1961)

SECTION 1. The District constituting the seat of Government of the United States shall appoint in such manner as the Congress may direct:

A number of electors of President and Vice President equal to the whole number of Senators and Representatives in Congress to which the District would be entitled if it were a State, but in no event more than the least populous State; they shall be in addition to those appointed by the States, but they shall be considered, for the purposes of the election of President and Vice President, to be electors appointed by a State; and they shall meet in the District and perform such duties as provided by the twelfth article of amendment.

SECTION 2. The Congress shall have power to enforce this article by appropriate legislation.

Amendment XXIV
(Ratified January 23, 1964)

SECTION 1. The right of citizens of the United States to vote in any primary or other election for President or Vice President, for electors for President or Vice President, or for Senator or Representative in Congress, shall not be denied or abridged by the United States or any State by reason of failure to pay any poll tax or other tax.

SECTION 2. The Congress shall have power to enforce this article by appropriate legislation.

Amendment XXV
(Ratified February 10, 1967)

SECTION 1. In case of the removal of the President from office or of his death or resignation, the Vice President shall become President.

SECTION 2. Whenever there is a vacancy in the office of the Vice President, the President shall nominate a Vice President who shall take office upon confirmation by a majority vote of both Houses of Congress.

SECTION 3. Whenever the President transmits to the President pro tempore of the Senate and the Speaker of the House of Representatives his written declaration that he is unable to discharge the powers and duties of his office, and until he transmits to them a written declaration to the contrary, such powers and duties shall be discharged by the Vice President as Acting President.

SECTION 4. Whenever the Vice President and a majority of either the principal officers of the executive departments or of such other body as Congress may by law provide, transmit to the President pro tempore of the Senate and the Speaker of the House of Representatives their written declaration that the President is unable to discharge the powers and duties of his office, the Vice President shall immediately assume the powers and duties of the office as Acting President.

Thereafter, when the President transmits to the President pro tempore of the Senate and the Speaker of the House of Representatives his written declaration that no inability exists, he shall resume the powers and duties of his office unless the Vice President and a majority of either the principal officers of the executive department or of such other body as Congress may by law provide, transmit within four days to the President pro tempore of the Senate and the Speaker of the House of Representatives their written declaration that the President is unable to discharge the powers and duties of his office. Thereupon Congress shall decide the issue, assembling within forty-eight hours for that purpose if not in session. If the Congress, within twenty-one days after receipt of the latter written declaration, or, if Congress is not in session, within twenty-one days after Congress is required to assemble, determines by two-thirds vote of both Houses that the President is unable to discharge the powers and duties of his office, the Vice President shall continue to discharge the same as Acting President; otherwise, the President shall resume the powers and duties of his office.

Amendment XXVI
(Ratified July 1, 1971)

SECTION 1. The right of citizens of the United States, who are eighteen years of age or older, to vote shall not be denied or abridged by the United States or by any State on account of age.

SECTION 2. The Congress shall have power to enforce this article by appropriate legislation.

. . . BY THE UNANIMOUS CONSENT OF THE STATES[2]

On Wednesday, June 27, a muggy afternoon pressed down upon Philadelphia. It was the summer of 1787. Flies droned through the high-ceilinged room of the State House where more than 40 Convention delegates from the quarrelsome American confederation of states, the New England men sweltering in their woolen suits, braced for yet another round of contention. They got it, this time from Maryland's Luther Martin, who enhanced a reputation for tiresome bombast with a three-hour speech. His subject was the rights of the thirteen sovereign states with which

[2]Reprint of an article by Ezra Bowen, senior writer at *Time* magazine. *Smithsonian.* 18:32–43. Jl. '87. Copyright © 1987 by Ezra Bowen.

this Convention, said he ad infinitum, had neither legal power nor fair reason to tamper.

Already restive from five weeks of debate, his listeners could hardly bear it: Oliver Ellsworth of Connecticut later chided Martin, saying that the speech "might have continued two months, but for those marks of fatigue and disgust . . . strongly expressed on whichever side of the house you turned your mortified eyes."

Two days later brilliant Alexander Hamilton, one of the men who at various times left the Convention to return or not, walked out. He might come back, he said, but only if persuaded it would not be a "mere waste of time." Hamilton's position was clear. His discourses, described by some as "logic on fire," presented the case for strong, central government—a near kin to the British monarchy, in fact—that the states felt most threatening.

And as it happened, Hamilton's vote didn't matter much to the Convention just then. He was one of three New York delegates and the other two hated the idea of federal government. Since Convention rules permitted each state only a single vote, they steadily overrode him. But soon it would be very much worth Hamilton's while to return. For during the first two weeks in July the proceedings dramatically neared complete collapse. And then, perhaps frightened by the possibility of total failure, the Convention finally hammered out a deal that not only held the delegates to the end but ultimately produced a daring blueprint for a federal constitution. It would, in time, substantially govern the most powerful nation on Earth.

From the viewpoint of high statesmanship, the pressure for compromise was strong. All the delegates knew they were laboring under the critical eye of history in the cause of as yet untried liberties. "What a triumph for our enemies . . . to find that we are incapable of governing ourselves," George Washington wrote, "and that systems founded on the basis of equal liberty are merely ideal and fallacious." No delegate doubted that stronger government of some sort was needed to replace the toothless Articles of Confederation. After the Revolution, national authority had become almost a joke. The Congress had no real power to tax, regulate commerce, enforce foreign treaties; and criminals who crossed state lines were likely to go scot-free, since extradition was almost unheard of.

Worse still, the beggar government had gone virtually broke. Seven of the states, and the Congress as well, had been churning out paper money until, as pamphleteer Tom Paine once memorably put it, their paper was worth less than hobnails and wampum. Delegates to the Philadelphia Convention, some of whom had to ride or sail as much as 600 miles through spring mud or tides to get there, were obliged to change money into Pennsylvania shillings, the local coinage, as though entering a foreign country. Shipping states in the North wanted more laws to help them compete for world commerce against cut-rate British cargo rates. But most of the agricultural South was opposed to any protective ordinance that would drive up costs for its comfortable export trade in tobacco, indigo and rice.

Division and danger were everywhere. Beyond their economic squeeze the British were still a clear potential threat to American nationhood. The Union Jack still flew over the western posts where fur traders gathered pelts for London glove and hat makers. Former ally France desperately wanted to collect its wartime loans. Spain, another wartime friend, still controlled Florida, and was conniving for control of trade in the wild, fast-growing western reaches that stretched to the Mississippi, America's border under the terms of the 1783 Treaty of Paris. Spain had closed the Mississippi to American trade at New Orleans, and the river was the only shipping route from much of the western wilderness. Indeed, Georgia, which claimed land running from Savannah clear to the Mississippi, had just declared martial law in fear of Indians and Spaniards.

For more than a decade settlers had been flooding west over the mountains. Since early February 1787 alone, more than 1,000 flatboats had headed west on the Ohio carrying 18,000 pioneers, with 12,000 horses, cattle and sheep. These rude frontiersmen did not see eye to eye with the rich planters of Virginia or with the Eastern seaboard traders of New York, Philadelphia and Boston. Not at all. Would these immigrants to the west form into new states or, God forbid, new countries under the protection of some foreign power? If as states, would their votes be equal to those of the original thirteen? Would, say, Virginia's laws and contracts under the Confederation hold up in a separate, sovereign Kentucky, or separate, sovereign anywhere else, such as "Transylvania," part of what is now Kentucky and Tennessee, to name just one other would-be western state then taking shape? And might these new states hold slaves or be free? "I dread the cold and sower temper of the back countries," said peg-legged, urbane lawyer and Pennsylvania delegate Gouverneur Morris, sounding very like any sober Briton contemplating the surly, separatist mood of colonial immigrants 15 years earlier.

Here was a set of time bombs that a young nation with huge, unorganized territories, whatever government it chose, must try to defuse as quickly as possible.

Some central control was crucial, but how much would be enough and yet not too much? Fear of an executive, or any central government for that matter, was strong in most delegates. They had fought for more than six years to throw off the distant, and not too onerous, rule of George III and his ministry. That helped explain both the toothlessness of the Articles of Confederation, and why they now defined each former colony represented at this Convention as a "sovereign and independent" state. James Madison, idealistic, politically relentless, the man who more than any other had brought the Convention into existence, spoke for all of them when he observed that "all men having power ought to be distrusted to a certain degree."

Almost as much, though, they feared the tyranny of the majority, any majority. And they knew that earlier attempts at creating anything like a democratic republic had failed. They had it from the much-admired Montesquieu, the world's leading authority on stable government, that democracies were unstable, that anything like a large republic was impossible to govern. Trying to regulate so vast and diverse a land as the United States (if there ever were to be a United States), as one Yankee wit put it, would be a bit like attempting "to rule Hell by prayer."

Besides, the small states wanted to know, what would happen to them when they were at the mercy of their large and populous neighbors? The same was true of the Southern states vis-à-vis the North. Beyond that lay the question of slavery, mentioned by name at the Convention as little as possible because the delegates knew from the beginning that confrontation over it might wreck any chance they had of agreeing on *any* effective central power. They were there, after all, not to abolish slavery but to shape, against great odds, a stable government that could maintain democratic order as freedom evolved. Though slavery's existence contradicted the terms of the Declaration of Independence they did not seriously discuss abolition. However hotly individual delegates might inveigh against it, slavery was still legally practiced in all but one of the sovereign states; the obnoxious slave trade itself had been outlawed, or sharply discouraged, by only seven. Every delegate understood that slaves were legally private property and, in the South, worth millions. Every delegate understood that under English common law, the protection of property had served as the foundation of all political rights.

Yet at first the Convention moved swiftly, far faster than anyone had expected. Even when disagreements and contentious vote taking occurred (over the course of nearly four months there would be more than 569 votes taken), the proceedings, early on at least, did not bog down.

Mostly this was due to the advance lobbying and planning of Madison, a Virginia planter by birth, but by trade perhaps the most farsighted and perceptive politician and political analyst alive. From 1780 to 1783 he served as a hardworking delegate in the Continental Congress, and from bitter experience while confronting petty state rivalry as he tried to get the states to pay for the war against Britain, Madison had come to the conclusion that the country might not survive at all without a drastic change in the "partition of power" between the states and the nation. To save the tottering Union he had studied past attempts at democracy; made himself an expert economist; helped enlist the reluctant Washington's support for this Convention; and nurtured an outline, condensed into 15 "resolves," officially known as the Virginia Plan, for totally overhauling the Articles of Confederation.

Madison was small, some said no more than five feet tall, with a voice that could scarcely carry across a crowded room. So a friend and fellow Virginian, Edmund Randolph, was chosen to speak for the resolves—to be, as Madison later put it, the "organ on the occasion." Six feet tall, handsome, a man "of distinguished talents, and in the habit of public speaking," Randolph was already, at 33, the Governor of Virginia, the most important state for any such Convention, being as it was both large and at the same time Southern and agricultural and so able to influence states least likely to favor strong central government. Hardly had the Convention opened than Randolph had the floor, and variously shocked and delighted the delegates with Madison's distilled ideas.

The rough structure of what Madison (and Randolph) urged is familiar to us today—indeed, at the time, six of the states had constitutions roughly similar in shape. A government divided into three parts: executive, legislative and judicial, variously elected and appointed. And as a rough form the Convention swiftly agreed to it. Easy passage was also given to the idea of a bicameral legislature, a fixture everywhere but Georgia and Pennsylvania. The Virginia Plan's provision for popular election of the lower house also was accepted, though it would come up again for bitter dispute. So, in fact, would virtually everything else. The real trouble, though, lay in the proposals for what sort of power each house would have, and on what numerical (and voting) basis representatives would be chosen.

"An individual independence of the States," Madison had written, "is utterly irreconcilable. . . . Let national Government be armed with positive and complete authority." He wanted to extend this "national supremacy" to the judiciary as well, and noted that in order "to give the new system its proper energy," all this executive power should be "ratified by the authority of the people."

The words "national" and "supreme" exploded through the hall when Randolph read them, imperiling sacred creeds. During the war with Britain, New Jersey troops had refused to swear allegiance to the Confederation, declaring "New Jersey is our country." New York delegate John Lansing, dead set against a new constitution anyway, promptly scalded this "triple-headed monster, as deep and wicked a conspiracy as ever was invented in the darkest ages against the liberties of a free people." Rising to challenge Randolph, South Carolina's Charles Pinckney, a dandy and later a Congressman, demanded: I wish to know if you "mean to abolish the State Governments altogether."

With characteristic mildness and courtesy, Randolph explained that he had merely "meant to introduce" some general propositions. And indeed, to others, this nationalist concept seemed exactly what anarchic America needed. Among them, Pennsylvania's James Wilson declared: "We must bury all local interests and distinctions."

The Convention might have broken down right there, except for two procedural devices that the delegates wisely adopted. The first was that no vote on any matter would be binding until a final vote was taken on a full, finished text of the Constitution. That way, no delegate would feel he was being pressured, and collectively, with a chance to reflect and reexamine, they all might produce a better document to place before the judgment of their countrymen.

Through another bit of cautious wisdom, they decided to keep the debates secret. Thomas Jefferson, in France as American Minister, protested in a letter "so abominable a precedent," yet not a single delegate objected. Guards were posted every day at the door. And at one point Washington, who hardly spoke in his role as President of the Convention, rose with a piece of paper in his hand. It was, he said sternly, a copy of their proceedings someone had dropped on the State House floor. If the newspapers ever got hold of such documents, the General scolded, their revelations could "disturb the public repose by premature speculations. I know not whose Paper it is," he continued, "but there it is." He tossed the paper on a table with the comment "let him who owns it take it," then bowed and walked out.

"It is something remarkable," delegate William Pierce of Georgia recalled, "that no Person ever owned that Paper."

As a result of what was essentially a gentleman's agreement about tight security, no one but the delegates really knew what was said in the hall until 53 years later when Madison's widow released the meticulous notes he had copied out each night, a record of the debate that, translated into direct dialogue, has been used ever since in dramatic accounts of the Convention. Madison was convinced to the end that secrecy had given delegates freedom to speak with nearly complete candor, and even to change their minds, often several times, as they never would have done if each word had been shared with the press or with their volatile constituencies. "If the debates had been public," Madison later wrote, "no constitution would ever have been adopted."

Indeed the public might have erupted early over some of the arguments about the power and structure of the proposed executive branch. When Wilson put forward a motion for a single President, even Randolph boggled; he preferred an executive council. Of special concern, too, was the proposition that the President have veto power over laws written by the proposed National Legislature. "But why might not a Catiline or a Cromwell arise in this Country as well as in others?" South Carolina's Pierce Butler wanted to know. George Mason spoke darkly about "hereditary Monarchy."

Benjamin Franklin was worried too. Pennsylvania, after all, had an 11-man Executive Council. But everyone knew that if a national government were devised, George Washington would be elected the first President of the United States. They knew, too, that he had once been offered virtual dictatorship of the troubled country and steadfastly refused. With that in mind, though still distrustful of human nature, Franklin concluded, "The first man, put at the helm will be a good one," but then added, "Nobody knows what sort may come afterwards." It took 60 different votes before the Convention finally agreed to a single President with a legislative veto—albeit a veto that two-thirds of the Congress could, as it still can, override.

Many men who arrived in Philadelphia fearful of executive power, and seeing states' rights as the best bulwark against an overreaching central government with a tendency to fall under the control of powerful interests, were impressed by Madison's reassurances. In a startling speech that contradicted Montesquieu's political theories, Madison refuted the argument that huge size and a large, diverse population were a hazard to stable democratic government. Quite the reverse. The unified Virginia Plan, he said, would so "enlarge the sphere and thereby divide the community into so great a number of interests . . . that . . . a majority will not be likely at the same moment to have a common interest . . . and . . . in case they should have such an interest, they may not be apt to unite in the pursuit of it."

Numerous standards were put forward as qualifications for serving as a national senator or representative. Many remain in the Constitution today. One that does not is the possession of property. If a man held property, it was estimated, the more substantial a citizen his interest would make him; he was likely to have a thoughtful, sober stake in stable government. After all, the delegates in the State House were mostly lawyers, bankers, merchants or plantation owners. Twenty-one of them had fought in the Revolution, 24 had served in the Continental Congress and, together with the leading figures from smaller states, they felt they had created the nation.

In June, debate began more and more to home in on the question over which the Convention soon almost foundered. Not only who would elect the representatives to the National Legislature, whatever their quality, but above all, how those representatives might be apportioned. According to the steadily evolving Virginia Plan, members of the first house (what we now call the House of Representatives) were to be chosen by the people for terms of three years.

For the other house (or Senate) representatives were to be chosen by the state legislatures for seven years. The aim was to create a lower house directly answerable to the people on a short-term basis, balanced by a less volatile, more elite body (a "House of Lords," opponents were to brand it) that did not need to worry about quick, popular complaint. Representation in both chambers would be portioned out roughly according to the number of people in each state, the slaves included, but with each slave to be counted as three-fifths of a person—a bizarre bit of arithmetic that the Continental Congress had first settled on in 1783.

Many delegates were still a long way from swallowing such a radical direct-election principle. "[I am] opposed to the election by the people," said Roger Sherman of Connecticut bluntly. A lean, sharp-nosed man, "cunning as the devil" (even his friends put it that way), Sherman was born poor but had risen by shrewd industry as a farmer and lawyer. The people, he continued, "want information and are constantly liable to be misled." Delaware's John Dickinson scornfully defined the people as "those multitudes without property and without principle, with which our Country like all others, will in time abound."

Present-day politicians would not dare say such things, even if they believed them. But in 1787 these views were widespread. The debates were secret, and to many men interested in stable government they seemed the essence of common sense. It was a time, after all, when not a single government in the world received its power directly from the people; two years later, in the name of "the people," the uncontrolled power of the mob in France would eventually lead to a bloodbath, followed by an emperor. Elbridge Gerry, the man who would one day give his name to the word gerrymander, had been a firebrand during America's struggle against George III. Now, he told the delegates, he was convinced that "The evils we experience flow from the excess of democracy."

Many delegates disagreed. Whatever they may have felt about the mob, it was clear to them that the power of any just government must derive from the people, however much they and all other contending political forces needed to be hedged around with checks and balances. Along with Madison, one apparently surprising proponent of power to the people turned out to be James Wilson of Philadelphia, a rich businessman and lawyer to the monied interests, including, during the Revolution, men accused of still being loyal to George III. George Mason of Virginia was another. Born to the privilege and responsibility of a 5,000-acre plantation, with more slaves than any delegate, he not only espoused abolition but now observed that since the "people will be represented; they ought therefore to choose the Representatives."

Gouverneur Morris, of course, disagreed. Other tempers were rising, along with the thermometer, as delegates fixed on points of conflict. Gunning Bedford of Delaware continued to denounce population-based representation as disastrous to the interest of small states. Virginia's population of 750,000 was almos 13 times that of Delaware; Pennsylvania, second largest of the original thirteen, had 430,000. How could the rights of a small state survive in such a government? "It seems as if Pennsylvania and Virginia . . . wished to provide a system in which they would have an enormous and monstrous influence," Bedford asserted. And later he thundered at the large-state delegates, *"I do not, gentlemen, trust you."*

But the Delaware delegate really jolted the Convention when he said, the "small [states] will find some foreign ally of more honor and good faith, who will take them by the hand and do them justice."

This dangerous turn in the arguments, raising the specter of a separate American confederacy under the thumb of Britain, Spain or France, brought the proceedings to their most desperate impasse. Madison said that the small states could depart if so inclined; they would have to join later, anyway. Wilson, equally out of patience, derided states, large and small, as "imaginary creatures," divisive, obsolescent. George Read, of Bedford's own delegation, grandly declared, "The State Governments must be swept away."

Small wonder, in the face of such wrangling, that delegates were all but ready to give up. Hamilton's conscience later brought him back. Mason, who stayed through to the end, declared that if he were doing this for money, a thousand pounds a day would not be enough pay. Even George Washington admitted, "I *almost* despair of seeing a favourable issue to the proceedings of the Convention, and do therefore repent having had any agency in the business."

Yet those days in early July, the worst times for the delegates, turned out to be the best times for the future United States of America. From them came a political compromise that saved the Convention and led to a Constitution that could be presented to the country with more than a fighting chance of ratification.

As the hot words flew, and proposals and counterproposals were voted on, one of the blows struck in the direction of possible compromise came from an unexpected quarter, Roger Sherman, who seemed to be changing his mind about the direct vote of the people.

According to Madison's notes, "Mr. Sherman proposed that the proportion of suffrage in the 1st branch should be according to the respective number of free inhabitants [a clear advantage for the large states]; and that in the second branch of Senate, each State should have one vote and no more." Thus could small states retain power beyond the size of their electorates. Like most useful ideas, the one Sherman presented was both simple and functional. But like all compromises it contained elements that each major faction—small states, large states, nationalists and states-righters—regarded either as imperfect or outright distasteful.

Also proposed by John Dickinson of Delaware and Oliver Ellsworth of Connecticut, the compromise was voted down. But the idea that "in *one* branch the *people*, ought to be represented; in the *other*, the *States*" did not disappear. Wilson and most other nationalists still wanted as little significant residue of state sovereignty as possible. Some delegates were outraged by the very idea that, say, tiny Rhode Island, which had boycotted the Convention and had been heavily engaged in smuggling before the Revolution, could vote with the august weight of Virginia or Massachusetts.

Like Wilson and Read, Madison was out of patience with state rivalries and petty fears of being dominated by neighbors. Such things seemed likely to destroy the dream of shaping the birth of a great republic. In his direct and prescient way he now let the delegates know where the real historic peril lay. "The great danger to our general government," said Madison, "is the great southern and northern interests of the continent being opposed to each other." The states, he also pointed out, are "divided into different interests not by their difference of size . . . but principally from their having or not having slaves."

It was true. Even with the help of a three-fifths count on slaves, if a National Congress based on proportional representation were put together right now, the North would have 31 votes to 25 for the South. Furthermore, during the same summer up in New York, the Confederation Congress was trying to put the finishing touches on an ordinance for the newly won Northwest Territories (previously claimed by Virginia, among others, and extending to the headwaters of the Mississippi) by which slavery was forbidden, currently and in the future, when these territories might become states.

Pierce Butler of South Carolina now offered an astonishing proposal—to add to the South's voting power by counting slaves equally with whites in apportioning the number of national delegates each state had. Gouverneur Morris riposted that Pennsylvanians, anyway, would not stand for "being put on a footing with slaves." Crusty Elbridge Gerry had already observed that property should not be involved in rules for political representation. Otherwise why should not horses and cattle in the North, like slaves in the South, count toward voting totals.

As the floor debate sank to the level of bitter farce, Wilson turned the discussion skillfully, in a slightly different direction. He spoke of taxation, but, as had been proposed earlier, taxation used as a way of measuring voting powers. Taxes came from property. Slaves were property. America had been founded on the principle that there be no taxation without representation.

The argument moved the debate forward. Delegates began working on various ratios whereby representatives of the South in the legislature would not be at the immediate mercy of the North. They sought ways of expanding the number of representatives in the future so as to preserve political balance as the country grew—and populous western states came in. And it was, indeed, this vision of a threatening future, when the large and powerful Eastern states might find themselves in the minority, that made them see there was merit in having at least one house in which all states had the same number of representatives regardless of population.

And at last, with the main issue so clearly defined, but with the regional voting blocks now slightly divided among themselves, the Convention gained momentum once more under the rising banner of compromise. When the strongest nationalists, including Madison and Wilson, clung to their objections about the proposed arrangement for the Senate, delegates thought of something Ben Franklin, ever the conciliator, had raised earlier—an idea made to order for propertied men. Why not have the first house control all money bills?

For the populous states this appeared to be a nice trade-off—dollars, and the power of appropriating public funds, against a loss of political clout in the Senate—and it became part of a package that was moving toward a floor vote.

Madison still did not like it. The dispute "ended in the compromise," Madison later wrote Jefferson, "but very much to the dissatisfaction of several members from the large States." The deal left the national government far weaker than Hamilton would have wanted, too, but he took a non-utopian view. It was not hard, he would suggest, to choose "between anarchy and Convulsion on one side," and the chance of good on the other. South Carolina's John Rutledge eventually voiced the changing mood toward accommodation when, noting that the delegates could not do what they all thought best, he added, "we ought to do something."

And they did. On Monday, July 16, by the narrow vote of five states to four, with one state divided, the Convention passed the Connecticut delegation's much-amended measure, which would soon become known as the Great Compromise. A strong, central government had been agreed upon, but the small states were protected from the large in the Senate, while in the House, the South, with slaves counted as part of population, could not easily be overborne by the North. It was clear that no other arrangement would be acceptable to a majority. Even so, Madison was openly angry. He had always insisted the supremacy of the central government in the proposed federation must be unequivocal. Beyond that the idea of Delaware as Virginia's equal in the Senate seemed antirepublican to him. But what could he do? The very fact of the Compromise seemed to prove his perception that in an enormous country only the free play of diverse and contending interests could lead to an acceptably balanced decision.

As a final concession, Southerners agreed that, after 1808, the slave trade could be prohibited by Congress. Sherman had noted that the "abolition of slavery seemed to be going on in the United States, and that the good sense of the several States would probably by degrees compleat it." Some conscience-troubled northern Southerns, like Washington, who hated slavery but lived off its production, agreed. They hoped that in 20 years the practice might fade away, a hope made somewhat more reasonable to them because their kind of mixed farming depended less on slaves than did the deep South's. Southerners may have been somewhat reassured by a clause in the Northwest Ordinances mandating the return of fugitive slaves who entered free territory.

Two more exhausting months would pass before their work was finished, but after July 16 the delegates were clearly minded to get the job done. Members of the House, they agreed, would serve two years, not three. There would be two Senators per state, with six-year terms. And they would, indeed, be elected by the state legislators. It was not until 1913 that the 17th Amendment conveyed their election directly to the people.

Though the Convention established a national judiciary, it never gave the courts specific authority to review legislative acts, or to strike them down as unconstitutional. That famous precedent was set in 1803, with the celebrated Marbury v. Madison case, when arch-federalist John Marshall, Chief Justice during the presidency of anti-federalist Thomas Jefferson, broadly interpreted the new Constitution's breadth and power by declaring an act of Congress unconstitutional. So doing, he balanced for all time the three branches of government. He also opened the debate that rages today on how far judges may properly go in interpreting the original text and intent of the Constitution.

In 1787 some delegates believed they had done well to lay down broad principles rather than an interminable list of strict instructions. Others felt the document they were completing was far too vague and would fail to be ratified. "I'll be hanged if ever the people of Maryland agree to it," declared Luther Martin.

Martin had company. George Mason had become seriously alienated. Now at the eleventh hour he chose to ask why the document had no Bill of Rights. Mason was the spokesman on the

point, though he surely had taken his sweet time about bringing
it up. He would sooner chop off his right hand, Mason said, "than
put it to the Constitution as it now stands." If some things were
not changed or added, he wanted "to bring the whole subject before another general Convention." Eager to be finished, the other delegates disagreed and the Convention hurried on.

On September 17, 1787, the day the document was signed,
Gouverneur Morris, a master of style to whom the final polishing
of prose had been assigned, listened proudly as the finished work
was read aloud to the 41 delegates who had stayed for the last act.
It began with the ringing phrase, "We the People." With Franklin's special blessing, Morris had also fashioned a particular
ending to the Constitution: "Done in Convention by the Unanimous Consent of the States present this Seventeenth Day of
September."

It was a neat device, with a double purpose. Once signed, the
Constitution would go to the Congress and then to state ratifying
conventions. To carry the country, it needed all the help it could
get and preferably should emerge from the State House with
unanimous approval. For, as one Philadelphian, not in the Convention but clearly in the know, had lately noted, "no sooner will
the chicken be hatch'd, but every one will be for plucking a
feather." Franklin hoped the insertion of the words "the States"
would keep the bird whole. As state delegates, he purred, gentlemen could approve the Constitution with their signatures while
as individuals they retained personal reservations.

The artful measure nearly succeeded. Delegate after delegate
stepped forward to sign. But some, most notably George Mason
and Randolph, refused their signatures. They held firm though
warned both of the "infinite mischief" the lack of their names
might do at the ratifying conventions, where nine of the thirteen
states would have to approve the document, and of the "anarchy
and Convulsions" that might well ensue if the Constitution were
rejected.

Predictably, it was in Virginia that one key ratification fight
took place. In Richmond, Madison spearheaded one side, Mason
and states' rightist Patrick ("give me liberty or give me death")
Henry the other. "Who authorized them to speak the language
of We the People," Henry roared, "instead of, We the States?"

If a bare majority of Congress could make laws, he argued,
the "situation of our western citizens is dreadful. You have a bill

of rights to defend you against state government [yet] you have none against Congress. . . . May they not pronounce all slaves free . . . ?" The torrent of Henry's words, steadily rebutted by Madison, lasted 23 days. Sometimes he made five speeches a day, and his list of proposed rights and amendments that must be added to the Constitution grew to 40. But eventually, though he didn't vote aye, he ceased fire, partly yielding to the promise that a Bill of Rights would be added after ratification.

Within two years, the national Congress under the new Constitution proposed the first ten amendments that make up the present Bill of Rights. But the historic issue of whether a young nation, so dedicated and so constituted, could long endure, was anything but settled.

THE ARK OF AMERICA[3]

The Constitution has the aura of the sacred about it. It occupies a shrine up in the higher stretches of American reverence. A citizen imagines sun-shot clouds, the founders hovering in the air like saints in religious art.

But the Constitution has its other, mundane life. Down at sea level, where people struggle along in law courts and jailhouses and abortion clinics, where lives and ideas crash into each other, the Constitution has a more interesting and turbulent existence. There the Constitution is not a civic icon but a messy series of collisions that knock together the arrangements of the nation's life. Those arrangements become America's history—what its people do, what they are, what they mean. Walt Whitman wrote, "I contain multitudes." That is what the Constitution does—an astonishing feat considering the variety of multitudes that have landed on American shores, and continue to land.

May a man be detained in jail before being tried? Is prayer to be permitted in the public schools? Or a Christmas crèche in the town square? What of the Reagan Administration's arranging military help for the Nicaraguan *contras* when Congress has for-

[3]Reprint of an article by senior writer Lance Morrow. *Time.* 130:22+. Jl. 6, '87. Copyright © 1987 Time Inc. All rights reserved. Reprinted by permission from TIME.

bidden it? If a man murders someone, may the state kill the killer in retribution? May government employees be forced to have their urine tested to search for the trace of drugs? May American Nazis march in an Illinois suburb that is home to Jewish survivors of the Holocaust? May a man be arrested for performing a homosexual act in his own home? Is it right to promote a woman ahead of an equally qualified man in order to redress past inequities toward women?

Issues passionate and human and difficult surge up against the Constitution. Every day it attends to the pleas of lust, rage, unborn life, the killer's remorse, the President's prerogatives, the First Amendment rights of a Ku Klux Klansman. The Constitution even makes a ritual appearance in the American television cop show: there comes a moment of denouement when the detective, triumphant but sardonically obedient to the *Miranda* decision, snaps the cuffs on a suspect and growls, "You have the right to remain silent. You have the right to . . . "

The Constitution forces Americans to think about uncongenial matters, to think about tolerating everything they may hate. It is the American superego. It holds Americans to a high standard, even though it has sometimes countenanced filthy deeds—most notoriously, the owning of slaves.

In this Bicentennial year, fiestas are swirling around the shrine of the Constitution. In Philadelphia there are endless parties, picnics and explications. The pageantry is perfectly American. Yet the nation may have grown a little weary of such celebrations. The skies of the '80s have been filled with red, white and blue balloons. In the waning Reagan years, the note of national self-congratulation sounds hollow.

Celebrations of the Constitution are inherently different in any case. The bunting and period costumes are accompanied this time by processions of scholars, by seminars on Public Television, by a different public mood. The Constitution is more complex than a Fourth of July, more technical, more cerebral and, in its intricacies, subtleties and silences, even enigmatic. A Fourth of July is fireworks and rhetoric, the old ritual romance of liberty. The Constitution is thought and legalism.

A few weeks ago, Supreme Court Justice Thurgood Marshall objected to some of the pietism attending the 200th anniversary of the Constitution. Speaking to a lawyers' group in Hawaii, Marshall said the document had been "defective from the start." The fact that Marshall is the great-grandson of a slave sharpened his point.

"I do not believe," Marshall went on, "that the meaning of the Constitution was forever 'fixed' at the Philadelphia convention." The document required "several amendments, a civil war and momentous social transformation to attain the system of constitutional government, and its respect for the individual freedoms and human rights, we hold as fundamental today."

In 1919 Justice Oliver Wendell Holmes observed, "Our Constitution is an experiment, as all life is an experiment." The Constitution is an experiment as the U.S. is an experiment. It was flawed from the beginning as the nation was flawed. But the Constitution has also been the genius of America, the life of its laws and the conscience of its power. The Constitution and the country formed each other. The genius lay in the hermeneutical life of the document, the complicated, brilliant, sometimes disgraceful unfolding of America.

In retrospect, Americans have often believed that their nation was inevitable. It did not seem so at the start. The 13 colonies that fought the Revolution had formed a loose confederation, a flimsy arrangement, each state in business for itself, guarding its sovereignty. By 1785 it looked as if the arrangement would disintegrate, that the colonies would at best turn into separate national entities connected only by more or less friendly treaties with one another.

The founders meeting in Philadelphia in the summer of 1787 invented a true U.S. Ever since, the country has gone on inventing and reinventing itself—the Constitution shaping the nation, a changing America rethinking the Constitution. The one time the Constitution proved inadequate to the task, in the 1860s, half a million died in order to improve the document. The Civil War amounted to a Second Constitutional Convention.

The U.S. as a nation is famously lucky. Its primal luck was geography and timing: a wild natural abundance that was encountered by gifted men and women in the clear rational blue of the Enlightenment. The Constitution was drafted in a moment of ascendant science—political science preached by Locke and Montesquieu, for example—and belief in the power of reason to subdue the savage and ignorant regions of the mind.

A few generations after the Constitutional Convention, Ralph Waldo Emerson wrote his essay *History*, with one of his lines of crystal meditation: "It seems as if heaven had sent its insane angels into our world as to an asylum, and here they will break out in their native music and utter at intervals the words they have heard in heaven; then the mad fit returns and they mope and wallow like dogs." The founders of 1787 knew all about the moping dogs. They designed their instrument to break out of the dark alternations of anarchy and tyranny, to manage power and preserve freedom.

Philadelphia 200 years ago was the real morning in America. In the beginning were the words, and they were made flesh—Presidents, Senators, Justices. The imagery of creation and divine sponsorship hovered over the enterprise. As Lincoln said at Gettysburg, the U.S. was a new nation, "brought forth" and dedicated to a proposition, an idea. America was not a pre-existing cohesion, like Japan, which had its origins back in the Shinto mists of its prehistory. America was a conscious creation of the mind, of science. It was creatively assembled out of ideas, traditions and genes rounded up elsewhere and unloaded in a New World.

Most of history is passivity, or lashing reaction. The Constitution represented a wonderfully energetic and active moment, the mind alive and assertive, yet amazingly self-knowing. The founders created government as an exquisite system of self-control and self-examination. The Constitution is, among other things, the model of a fine 18th century mind, with checks and balances that are both delicate and strong, a splendid mind that designed into itself the mechanisms of civilized change. As W. H. Auden once said, Americans are great moral improvisers.

The founders were élitists and realists about human nature, a configuration stamped upon the document they wrote. Their task was to make passion subject to reason. If men could be expected to be selfish, or worse, then, said James Madison, "ambition must be made to counteract ambition." The Newtonian principles of action and reaction were applied to politics. The founders mistrusted human nature (not a bad call) but harbored great ambitions for mankind nonetheless.

The U.S. owes much to the patriarchal authority of its Constitution. Its citizens have almost always believed that men may be wrong (transient politicians, bigots, mortal fools temporarily in power), but that the Constitution is the repository of truth, if only citizens are wise enough to discover it. Is it constitutional? It is moving that the question is asked so often in America, so seriously, so indignantly, so hopefully. The asker may be angry but nonetheless believes he has knocked at the door where justice lives. (Justice, of course, is not invariably at home.)

The 7,567 words of the Constitution and amendments, mostly dry and functional prose, are sometimes cryptic and elusive, and Americans have suggested a variety of similes and metaphors to describe the document. In the early 19th century, a Congressman named Caleb Cushing hinted at the Constitution's divine inspiration when he called it "our Ark of Covenant." (Abolitionists a little later called it the handiwork of Satan.)

Writers have often thought of the Constitution in nautical terms, a motif probably suggested by the image of the ship of state. In 1857 Macaulay told an American, "Your Constitution is all sail and no anchor." (A foreigner's elegant remark. Others suspect that the Constitution has entirely too much anchor—too many checks and balances—to make any headway at all.) The sociologist David Riesman likens the Constitution to the shallow keel of the national ferryboat, on which the passengers keep shifting from port to starboard and back again. One might also suggest the image of a trimaran—a craft with three hulls (Legislative, Executive and Judicial) that is both stable and fast. Harvard's Paul Freund likes to think of the whole arrangement as a symphony orchestra or a jazz band.

A Newtonian, mechanical metaphor was prevalent during the Industrial Revolution. As America was celebrating the 100th anniversary of the document, James Russell Lowell observed, "After our Constitution got fairly into working order, it really seemed as if we had invented a machine that would go of itself, and this begot a faith in our luck."

Eventually, the Newtonian notion of the Constitution came to seem static. Thinkers like Woodrow Wilson and Oliver Wendell Holmes began referring to it as an animate thing. Wrote Wilson: "Society is a living organism, and must obey the laws of life, not of mechanics; it must develop."

A living thing grows and changes. In a speech in July 1985, Attorney General Edwin Meese argued that the Supreme Court had allowed the Constitution to become far too organic. He criticized the court for making the law rather than merely applying the law as it had been set down by the founders. The Justices, said Meese, should stick closely to the views of the men who wrote the

Constitution; they should practice today a "jurisprudence of original intention."

The framers of the Constitution could not possibly have foreseen the America of the late 20th century, with its enormous national Government, its multinational corporations, its crime, computer technology, genetic engineering, pollution, mass media, nuclear weapons and the rest. Madison did not permit the notes that he made during the Constitutional Convention to be published until after his death, believing that the Constitution must stand alone, that the specific thoughts of individual framers were essentially irrelevant and might even be mischievous in later times.

"Original intent has a strong gravitational pull," acknowledges Columbia Law Professor Henry Monaghan. But how specific an intent are we looking for? Today's interpreters of the Constitution, for example, would never tolerate the brutality of the criminal punishments that were prevalent 200 years ago—brandings, say, or the puncturing of nostrils. Notes Federal Appeals Court Judge Irving Kaufman: "I regard reliance on original intent to be a largely specious mode of interpretation. I often find it instructive to consult the framers when I am called upon to interpret the Constitution. But it is the beginning of my inquiry, not the end. . . . The framers' legacy to modern times is the language and spirit of the Constitution, not the conflict and dated conceptions that lay beneath that language."

Anyone who doubts that the Constitution is a living thing that changes and evolves should think about the difference between the document then and now. As framed 200 years ago, the Constitution was virtually paranoid on the subject of democracy. James Madison wrote in *The Federalist* about his view of democracy and direct government. If every Athenian citizen had been a Socrates, he thought, every Athenian assembly would still have been a mob. The founders began, "We the People." And yet "the People" had very little to do with writing the thing. The framers, working behind closed doors and shut windows, were highly literate white males—landowners, military heroes, merchants, accomplished lawyers. Hardly a word was heard from the common folk. Only 133 years later, with the 19th Amendment, did women acquire the right to vote.

If there is any matter on which the original intent of the founders is clear, it is the issue of slavery. Says Columbia Law

Professor Jack Greenberg, former director-counsel of the N.A.A.C.P. Legal Defense and Educational Fund: "The original Constitution not only accepted slavery, but it gave the South a bonus for it"—the stipulation in Article I, Section 3 that in apportioning Representatives for the House, "three fifths of all other persons" should be added to the "whole number of free persons."

Deeds as well as words have made the Constitution—sometimes deeds that were considered illegal. As Harvard Law Professor Laurence Tribe remarks, "The framing of the Constitution has been a continuous process rather than a purely episodic one. I think the real framers were not only the gentlemen who met in Philadelphia and those who drafted and ratified the crucial amendments, such as the amendments following the Civil War, but also the many people who often in the roles of dissent and rebellion, sat in, or marched and sang, or sometimes gave their lives, in order to translate their vision of what the Constitution might be and how it should be understood into political and legal reality."

The law of the land evolves, sometimes from grotesque early versions. In its Dred Scott decision in 1857, the Supreme Court declared that blacks do not have the rights of citizens. The law has been changed at barricades, in the streets, by a procession of Americans like John Brown, Rosa Parks, Martin Luther King Jr. Women struggled for two or three generations to acquire the right to vote.

A dozen years ago, Supreme Court Justice Potter Stewart gave a speech to a group of journalists regarding the First Amendment's protection of a free press. "The Constitution," he said, "is not a self-executing document. . . . If you went back to the original understanding of our ancestors, back in the early years of the 19th century, you would find that their understanding of this clause and the Constitution in their judgment allowed them to enact the Alien and Sedition laws. And if those laws were still on the books, Richard Nixon would still be President of the U.S. and Spiro Agnew would still be Vice President, and all of you people would probably be in prison."

America now is incomparably more democratic than it was 200 years ago. Originally, only the House of Representatives was elected directly by the people. Now the Senate is directly elected, and sees itself as responsive to the people. The President is in effect directly elected by the people, not by the vestigial Electoral

College that the founders invented. Even the Supreme Court has long since taken on a representative character. Said Justice Thurgood Marshall of the founders: "They could not have imagined, nor would they have accepted, that the document they were drafting would one day be construed by a Supreme Court to which had been appointed a woman and the descendant of an African slave."

But where does salutary reinvention of America leave off and dangerous tampering with the nation's governmental structure begin? Today, various forces have been agitating for changes. Some have called for a constitutional convention or a constitutional amendment to force the Federal Government to balance its budget.

In Congress a group of conservative Republicans, led by Jesse Helms of North Carolina and Orrin Hatch of Utah in the Senate and by Philip Crane of Illinois in the House, has been trying to reduce the Supreme Court's authority by introducing so-called court-stripping bills. The bills may be constitutional, under Article III, Section 2, which provides that Congress may set limits on the Supreme Court's appellate jurisdiction. "At stake in all of this," writes Historian Michael Kammen, "is nothing less than a campaign against the system of checks and balances intended by the founders."

Helms proclaims his purposes clearly: "Article III, Section 2 is the fundamental key for congressional efforts to restrain federal judges who distort rather than enforce the Constitution." A prime target: abortion cases. "Through similar legislative enactments," Helms said, "Congress could restore voluntary school prayer and severely limit enforced busing. There are other areas in which Congress could act as well." Barry Goldwater, hardly a liberal, is enraged by the tactic: "I've spent my whole life railing against those who use any excuse to get around the law or the Constitution." For the moment, however, the stripper bills are going nowhere in a Congress controlled by the Democrats.

In another part of the forest, some Anglophile theorists would like to see the American system take on the British parliamentary form. Not long ago in *American Heritage* magazine, Historian James MacGregor Burns declared, "I would favor a constitutional amendment permitting the President not only to choose members of his Cabinet or top executive officers from the Senate or the House, but allowing those appointees to retain their seats in Congress. This not only would draw the President and Congress into somewhat closer teamwork, but would serve as a stabilizing force in the Executive and an enhancement of executive leadership in Congress."

The parliamentary form would effectively destroy the Congress as an equal and separate branch of the Federal Government. That, of course, is the intent. Congress tends to be a nuisance to Presidents. Those favoring the parliamentary arrangement want to make a majority-party President more powerful, influential and effective—precisely what the founders feared to do.

Moreover, the parliamentary idea might dramatically shift the ballast and introduce considerable instability. Even in the stable British system, governments can be voted out of office by Parliament. Would Americans in the midst of a crisis—the Iran-*contra* scandal, for example—wish to subject the Administration to no-confidence votes?

It is a tribute to the Constitution's adaptability that since the Bill of Rights was added in 1791, only 16 more amendments have been ratified. Yet new contexts have arisen that Madison and his contemporaries could not foresee. The Bill of Rights, for example, says nothing directly about the right of privacy, what Supreme Court Justice Louis Brandeis called the "right to be let alone." In the 18th century, the power of Government to intrude on the individual was acknowledged in the Fourth Amendment ban on unreasonable searches and seizures. But the bureaucracies, technologies—and social problems—of the late 20th century make the issue of privacy considerably more complex and important. Government is not the only intrusive agent. Says Harvard Law Professor Arthur Miller: "Whether you are talking about computer data banks or AIDS testing or drug testing or surveillance, the notion that the only threat to the individual in our society comes from the nation-state is nuts. The primary threat to individual privacy in this country comes from entities that are not governmental: hospitals, corporations, each other." The Constitution contains no guarantees against nongovernmental threats to privacy.

There are other contexts in which the Constitution offers little guidance: in genetic engineering, in the issues of the right to die and the right to life. At a time when doctors can perform surgery on a fetus before delivery, when exactly does the law consider that life has begun? Does that fetus have constitutional rights? What is death? Who has the right to be alive, and who has the right to choose death?

Another area of silence in the Constitution: economic rights, the right to a job, the right to shelter, the right to food. The first constitution to address such rights was the Mexican constitution of 1917. Since then, the idea has spread to many 20th century constitutions around the world. But as Rutgers Law Professor Albert Blaustein points out, "civil and political rights are rights of abstinence. They are rights against the state. When you start talking about social and cultural rights, you are asking for rights of action, affirmative rights."

Most well-drafted constitutions of this century—those of India, Nigeria and Liberia, for example—have separated economic rights from political rights and placed them in different sections. Political rights are justiciable. Economic rights are "aspirational" or "programmatic," which is touching but perhaps no more than that. Aspirational clauses are impossible to enforce unless the government runs the economy. Food, jobs, shelter and other needs of that kind are most acute in countries that can least afford to supply them, however handsomely a constitution is composed. Besides, countries like Liberia and Nigeria may cherish the most articulate aspirations, but as T. S. Eliot wrote, "between the idea and the reality . . . falls the shadow." The reality may be one of coups, civil wars and misery.

The Constitution is endlessly unfinished business. The founders worried intensely about protecting property. Americans now worry intensely about protecting individual rights. The morale of the tribe must be considered, along with the rights of the individual and the appetites of the lawyer. In many ways, the U.S. is a hopelessly overlawyered society, the air thick with litigating birds of prey.

One of the *Federalist* papers, in a grandiose moment, predicted that the Constitution would "vindicate the honor of the human race." What the founders created, at any rate, was an extraordinary civilizing program, and a moral style in which conscience— the Judiciary, the third eye—was turned into an institution. The genius of the Constitution has been the moral restlessness it embodies, and its capacity to change even while its basic structure abides. Today, all but six of the world's nations either have or are committed to having a single-document constitution. That idea was born in Philadelphia. Reverence is due to those men in the hot summer of the Enlightenment. They changed the world.

A CITIZEN READS THE CONSTITUTION[4]

Not including the amendments, it is approximately 5,000 words long—about the length of a short story. It is an enigmatically dry, unemotional piece of work, tolling off in its monotone the structures and functions of government, the conditions and obligations of office, the limitations of powers, the means for redressing crimes and conducting commerce. It makes itself the supreme law of the land. It concludes with instructions on how it can amend itself, and undertakes to pay all the debts incurred by the states under its indigent parent, the Articles of Confederation.

It is no more scintillating as reading than I remember it to have been in Mrs. Brundage's seventh-grade civics class at Joseph H. Wade Junior High School. It is 5,000 words but reads like 50,000. It lacks high rhetoric and shows not a trace of wit, as you might expect, having been produced by a committee of lawyers. It uses none of the tropes of literature to create empathetic states in the mind of the reader. It does not mean to persuade. It abhors metaphor as nature abhors a vacuum.

One's first reaction upon reading it is to rush for relief to an earlier American document, as alive with passion and the juices of outrage as the work of any single artist:

We hold these truths to be self-evident, that all men are created equal, that they are endowed by their Creator with certain unalienable Rights, that among these are Life, Liberty and the pursuit of Happiness. That to secure these rights, Governments are instituted among Men, deriving their just powers from the consent of the governed. That whenever any Form of Government becomes destructive of these ends, it is the Right of the People to alter or to abolish it, and to institute new Government.

Here is the substantive diction of a single human mind—Thomas Jefferson's, as it happens—even as it speaks for all. It is engaged in the art of literary revolution, rewriting history, over-

---

[4]Reprint of an address by novelist E. L. Doctorow. *The Nation.* 244:208+. F. 21, '87. Copyright © 1987 by The Nation Company, Inc.

throwing divine claims to rule and genealogical hierarchies of human privilege as cruel frauds, defining human rights as universal and distributing the source and power of government to the people governed. It is the radical voice of national liberation, combative prose lifting its musketry of self-evident truths and firing away.

What reader does not wish the Constitution could have been written out of something of the same spirit? Of course, we all know instinctively that it could not, that statute-writing in the hands of lawyers has its own demands, and those are presumably precision and clarity, which call for sentences bolted at all four corners with *wherein*'s and *whereunder*'s and *thereof*'s and *therein*'s and notwithstanding the *foregoing*'s.

Still and all, our understanding of the Constitution must come of an assessment of its character as a composition, and it would serve us to explore further why it is the way it is. Here is something of what I have learned of the circumstances under which it was written.

The Background

The Constitutional Convention was called in the first place because in the postwar world of North America influential men in the government, in the Continental Congress, were not confident that the loosely structured Articles of Confederation, as written, could make permanent the gains of the Revolution. Without the hated British to unite them the states would revert to bickering and mutual exploitation. They had as many problems with one another as the classes of people in each state had among themselves, and men like George Washington and James Madison foresaw a kind of anarchy ensuing that would lead to yet another despotism, either native or from foreign invasion by the Spanish or again by the English. Many competing interests were going unmediated. The agrarian Southern states, with their tropical rice and cotton plantations, saw danger to themselves in export taxes applied to all their goods by the North Atlantic port states. The small states, like Delaware, felt threatened by their bigger neighbors, such as Pennsylvania. There was immense debt as a result of the Revolution, which debtors wanted to pay off with state-issued paper money—and which creditors, security holders, bankers, merchants, men of wealth, wanted returned in hard currency. There were diverse ethnic and religious communities, black slaves, white indentured servants. And there were Indians in the woods. The states not contiguous had little in common with one another. To a New Yorker, South Carolina was not the South; it was another kingdom entirely, with people of completely different backgrounds and with bizarre manners in speech and deportment—foreigners, in short. Georgia and South Carolina depended on slave labor to run their plantations. Slavery was abhorrent to many Northerners in 1787, and an economy of slaves was morally detestable.

It is important to remind ourselves in this regard that colonial society had existed for 150 years before the idea of independence caught on. That's a long time, certainly long enough for an indigenous class of great wealth to arise and a great schism to emerge between the rich and the poor. A very few people owned most of the land and were keenly resented. Three percent of the population controlled 50 percent of the wealth. People were not stupid; there was general knowledge of the plunder, legal chicanery, favoritism, privilege of name and corruption of government officials that had created such inequity. In fact, it is possible that organization of public sentiment against King George is exactly what saved the colonies from tearing themselves apart with insurrections of the poor against the rich; that events like the Boston Tea Party and calls to arms by Jefferson and Tom Paine created the common enemy, the British, to unify all the classes in America and save, by diversion of anger and rage to the redcoats, the fortunes and hides of the American upper class. This was the class, as it happened, of most of the fifty-five men who convened in Philadelphia. Washington was perhaps the largest landowner in the country. Benjamin Franklin possessed a considerable fortune, and Madison owned several slave plantations.

There was an additional factor to make them sensitive. The convention had been called to consider amendments to the Articles of Confederation. The Continental Congress was even now sitting in New York City and doing government business, and not all that ineffectually. It was, for example, passing legislation outlawing slavery in the western territories. But rather than amending the Articles, the convention in Philadelphia was persuaded to throw them aside entirely and design something new—a federal entity that would incorporate the states. The agenda for this course of action was proposed by Governor Edmund Randolph of Virginia, who presented a number of resolutions for debate, and so it has come to be called the Virginia plan. But the sentiment for something new, a new federal government over and above state sovereignties, had the strong support of influential delegates from several venues. And so the convention got down to business that was actually subversive. It violated its own mandate and began to move in the direction the federalists pushed it. It was because of this and because no one participating wanted, in the vigorous debates that were to ensue over the next months, to be confronted with a record of his remarks or positions, that the conventioneers agreed to make their deliberations secret for the entire time they sat, permitting no official journal of the proceedings and swearing themselves to a press blackout, as it were. That was to upset Jefferson greatly, who was off in France as a minister; the idea of such secrecy repelled him. Only Madison, fortunately for us, kept a notebook, which did not come to light until 1843 but which provides us the fullest account of those secret deliberations and the character of the minds that conducted them.

The Convention

What a remarkable group of minds they were. The first thing they did was constitute themselves as a Committee of the Whole, which gave them the power of improvisation and debate, flexibility of action, so that when the collected resolutions were decided on they could present them to themselves in plenary session.

Methodically, treating one thorny question after another, they made their stately way through the agenda. If something could not be resolved it was tabled and the next issue was confronted. Nothing stopped their painstaking progress through the maze of ideas and resolutions from which they slowly constructed a new world for themselves: who would make the laws, who would execute them, who would review their judicial propriety; should the small states balk at proportional representation, then the Senate would be created to give equal representation to every state. Some matters were easy to agree on—the writ of *habeas corpus*, the precise nature of treason. If one reads any of the dramatic reconstructions of their work, and there are several good books that provide this, one has the thrill of watching living, fallible men composing the United States of America and producing its ruling concept of federalism, a system of national and local governments, each with defined powers and separate legal jurisdictions.

Through it all Washington sat up at the front of the room, and he never said a word. The less he said the more his prestige grew. They had settled on one chief executive, to be called a President, and everyone knew who it would be. He had only to sit there to give the delegates courage to persevere. Franklin, too, lent the considerable weight of his presence, only occasionally saying a few soft words or passing up a note to be read by the speaker. Franklin was an old man at the time, over 80. At one point, when the proceedings were bogging down in dissension, he offered the recommendation that everyone stop and pray. The lawyers were so stunned by this idea that tempers cooled, probably just as he had intended, and the meeting went on.

And as the weeks wore on there slowly emerged among the delegates—or must have—a rising sense of their identity not only as Carolinians or Virginians or New Yorkers but as American nationals. A continental vision of nationhood lit their minds, and a collaborative excitement had to have come over them as day after day, month after month, they fantasized together their nation on paper. One cannot read any account of their deliberations without understanding how they made things up as they went along from their own debated differences, so that a sort of group intellect arose. It was wise with a knowledge of the way men act with power and from what motives. This objectification of separate personalities and interests came of a unanimous familiarity with parliamentary method and was finally self-propelling. These men invented a country of language, and that language celebrated— whether in resolutions of moral triumph or moral failure—the idea of law. The idea of a dispassionate law ruling men, even those men who were to make and effect the law.

Enough resolutions having been put forth, a Committee of Detail was formed to get them into an orderly shape, and that was accomplished with the scheme of articles, and sections under the articles, grouping the resolutions about legislative, judicial and executive branches, the rights and obligations of the states, the supremacy of the Constitution as law, etc.

When the Committee of Detail had structured the composition and it was duly examined and considered and amended, a Committee of Style was formed. That is my favorite committee.

It comprised William Samuel Johnson of Connecticut, Alexander
Hamilton of New York, Madison of Virginia, Rufus King of Massachusetts, and Gouverneur Morris of Pennsylvania. Apparently
Morris did the actual writing. And it is this document, produced
by the Committee of Style and approved by the convention, that
was called the Constitution of the United States. And for the first
time in the various drafts there appeared in the preamble the
phrase "We the people of the United States," thus quietly absorb-
ing both the seminal idea of the Declaration of Independence and
the continental vision of federalism.

The Voice of the Constitution

So we come back to this question of text. It is true but not sufficient to say that the Constitution reads as it does because it was
written by a committee of lawyers. Something more is going on
here. Every written composition has a voice, a persona, a character of presentation, whether by design of the author or not. The
voice of the Constitution is a quiet voice. It does not rally us; it
does not call on self-evident truths; it does not arm itself with philosophy or political principle; it does not argue, explain, con-
demn, excuse or justify. It is postrevolutionary. Not claiming
righteousness, it is, however, suffused with rectitude. It is this way
because it seeks standing in the world, the elevation of the unlawful acts of men—unlawful first because the British government
has been overthrown, and second because the confederation of
the states has been subverted—to the lawful standing of nationhood. All the *herein*'s and *whereas*'s and *thereof*'s are not only legal-
isms; they also happen to be the diction of the British Empire, the
language of the deposed. Nothing has changed that much, the
Constitution says, lying; we are nothing that you won't recognize.

But there is something more. The key verb of the text is *shall*,
as in "All legislative powers herein granted shall be vested in a
Congress of the United States which shall consist of a Senate and
a House of Representatives," or "New States may be admitted by
the Congress into this Union; but no new State shall be formed
or erected within the jurisdiction of any other State." The Constitution does not explicitly concern itself with the grievances that
brought it about. It is syntactically futuristic: it prescribes what
is to come. It prophesies. Even today, living 200 years into the
prophecy, we read it and find it still ahead of us, still extending

itself in time. The Constitution gives law and assumes for itself the power endlessly to give law. It ordains. In its articles and sections, one after another, it offers a ladder to heaven. It is cold, distant, remote as a voice from on high, self-authenticating.

Through most of history kings and their servitor churches did the ordaining, and always in the name of God. But here the people do it: "We the People . . . do ordain and establish this Constitution for the United States." And the word for God appears nowhere in the text. Heaven forbid! In fact, its very last stricture is that "no religious test shall ever be required as a qualification to any office or public trust under the United States."

The voice of the Constitution is the inescapably solemn self-consciousness of the people giving the law unto themselves. But since in the Judeo-Christian world of Western civilization all given law imitates God—God being the ultimate lawgiver—in affecting the transhuman voice of law, that dry monotone that disdains persuasion, the Constitution not only takes on the respectable sound of British statute, it more radically assumes the character of scripture.

The ordaining voice of the Constitution is scriptural, but in resolutely keeping the authority for its dominion in the public consent, it presents itself as the sacred text of secular humanism.

I wish Mrs. Brundage had told me that back in Wade Junior High School.

I wish Jerry Falwell's and Jimmy Swaggart's and Pat Robertson's teachers had taught them that back in their junior high schools.

The Sacred Text

Now, it is characteristic of any sacred text that it has beyond its literal instruction tremendous symbolic meaning for the people who live by it. Think of the Torah, the Koran, the Gospels. The sacred text dispenses not just social order but spiritual identity. And as the states each in its turn ratified the Constitution, usually not without vehement debate and wrangling, the public turned out in the streets of major cities for processions, festivities, with a fresh new sense of themselves and their future.

Every major city had its ship of state rolling through the streets, pulled by teams of horses—a carpentered ship on wheels rolling around the corners and down the avenues in full sail, and perhaps with a crew of boys in sailor uniforms. It was called, inevitably, The Constitution or Federalism or Union. Companies of militia would precede it, the music of fifes and drums surround it, and children run after it, laughing at the surreal delight.

Of all the ratification processions, Philadelphia's was the grandest. There was not only a ship of state, the Union, but a float in the shape of a great eagle, drawn by six horses bearing a representation of the Constitution framed and fixed on a staff, crowned with the cap of Liberty, the words THE PEOPLE in gold letters on the staff. Even more elaborate was a slow-rolling majestic float called the New Roof, the Constitution being seen, in this case, as a structure under which society took secure shelter. The New Roof of the Constitution stood on a carriage drawn by ten white horses. Ornamented with stars, the dome was supported by thirteen pillars, each representing a state; at the top of the dome was a handsome cupola surmounted by a figure of Plenty, bearing her cornucopia. If you like the quaint charm of that, I remind you that today we speak of the framers of the Constitution, not the writers, which is more exact and realistic and less mythologically adequate.

Behind the New Roof came 450 architects, house carpenters, saw makers and file cutters, just to let people know there was now a roof-building industry available for everyone.

A thirty-foot-long float displayed a carding machine, a spinning machine of eighty spindles, a lace loom and a textile printer. There were military units in this procession, companies of light infantry and cavalry, and there were clergymen of every denomination. There were city officials and schools in their entire enrollments, but more prominent were the members of various trades, each dressed in its working clothes and carrying some display or pulling some float in advertisement of itself—sail makers and ship chandlers, cordwainers, coach builders, sign painters, clock- and watchmakers, fringe and ribbon weavers, bricklayers, tailors, spinning-wheel makers, carvers and guilders, coopers, blacksmiths, potters, wheelwrights, tinplate workers, hatters, skinners, breeches makers, gunsmiths, saddlers, stonecutters, bakers, brewers, barber-surgeons, butchers, tanners, curriers and, I am pleased to say, printers, booksellers and stationers.

So heavily weighted was the great Philadelphia procession with those tradesmen and artisans, it could just as easily have been a labor day parade. The newly self-determined America was showing its strength and pride as a republic of hard work, in contrast to the European domains of privilege and title and their attendant poverty system. The Constitution was America de-Europeanizing itself. A kind of fission was taking place, and now here was a working-class republic, carried on the backs first of its citizen-soldiers dressed in rough brown and sober black, and then on the shoulders of its artisans and skilled workers. That anyway was the symbolic idea, the mythology that almost immediately attached itself to the ratified Constitution. From the very beginning it took on a symbolic character that its writers, worried always that they might never get it ratified, could not have foreseen. We speak of the "miracle at Philadelphia." That same impulse was working then: the celebration of the sacred text, miracles being beyond mere human understanding, a cause for wonder and gratitude—in a word, the supernatural.

The Subtext

Yet it is true also of sacred texts that when they create a spiritual community, they at the same time create a larger community of the excluded. The Philistines are excluded or the pagans or the unwashed.

Even as the Constitution was establishing its sacred self in the general mind, it was still the work, the composition, of writers; and the writers were largely patrician, not working class. They tended to be well educated, wealthy and not without self-interest. The historian Carl Degler says in *Out of Our Past*: "No new social class came to power through the doors of the American Revolution. The men who engineered the revolt were largely members of the colonial ruling class." That holds for the Philadelphia 55. They themselves were aware of the benefits, if not to themselves then to their class, of the provision guaranteeing the debts incurred under the Confederation: the security holders, the creditors of America, stood to make a lot of money; at the same time, the debtors—the free holders, the small farmers—stood to lose everything. It was a practical document in their minds. They did not think of themselves as founding fathers or framers or anything more august than a group of men who held natural stewardship of the public welfare by virtue of their experience and background. They were concerned to establish a free and independent nation, but also a national economic order that would allow them to conduct business peaceably, profitably and in the stable circumstances deriving from a strong central government.

The ideals of political democracy do not always accord with the successful conduct of business. Thus, as conceived in 1787 only the House of Representatives would be elected by popular vote. Senators were to be elected by state legislatures, and the President by an electoral college, meaning men like themselves who would command the votes of their localities. There was the sense in these strictures of a need for checks and balances against popular majorities. Furthermore, to come up with a piece of paper that diverse regional business interests could agree on meant cutting deals. One such deal was between the Northeastern states and the Southern. Importation of slaves would be allowed for twenty more years; in return only a simple majority in Congress would be required to pass navigational commerce acts that the seagoing Atlantic states much wanted. That odious deal appears, in part, in Article Four of the original Constitution. The exactness and precision of statute language in this case is used not to clarify but to euphemize a practice recognizably abhorrent to the writers:

No person held to service or labour in one State under the laws thereof, escaping into another, shall, in consequence of any law or regulation therein, be discharged from such service or labour, but shall be delivered up on claim of the party to whom such service or labour may be due.

There is no mention of the word *slave*, yet a slave in one state became a slave in all. The Virginia delegate, George Mason, to my mind the great underrated hero of the convention, warned his colleagues: "As nations cannot be rewarded or punished in the next world they must in this. By an inevitable chain of causes and effects, Providence punishes national sins by national calamities." If you affect the scriptural voice, he could have been telling them, you had better aspire to enlightenment, or the power of prophecy of your speech will work against you. And so it came to pass. That odious article worked through a historic chain of cause and effect like a powder fuse, until the country blew apart seventy-five years later in civil war. Not until 1865, with the passage of the Thirteenth Amendment, was slavery outlawed in the United States. And the monumental cost in lives, black and white, of that war, and the cost to the black people, the tragedy of their life in the antebellum South, and to American blacks everywhere since then (the state poll taxes that kept black people from voting in the

South were not outlawed until the Twenty-fourth Amendment was ratified, in 1964), shows how potent, how malignly powerful, the futuristic, transhuman Constitution has been where it has been poorly written. What was sacred is profane; there is a kind of blasphemous inversion of the thing.

In this formulation it is the power of the Constitution to amend itself, or, in writers' terms, to accept revision, that shows the delegates at their best. They knew what they had was imperfect, a beginning; Franklin and Washington said as much. Nevertheless, Mason refused to put his name to the constitutional document even after Franklin urged a unanimous presentation to the states, because of the slavery article and also because there was no Bill of Rights—no explicit statutes on the rights of American citizens to free speech and assembly and religious practice, and to speedy trial by jury of defendants in criminal charges; no prohibition against government search and seizure without judicial warrant; no guarantee of a free press and so forth. Alexander Hamilton argued that those things were implicit in the Constitution and did not have to be spelled out, much as people now say the Equal Rights Amendment is unnecessary, but Mason, to his credit, knew that they must be spelled out, which is to say written. Imagine where we would be today if Mason had not held his ground and if the lack of a Bill of Rights had not been taken up as the major concern of the antifederalists, such as Patrick Henry. We would be trusting our rights and liberties to the reading of the Attorney General, who today believes that people who are defendants in criminal trials are probably guilty or they would not be defendants, and who has said that the American Civil Liberties Union is essentially a criminals' lobby. George Mason's amendments, the first ten, were passed on to the states for ratification by the first elected Congress in 1791.

It is true of most of the sacred texts, I think, that a body of additional law usually works itself up around the primary material, and also achieves the force of prophecy. The Torah has its Talmud, and the Koran its *hadith*, and the New Testament its apostolic teachings. In like manner we have our sacred secular humanist amendments. Mythic or sacred time is endless, of course, and it was not until 1920, with the passage of the Nineteenth Amendment, that the women of the United States achieved suffrage. (I am told that this amendment has still not been ratified by the state of Georgia.)

Hermeneutics

Notice at this point a certain change of tone: my song of the miracle of Philadelphia has wobbled a bit; my voice has broken, and here I am speaking in the bitter caw of the critic. Yet there is a kind of inevitability to this. One cannot consider the Constitution of the United States without getting into an argument with it. It is the demand of the sacred text that its adherents not just believe in it but engage to understand its meanings, its values, its revelation. One finds every day in the newspapers the continuing argument with the Constitution, as different elements of society represent their versions of its truth. President Reagan argues with it, Attorney General Edwin Meese argues with it, and so, as a defenseless citizen from a different point of view, do I. And, of course, the Federal judiciary has amended, interpreted and derived law from it. From the days of the great John Marshall on down—way down—to the days of William Rehnquist, the courts have not just worshiped the Constitution; they have read it. Their readings are equivalent to the priestly commentaries that accrue to every sacred text, and the commentaries on the commentaries, and we have 200 years of these as statute and opinion.

It is the nature of the sacred text, speaking from the past to the present and into the future in that scriptural voice that does not explain, embellish itself, provide the source of its ideas or the intentions from which it is written, but which is packed with wild history—the self-authenticating text that is pared of all emotions in the interest of clear and precise law-giving—it is the nature of such a text, paradoxically, to shimmer with ambiguity and to become finally enigmatic, as if it were the ultimate voice of Buddhist self-realization.

And so I find here in my reflections a recapitulation of the debate of American constitutional studies of the past 200 years, in the same manner that ontogeny recapitulates phylogeny. Thus it was in the nineteenth century that historians such as George Bancroft celebrated the revolutionary nature of the Founding Fathers' work, praising them for having conceived of a republic of equal rights under law, constructed from the materials of the European Enlightenment but according to their own pragmatic Yankee design—a federalism of checks and balances that would withstand the worst buffetings of history, namely the Civil War, in the aftermath of which Bancroft happened to be writing.

Then in the early part of the twentieth century, when the worst excesses of American business were coming to light, one historian, Charles Beard, looked at old Treasury records and other documents and discovered enough to assert that the Fathers stood to gain personally from the way they put the thing together, at least their class did; that they were mostly wealthy men and lawyers; and that the celebrated system of checks and balances, rather than insuring a distribution of power and a democratic form of government, in fact could be seen as having been devised to control populist sentiment and prevent a true majoritarian politics from operating in American life at the expense of property rights. Madison had said as much, Beard claimed, in *Federalist* number 10, which he wrote to urge ratification. Beard's economic interpretation of the Constitution has ever since governed scholarly debate. At the end of the Depression a neo-Beardian, Merrill Jensen, looked again at the post-Revolutionary period and came up with a thesis defending the Articles of Confederation as the true legal instrument of the Revolution, which, with modest amendments, could have effected the peace and order of the states with more democracy than a centralist government. In fact, he argued, there was no crisis under the Articles or danger of anarchy, except in the minds of the wealthy men who met in Philadelphia.

But countervailing studies appeared in the 1950s, the era of postwar conservatism, that showed Beard's research to be inadequate, asserting, for instance, that there were as many wealthy men of the framers' class who were against ratification as who were for it, or that men of power and influence tended to react according to the specific needs of their own states and localities, coastal or rural, rather than according to class.

And in the 1960s, the Kennedy years, a new argument appeared describing the Constitutional Convention above all as an exercise of democratic politics, a nationalist reform caucus that was genuinely patriotic, improvisational and always aware that what it did must win popular approval if it was to become the law of the land.

In my citizen's self-instruction I embrace all of those interpretations. I believe all of them. I agree that something unprecedented and noble was created in Philadelphia; but that economic class self-interest was a large part of it; but that it was democratic and improvisational; but that it was, at the same time, something of a coup. I think all of those theories are true, simultaneously.

The 200th Year

And what of constitutional scholarship today, in the Age of Reagan?

Well, my emphasis on text, my use of textual analogy, responds to the work over the past few years of a new generation of legal scholars who have been arguing among themselves as to whether the Constitution can be seen usefully as a kind of literary text, sustaining intense interpretive reading—as a great poem, say—or better perhaps as a form of scripture. I have swiveled to embrace both of those critiques too, but adding, as a professional writer, that when I see the other professions become as obsessively attentive to text as mine is, I suspect it is a sign that we live in an age in which the meanings of words are dissolving, in which the culture of discourse itself seems threatened. That is my view of America under Reagan today: in literary critical terms, I would describe his Administration as deconstructionist.

And so, by way of preservation, text consciousness may have arisen among us, law professors no less than novelists, as in medieval times monks began painstakingly copying the crumbling parchments to preserve them.

All told, it is as if the enigmatic constitutional text cannot be seen through, but, shimmering in ambiguity, dazzles back at each generation in its own times and struggles. It is as if the ambiguity is not in the text but in us, as we struggle in our natures—our consciences with our appetites, our sense of justice with our animal fears and self-interests—just as the Founding Fathers struggled so with their Constitution, providing us with a mirror of ourselves to go on shining, shining back at us through the ages, as the circumstances of our lives change, our costumes change, our general store is transformed into a mile-long twenty-four-hour shopping mall, our trundle carts transmogrify into rockets in space, our country paves over, and our young republic becomes a plated armory of ideological warfare: a mirror for us to see who we are and who we would like to be, the sponsors of private armies of thugs and rapists and murderers, or the last best hope of mankind.

It may be that as a result of World War II and the past forty years of our history we are on the verge, as a nation, of some characterological change that neither the federalists of the convention nor the antifederalists who opposed them could have foreseen or endorsed. We are evolving under *Realpolitik* circumstances into a national military state—with a militarized economy larger than, and growing at the expense of, a consumer economy; a militarized scientific-intellectual establishment; and a bureaucracy of secret paramilitary intelligence agencies—that becomes increasingly self-governing and unlegislated. There may be no news in any of this. What may be news, however, is the extent to which the present Administration has articulated a rationale for this state of being, so that the culture too, both secular and religious, can be seen as beginning to conform to the needs of a national security state. More than any previous Administration this one apotheosizes not law but a carelessness or even contempt of law, as internationally it scorns the World Court and domestically it refuses to enforce Federal civil rights statutes or honor the decrees of judicial review, or gives into private hands the conduct of foreign policy outlawed by the Congress. And more than any previous Administration this one discourses not in reason and argument but in demagogic pieties. Its lack of reverence for law and contempt for language seem to go hand in hand.

By contrast, I call your attention to the great genius of the convention of 1787, which was its community of discourse. The law it designed found character from the means of its designing. Something arose from its deliberations, however contentious, and that was the empowering act of composition given to people who know what words mean and how they must be valued. Nobody told anybody else to love it or leave it; nobody told anybody else to go back where they came from; nobody suggested disagreement was disloyalty; and nobody pulled a gun. Ideas, difficult ideas, were articulated with language and disputed with language and took their final fate, to be passed or rejected, as language. The possibility of man-made law with the authority, the moral imperative, of God's law, inhered in the process of making it.

That is what we celebrate as citizens today. That is what we cherish and honor, a document that gives us the means by which we may fearlessly argue ourselves into clarity as a free and unified people. To me the miracle at Philadelphia was finally the idea of democratic polity, a foot in the door of the new house for all man and womankind. The relentless logic of a Constitution in the name of the people is that a national state exists for their sake, not the other way around. The undeviating logic of a Constitution in the name of the people is that the privilege of life under its domain is equitable, which is to say, universal. That you cannot have democracy only for yourself or your club or your class or your church or your clan or your color or your sex, for then the word doesn't mean what it says. That once you write the prophetic text for a true democracy—as our forefathers did in their draft and as our amending legislators and judiciary have continued to do in their editing of its moral self-contradictions and methodological inadequacies—that once this text is in voice, it cannot be said to be realized on earth until all the relations among the American people, legal relations, property relations, are made just.

And I reflect now, in conclusion, that this is what brought the people into the streets in Philadelphia 200 years ago, those wheelwrights and coach builders and ribbon and fringe weavers: the idea, the belief, the faith that America was unprecedented.

I'd like to think, in this year of bicentennial celebration, that the prevailing image will be of those plain people taking to the streets, those people with only their wit and their skills to lead them through their lives, forming their processions: the wheelwrights and ribbon makers, the railroad porters and coal miners, the garment workers, the steelworkers, the automobile workers, the telephone operators, the air traffic controllers, the farm workers, the computer programmers and, one hopes, the printers, stationers and booksellers too.

II. A LIVING DOCUMENT

EDITOR'S INTRODUCTION

Despite the quasireligious reverence in which the Constitution is held, the political system that it establishes is, like all others, doomed to imperfection. It can never entirely reconcile the competing rights claimed by the disparate groups that make up the citizenry. At best, it holds these rights temporarily in balance, until pressure from one or another source forces their reevaluation and redistribution.

This balancing act has succeeded in holding the nation together for the better part of 200 years. It has had one breakdown, the one that produced the Civil War, after which the balance was restored on terms that have allowed the extension of political and other rights to new classes of citizens. As Nathan Glazer points out in his article "The Constitution and American Diversity," reprinted from *The Public Interest*, the transformation of American society in this century has given rise to an ever more complicated web of conflicting rights, including "individual rights against group rights, group rights against group rights, both individual and group rights against the state, and, most intriguingly, individual and group rights against the right of the state to embody community values in its legislation and action." One of the examples discussed by Glazer—the consequences to American blacks and their neighbors of school busing and other integration efforts—is viewed from another, more partisan, perspective in Diane Camper's "The Quest for Liberty," an article reprinted from *Black Enterprise*.

Camper notes that the Constitution has been criticized for countenancing slavery and for excluding blacks and other people from power. In his careful analysis of the Constitution's phrasing, Robert A. Goldwin, in an article from *Commentary*, explains "Why Blacks, Women & Jews Are Not Mentioned in the Constitution." His conclusion—that "rights are inherent in individuals, not in the groups they belong to; that we are all equals as human beings" under the Constitution—helps to explain why the diversity described by Glazer has been able to flourish so vigorously in the

73

United States despite the long-lasting effects of traditional prejudices. "The Founders," Goldwin writes, "designed a better way to
make sure that no one was left out."

It is this visionary quality of the chief Founders, their ability
to transcend the limitations of their own historical circumstances
and to plan for an imagined society of the future, that commands
the respect of modern-day Americans who are their beneficiaries.
Walter F. Murphy, in his essay "The Constitution and the 14th
Amendment," reprinted from *The Center Magazine*, examines
some of the fundamental issues involved in the conception, formation, and functioning of a constitutional document. The
American Constitution, in his view, incorporates "democratic
and constitutional theory"—a set of assumptions about human
equality and about the legitimacy of governmental authority—as
well as the guiding principles set forth in the Declaration of Independence. The addition, during Reconstruction, of the 13th and
14th Amendments brought the Constitution further under the
dominance of these essential principles.

Radical changes in the Constitution have been rare, but demands for change have been persistent. During the first half of
the 1980s, three amendments were proposed—to authorize
prayer in the public schools, to make abortion illegal, and to require a balanced federal budget—and a movement was launched
to call a new constitutional convention. All three of these amendments met with the obstacles described by Mary Frances Berry in
"How Hard It Is to Change," a *New York Times Magazine* article.
Her article is followed by excerpts from the Senate debate over
the proposed school prayer amendment. Both speakers, Strom
Thurmond and Mark O. Hatfield, agree that prayer in public
schools is permitted by the Constitution; they differ over the
proper form of legislation to achieve it and on how much care
should be taken to avoid infringing on minority rights.

The final selection, "Move Over, James Madison," is a sam-
pling of suggestions from *The New Republic*, some whimsical and
some serious, for amending the Constitution.

THE CONSTITUTION AND AMERICAN DIVERSITY[1]

The celebration of the framing of the American Constitution comes close upon the heels of the celebration of the hundredth anniversary and rededication of the Statue of Liberty. This is, of course, sheer accident: The Statue was originally intended to celebrate the hundredth anniversary of the Declaration of Independence, and it was only the difficulty of raising the money to finish it and erect the pedestal on which it was to stand that delayed its completion ten years, almost in time for it to mark the hundredth anniversary of the other great founding document of the American Republic, the Constitution. And one might well think that if the Statue were to celebrate the Constitution, there would be an interesting clash between what the Constitution says (or rather does not say) and what the Statue has come to symbolize in the popular mind.

The Statue stands for free immigration, the gathering in of the tired, poor, and huddled masses. It stands for American ethnic and racial diversity, as was so insistently drummed into us in the course of the celebrations. Yet on this the Constitution is silent. Regarding racial diversity, it has only those now obsolete provisions on how long the slave trade could continue, on how slaves were to be counted for purposes of electoral representation, and on the exclusion of Indians in determining the basis of electoral representation. Concerning ethnic diversity, it says nothing. The Constitution was framed by "Anglo-Americans" (not a single signer comes from any other ethnic group). It is silent as to immigration, and it was not until 1876 that the Supreme Court ruled that control over immigration was exclusively in the hands of the federal government. That it was expected there would be immigration is indicated in the provisions giving Congress the power to "establish an uniform rule of naturalization," and other provisions requiring that the president be a native citizen, and that members of Congress and the Senate be citizens for a certain number of years. But as to any right to immigration or asylum, or any restriction on the power of Congress to limit immigration by race and ethnicity, it is of course silent.

[1]Reprint of an article by Nathan Glazer, coeditor of *The Public Interest* and professor at the Graduate School of Education, Harvard University. Reprinted with permission of the author from *The Public Interest*, No. 86 (Winter, 1987), pp. 10–22. Copyright © 1987 by National Affairs, Inc.

On religious diversity, we find the provision that no religious test could be set for public office and the pregnant opening phrases of the First Amendment, "Congress shall make no law respecting an establishment of religion, or prohibiting the free exercise thereof," phrases which come before those on freedom of speech, press, or assembly. But as a protection of diversity, one may doubt its (initial) efficacy. Indeed, one school of thought argues that the prohibition of establishment was meant to *protect* the establishments that existed in the states. "At least some evidence exists," writes Laurence Tribe in his authoritative treatise on the Constitution, "that, for the framers, the establishment clause was intended largely to protect state religious establishments from national displacement." A foot-note continues: "Until 1844, New Jersey limited full civil rights to Protestants. Pennsylvania and Maryland required belief in God of public office holders, Maryland until 1961. Connecticut taxed for the support of the Congregational establishment until 1818. The Massachusetts constitution, until 1833, authorized towns to maintain ministers where voluntary contributions were inadequate; New Hampshire did so until the twentieth century."

Diversity before the Court

The Constitution, with the Bill of Rights, may have been well-designed to protect individual rights. But little of the then existing religious, racial, and ethnic diversity of the United States was reflected in it, and no grand plan was laid down for any diversity that might be expected in the future. The diversity that concerned the Framers was that between large and small states; and "diversity" in American constitutional law refers to differences among the laws of the states, not to the diversity of religion, race, and ethnicity. The protection that religious, ethnic, and racial groups needed and sought they found, until after the Civil War, if they found it at all, in the political processes of the states, not in the Constitution, and in the widespread favorable attitude toward free immigration—until the Chinese, that is, were banned in 1882, and restrictionist sentiments led to further limitations on what races and what groups could enter. Blacks, as we know, received no protection under the Constitution until a bloody war led to the addition of the Thirteenth, Fourteenth, and Fifteenth Amendments. Even then a rather strange line of interpretation of the Fourteenth Amendment's "due process" clause meant that it served more as a protection of business than of blacks for sixty years.

Nevertheless, it is on the basis of the key phrases in the Fourteenth Amendment, with their direct imposition of restrictions on the states (to "deprive any person of life, liberty, or property without due process of law" or "deny to any person within its jurisdiction the equal protection of the laws"), that the religious, racial, and ethnic groups of the United States are ensured equal treatment and independence in a vast range of activities—education, religion, philanthropy, political action. And despite a restrictive line of interpretation regarding what limits these provisions imposed on the states, and on how much they protected the blacks, quite early the Supreme Court expanded their protection to other groups. In 1886, it struck down a California law that was applied only to the Chinese, and in 1906 it declared of the Thirteenth Amendment, "Slavery or involuntary servitude of the Chinese, the Italian, the Anglo-Saxon were as much within its compass as slavery or the involuntary servitude of the African." It is not until the 1920s that we find any protection at the federal level for the right of ethnic or religious groups to maintain their differences and distinctiveness through education: in *Meyer* v. *Nebraska* (1923), the Court struck down a Nebraska state law prohibiting the teaching of foreign languages in schools before the eighth grade, and in *Pierce* v. *Society of Sisters* (1925) it struck down an Oregon statute requiring all children to attend public schools. This decision borrows from the Fourteenth Amendment's guarantee of due process, and emphasizes the teacher's and parent's liberty to pursue a vocation and conclude contracts: The infamous "substantive due process" that had been used to strike down so much social legislation here served to protect a key right of ethnic and religious groups.

This cautious use of the Fourteenth Amendment was abandoned in the postwar period, and particularly since the *Brown* decision on the segregation of blacks in public schools in 1954. But no obvious resting place can be discerned in the expansion of the protection of religion, racial, and ethnic diversity in a country of enormous diversity. The picture presented by the constitutional protection of diversity today is no longer one of rights inadequately and insufficiently established but one rather of rights clashing with each other: individual rights against group rights, group rights against group rights, both individual and group rights against the state, and, most intriguingly, individual and group rights against the right of the state to embody community values in its legislation and action.

As a first cut at the problems that have arisen, it is necessary to understand that the provisions of the Constitution we have referred to, and almost all of the legislation that implements them, defend *individual* rights. This is true of the clauses dealing with the free exercise of religion, the nonestablishment of religion, religious tests for office, the guarantee of due process, and the equal protection of the laws. These are all matters of the defense of an individual's claim: Every case sets an individual against an agent of government or a level of government. The rights that are protected may indeed be hardly connected with the life of any group—religious, ethnic, or racial. They may be rights to individual conscience unconnected to any group belief or loyalty or culture: the right to be an atheist, and yet hold public office; the right to maintain a personal opposition to war, and not be subject to the draft.

Despite the language that frames them, however, all these clauses refer, by implication, to the rights of groups, religious, racial, and ethnic. Similarly, the rights that follow the free exercise and establishment clauses in the First Amendment (Congress may also not make a law "abridging the freedom of speech, or of the press; or the right of the people peaceably to assemble, and to petition the government for a redress of grievances") are individual rights. But clearly groups lay claim to them (particularly political groups), and they serve to protect group freedoms. The connection between individual rights and group rights, however, is complex: The interests of the group and of the individuals that make it up are not identical, and conflict between them is indeed possible. Religious, racial, ethnic, and political groups (parties, movements) in the United States are voluntary, with no power of state action. They may find it necessary on occasion to defend themselves against the state. But at the same time the individuals within them, despite their voluntary character, may find it necessary to defend themselves against the group.

Individuals, Groups, and the State

The rights of an individual may thus also be threatened by one of those diverse groups whose freedom of action we want to preserve in our diverse society. Religious groups have no state power, but they have the power that comes from the ownership of property, the strength of organization, the ability to mold the opinions and the actions of adherents. In all these ways, they inevitably have the power to act against the interests of individuals. The civil liberties and civil rights we have discussed in a somewhat amalgamated fashion may thus stand against each other. Individual conscience may stand against group power—and group conscience.

One of the major cases setting the limits of state power against the group also raises the question of group power over the individual. It arises, as so many cases involving group rights and limits do, in the context of education. In *Wisconsin* v. *Yoder* (1972), the question was raised whether the state of Wisconsin could require the children of members of the Old Order Amish religion and the Conservative Amish Mennonite religion to attend school until the age of sixteen, as state law required. The issue was not whether they would have to attend a public school—that was settled by *Pierce* v. *Society of Sisters* in 1925. But they were required to have schooling of some kind. Parents of children not in school were tried and convicted of violating the compulsory-attendance law and fined. They argued in their defense that under the "free exercise of religion" clause of the First Amendment, incorporated into the Fourteenth, they had the right to refuse to send their children to high school beyond the age of fourteen or fifteen. They believed that their children's attendance at high school, public or private, "was contrary to the Amish religion and way of life." They believed that by sending their children to high school, they would not only expose themselves to the censure of the church community, but, as found by the county court, "endanger their own salvation and that of their children."* The Supreme Court upheld their right to keep their children out of school.

But what of the rights of the children? Justice Douglas in dissent argued they would have to be taken into account: "If the parents in this case are allowed a religious exemption, the inevitable effect is to impose the parents' notion of religious duty upon their

Wisconsin v. *Yoder*, 406 U.S. 205 (1972).

children. Where the child is mature enough to express potentially conflicting desires, it would be an invasion of the child's rights to permit such an imposition without canvassing his views. . . . Religion is an individual experience."

The American voice and one American dilemma are heard in that last sentence: "Religion is an individual experience." Yes, but religion is even more a group experience. The *Yoder* case brings up the issue of group versus individual rights in an exceptional situation, that of a small religious group whose family life is exemplary and highly admired. The situation arises in other contexts, where the group does not enjoy such high public repute, as in the many cases where parents whose children have been, as they would put it, "captured" by new sects that separate them from their families, forcibly take possession of them in an effort to change their views. The United States remains a country of continual group creation, particularly in the sphere of religion. It has spawned hundreds of sects, some of which have been strong and respectable. The free exercise of religion does not give them unlimited rights—the Supreme Court stood with Congress in denying the Mormons the right to polygamy under the free exercise clause, and polygamy was stamped out by force.

The Clash over Rights

As American diversity expands, under the impact of six hundred thousand immigrants a year, primarily from Asia and Latin America, issues in which individual rights clash with the maintenance of group authority—and thus with the opportunity to maintain "diversity"—will undoubtedly become more complex. Consider the implications of an increase, for example, in the Muslim population (fortunately for problems of diversity, this is only a very small part of recent immigration). The problem here is less one of polygamy—I am not aware whether it has created conflicts with civil law in the United Kingdom, France, and Germany, where Muslims are more numerous than in the United States—than one of the rights of women and female children. American law now, in its expansion of the rights of women, has made it difficult to maintain single-sex schools. Indeed, in the public-sector schools, this is all but impossible. What then if Muslims raise the same claims as the Old Order Amish in order to protect their female children?

But we need not go to such exotic possibilities to see the clash between group rights and individual rights, state versus group, and group versus group exhibited. The individual rights of the Constitution envisage as the chief danger an abstract state enforcing uniformity on diverse individuals (or, by extension, as we have seen, on groups and peoples). But the state is restrained by constitutional protections from interfering with a community, racial, religious, or ethnic group that participates in a certain way of life, holds certain beliefs, or engages in some organizational activity. The state, though, in its specific manifestation also embodies, to some degree, such a community. A school district, a village, a town, even a city, may not be marked by the diversity common to the United States in general. Its homogeneity may be ethnic or religious or racial. When it wishes to express or symbolize, through public action, a religious or group practice or belief, another kind of conflict between community and individual—or community and community—is involved. One community has the power to pass laws, to compel uniform behavior. An individual or another community resists this. The present thrust of constitutional law strongly limits the community acting as the state. It may not require (nor may an individual school district, school, or teacher) a prayer, or the reading of the Bible, or the placing of the Ten Commandments on the school walls. To those who want to do these things, this is the "free exercise" of religion guaranteed by the First Amendment, or perhaps the state simply upholding a conventional and universal morality. To those who oppose them, they are examples of the "establishment of religion" prohibited by the same amendment.

These actions are seen by those who want them returned to the schools as of the same order in helping to raise responsible and dutiful children as the actions of the Amish in withdrawing their children from the secular and godless and hedonistic high school. The latter is protected—this is the action of a voluntary community engaged in "free exercise." The former is prohibited—it is "establishment." Even when the action is voluntary (as in the case of a moment of silence for "meditation or voluntary prayer"), the law authorizing it has been held unconstitutional under the establishment clause. There is an answer to those who wish to exercise the practice of their community in the school—withdrawal of their children from the public school and placing them in a private religious school, where prayer is not only permitted, but, if they so wish, prescribed. But there is a cost to such an action, a cost to the "free exercise" of religion, which in other contexts may not be imposed.

Much of the most fiercely disputed constitutional litigation in the United States today revolves around this question of what a community of religion, ethnicity, and race may do in the way of protecting its values and its way of life when that is attempted through the medium of state action. American diversity and American constitutional protection make it very difficult to do this. For example, how far may a community go in restricting the sale of pornography, the exhibition of pornographic movies, and the like? To some extent they fall under the protection of the First Amendment. But to an extent far greater than communities, as represented in municipalities and other local governments, would like to allow. How much respect may a community grant its churches? May it reach the point of allowing a church a veto over the right to sell liquor in its neighborhood? The state of Massachusetts granted this right; the Supreme Court said no. Some major American religions oppose the sale of alcohol and public drinking: Combined with other reformers they were able, remarkably, to pass the Eighteenth Amendment to the Constitution prohibiting the making or selling of "intoxicating liquors," in 1920. Were they imposing their religious views on the American people ("establishment")? Were they, by placing restrictions on the religious practices of Jews and Catholics, limiting "free exercise"? These issues were constitutionally moot because Prohibition was embodied in an amendment to the Constitution itself. It created such problems that it was finally repealed by yet another amendment (the Twenty-first in 1933), but in this amendment full powers to control the transportation and importation of "intoxicating liquors" remained with the states, and thus we have the crazy-quilt of regulation from state to state, and from community to community.

For the past ten years or so we have seen a strong revival of the "fundamentalist" or evangelical trend in American religion, embodied principally in Southern Baptism, but reaching in varying degrees into most of the major Protestant denominations. In the 1920s, two key demands of this tendency were that evolution not be taught in schools in opposition to the Biblical account of creation, and that liquor be prohibited. They lost on both counts, and fundamentalism was subsequently considered a backwater of

American life that would not become nationally significant again. It has, basing itself now on new issues, issues in large measure created by a liberal and progressive trend in constitutional interpretation which defends the rights of individuals against locally dominant groups that can implement their view through state and local legislation. The prohibition of school prayer, of restrictions on abortion, of support to private schools (since they are mostly religious, this would violate the Establishment Clause), the defense of student rights against school-imposed discipline, the defense of "sexual preference" (the rights of homosexuals and lesbians) all fall within this general category. As a result, a true *kulturkampf* now rages in the United States, and the Constitution offers no guidance as to how it may be resolved.

Diversity and Discrimination

The issue of the protection of diversity is also raised by a very different set of conflicts pitting individual rights against group rights, those dealing with the attempt to overcome discrimination against blacks (and some other minority groups) through constitutional and legal prohibition of discrimination. The problem here is not so much the protection of a specific culture or religion. A regime of discrimination and prejudice against blacks and Asians coexisted very nicely with the maintenance by these groups of associations, churches, language schools, or whatever else they wished. Indeed, the complaint of blacks was that through segregation they had rather more of their own schools and churches than they wished: They wanted to overcome discrimination and prejudice so as to enter the mainstream of American life. This was done by means of constitutional interpretation and laws against discrimination, again phrased as the defense of individuals without regard to color, race, or national origin. That is the way the Constitution is interpreted ("equal protection of the laws"), that is the way the legislation is written. Once again, trying to deal with prejudice and discrimination against groups, we nevertheless refer to no group (except in rare cases) but defend *individuals*. The rights in question are to education in an unsegregated and integrated setting, to jobs and promotions and rental and purchase of housing and access to public facilities without discrimination on grounds of race, color, or national origin. But all this has implications for ethnic and racial diversity.

Consider, for example, the first consequence of effective integration of the segregated black schools of the South. Black principals and administrators and teachers were dismissed, found to be in "excess," as two different school systems were merged into one. The capacity (I am not sure it was ever much exercised) to create an education in some way reflecting or directed to the segregated group disappeared. One form of "diversity" declined. If blacks had been more interested or effective in entering white churches, another key protection of diversity for the black group, the black church, would have declined.

But other groups—and their ability to maintain their diversity—were also affected. The fierce conflicts that developed over school busing were largely over diversity, though they were not often presented, in the constitutional or scholarly or even popular literature, as a conflict of this type. The key *Brown* decision declared segregation by race in education unconstitutional, as denying the equal protection of the laws. But what was the right that was granted? Was it the right to admission to any school without racial restriction, or was it the right to an educational setting with a majority of the majority race and a more than token number of persons of one's own race? The argument for the latter was that if very few persons of the protected race chose a given school setting, it was demonstration that in effect segregated schooling continued (through intimidation or otherwise), and no further examination was required judicially as to why. And if too few members of the majority race were present, that was also a demonstration that segregation persisted. Under such circumstances, children could be assigned to school by race so that segregation was in fact overcome. Other arguments could have been added to this key one, but the Supreme Court did not go into any educational reasons why certain proportions of a minority group and a majority group were necessary in each school (to overcome their self-consciousness as a minority, to provide them with the power to demand better education, etc.).

Under Supreme Court decisions, assignment to schools by race for minority and majority children became common. Children content with their schools were assigned by race to other schools to create a balance in each school. These children could be from communities which desired their children to remain close to their homes, and which preferred them to be educated among those of their own group. Thus, the Chinese children and

Mexican-American children of San Francisco were bused in order to provide an integrated setting for blacks. These communities were affected in their opportunity to maintain certain close ties among themselves, to create conditions in which they would have a better chance of surviving as distinct communities. The latter rights are not defended by the Constitution, yet if we are sympathetic to community maintenance, we cannot be indifferent to the impact of sending a community's children to schools that are selected simply so that their group can provide a majority in that school for black children.

While these measures were developed primarily to implement the rights of blacks, many blacks doubted that this kind of dispersion was what they wanted for the education of their children. Indeed, some looked back nostalgically at some of the schools blacks had maintained during the period of segregation, in part because they *were* black community institutions.

This issue of community and its relationship to school integration could be raised in a different way. Communities differ in values, orientation, behavior. It may well be right that the primary objective in school assignment should be to mix communities so all should learn about each other. But if some of these differences relate to the use of language, or sexual attitudes, or religious attitudes, the parents in some communities will wish to protect their children and reject homogenization. Or they may simply reject closeness to blacks, and thus create private schools ("segregation academies") in response to judicial desegregation decisions. Sometimes it is perfectly clear that the only reason such schools have been established is because of racial objections to going to school with blacks; in other cases, motives are more mixed and may indeed be predominantly religious or moral, such as the fact that schools cannot provide religion, or prescribe modest dress rules, or impose a traditional discipline in the schools. These schools are often established directly by churches and meet on church property. Are these schools entitled to tax exemption as schools? Or does the fact that they have no or few black children demonstrate they are racially segregated and should not be eligible for tax exemption?

Containing the Conflict

There is no question that conservative communities in the United States now feel threatened as a result of the expansion of civil rights and civil liberties. And that liberal communities now feel threatened by the mobilization of the traditionalists. On one side, the expansion of rights may be seen as giving the greatest possible freedom to the individual—and in that freedom individuals can create the subcommunities they desire, whether traditional or radical, conventional or unconventional. On the other side, this expansion may be seen as the arrogant extension of values and behavior that threaten traditional communities so that they cannot protect their schools and their neighborhoods from intrusions they find offensive, and that prevent them from providing the environment they desire for their children. This was the claim *Yoder* made in refusing to comply with the compulsory attendance laws of the state of Wisconsin; it is a claim now raised by that very large section of the American population that adheres to traditional values. As a result, other individuals and communities, characterized by liberal and progressive values, feel that they are threatened in their lifestyles. The conflict breaks out everywhere: when New York City insists that its institutions that provide social services must not discriminate against homosexuals—and the Catholic Church, which provides such services, says its religion cannot allow it to accept this prohibition; when communities and states seek all sorts of means to get around the Supreme Court's constitutionalization of abortion; when communities and neighborhoods seek ways to keep "adult theaters" out, or books with explicit sexual language from their school libraries. And the list can be extended.

American diversity today is well protected. Association on religious, racial, and ethnic bases flourishes widely, with the protection of the Constitution. Individual choice to express this diversity raises few problems: At the margin, law can be invoked against extreme and dangerous claims made on grounds of race, religion, or ethnicity, but this is rare. But diversity is a matter of more than individual choice. It is a matter of community, which seeks for some type of control, whether voluntary or state, to defend its values, its distinctiveness, its ideals. On such questions, where the individual may be oppressed by the group, or the group may use state power to try to oppress others, there are no simple answers. A generally divided Supreme Court is the best we can do in setting legal norms. The system works, and it has means of change when many think it is not working—as we see in present movements to amend the Constitution to make English the national language, return control of abortion to the states, or remove the Supreme Court from making decisions on school prayer.

Where diversity prevails, there will always be conflict. The hard question is how it may be held within the bounds of law and the Constitution, and how its resolutions, inevitably temporary, may find general acceptance.

THE QUEST FOR LIBERTY[2]

[The Constitution of the United States was] intended to endure for ages to come, and consequently, to be adapted to the various crises of human affairs. To have prescribed the means by which government should, in all future time, execute its powers, would have been to change, entirely, the character of the instrument, and give it the properties of a legal code. It would have been an unwise attempt to provide, by immutable rules, for exigencies which, if foreseen at all, must have been seen dimly, and which can best be provided for as they occur.

CHIEF JUSTICE JOHN MARSHALL

These words uttered in 1819 by the venerable chief justice of the Supreme Court explain why the Constitution is revered by so many Americans. It has been the vital thread woven throughout the fabric of American democracy for 200 years, and its durability will be tested for centuries to come.

The key to the Constitution's success is its flexibility. And the evolution of its texture and meaning has been no less important to blacks than to other Americans. In fact, the recognition of the rights of blacks, which gradually evolved from counting each slave as three-fifths of a person who had no human rights to granting blacks full rights of citizenship, equal protection under the laws and the right to vote, attests to the Constitution's remarkable adaptability. From the adoption of civil rights legislation to Rev. Jesse Jackson's historic run for the presidency, the document has served as a guide for blacks trying to gain a foothold in the American mainstream.

[2]Reprint of an article by Diane Camper. *Black Enterprise.* 17:53–6. Jl. '87. Copyright © July 1987, The Earl G. Graves Publishing Co., Inc., 130 Fifth Avenue, New York, NY 10011. All rights reserved.

But such sweeping societal changes depend largely on government—especially the nine jurists who sit on the Supreme Court, each holding his or her own political ideology and philosophy of law. And, on this anniversary of the grand document, scholars and legal experts are raising some serious questions about the Constitution. Foremost among these is the ongoing dispute over the proper function of such a document in a democratic society. Should the Constitution reflect the thoughts of its original authors or be open to interpretation? Some argue that constant reinterpretation has already distorted its original meaning, while others see such changes as being vital to its survival.

The Raging Debate

The debate over the Constitution continues to rage among the nation's top jurists and attorneys. Justice Thurgood Marshall, the only black to sit on the high court, criticized the architects of the Constitution for devising a document that "sacrificed moral principles for self-interest."

In a speech delivered to the San Francisco Patent and Trademark Law Association in May, the 78-year-old justice asserted: "I do not believe that the meaning of the Constitution was forever 'fixed' at the Philadelphia Convention nor do I find the wisdom, foresight and sense of justice exhibited by the Framers particularly profound. To the contrary, the government was defective from the start, requiring several amendments, a civil war and momentous social transformation to attain the system of constitutional government and its respect for the individual freedoms and human rights we hold as fundamental today."

Attorney General Edwin Meese takes the "strict constructionist" view that the Supreme Court should adhere to the original intent of the Constitution. Speaking before the American Bar Association two years ago, Meese said, "It is [the Reagan Administration's] belief that only the sense in which the Constitution was accepted and ratified by the nation and only the sense in which laws were drafted and passed provide a solid foundation for adjudication. Any other standard suffers the defect of pouring new meaning into old words."

In a rare rebuttal from a sitting member of the high court, Associate Justice William J. Brennan, Jr. maintained that Meese's view "feigns self-effacing deference to the specific judgments [of the founding fathers]. But, in truth, it is little more than arrogance cloaked as humility." It was supercilious, he explained, for the attorney general to pretend that "from our vantage point we can gauge accurately the intent of the framers [in regard] to specific, contemporary questions."

Justice Brennan makes the same point opined by Chief Justice John Marshall in the early nineteenth century. The framers couldn't have possibly anticipated constitutional cases involving contraception, abortion, affirmative action or the implementation of and resistance to court-ordered busing.

Arguments regarding constitutional interpretation continue to be rooted in political debate and questions of national policy. Those who favor an expansive interpretation of the Constitution like that proposed by Justice Thurgood Marshall tend to be liberal, while conservatives are generally strict constructionists like Meese who advocate a more limited reading of the document.

The Implications for Blacks

For blacks, the implications of this debate reflect the extent to which the Constitution can be made to recognize what Justice Brennan calls "the claims of the minority to rights against the majority." He sees judges being caught up in the same "seething, roaring conflict" over minority rights as those faced by society at large. Brennan raises a critical question in the midst of this fray: "Will the new commitment, begun most dramatically in 1954, to enforce fundamental and equal rights for all be once again reduced to a 'feeble promise' of maybe, sometimes and only in some respects?" The reference, of course, is to the landmark decision in *Brown* v. *Board of Education* and its promise of equal treatment for black Americans.

The discussion of equal rights for minorities, however, has been broadened to include such issues as poverty and justice, which some constitutional scholars argue should be the primary interpretative thrusts in the future. After all, the preamble to the Constitution vows to "promote the general welfare" and the Declaration of Independence states that among citizens' inalienable rights are "life, liberty and the pursuit of happiness."

In a recent article in the *Columbia Law Review*, Charles Black, Sterling professor of law at Yale University, argues that economic rights have a constitutional basis. He recently wrote in the

Columbia Law Review: "[Poverty] is the commonest, grimmest, stubbornest obstacle we know to the pursuit of happiness. The right to the pursuit of happiness is the right to be in a situation where that pursuit has some reasonable and continually refreshed chance of attaining its goal. . . . The possession of a decent material basis of life is an indispensable condition . . . to this pursuit." This is by no means a new concept. In 1963, Martin Luther King, Jr. proposed that the federal government adopt a "Bill of Rights for the Disadvantaged" to protect and eventually uplift poor Americans.

These issues hold particular importance for black Americans, one-third of whom subsist below the poverty line. And as the nation heads toward the twenty-first century, blacks will have to continue to contend with barriers of race and class.

The Question of Race and Class

How can the Constitution help blacks free themselves from the morass of poverty and class? Does the Constitution establish an implicit or explicit right to a good job, a decent home or adequate health care?

The Supreme Court has already had an impact on poverty through its rulings on school desegregation, voting rights and affirmative action. Thousands of black children have been exposed to better educational opportunities during the past 25 years. Black Americans have gained greater political autonomy by exercising their right to vote, and affirmative action programs have increased employment opportunities for black workers. Eventually, this ability to make political and economic choices can free blacks from poverty's grip.

In order for this to happen, however, the federal government must deliver on its promise to give *all* citizens an equal opportunity to participate in all facets of society. Affirmative action has been one of the key instruments used by black Americans to achieve this lofty goal. Many of the affirmative action rulings rendered by the Supreme Court have involved the interpretation of Title VII of the 1964 Civil Rights Act. But in constitutional cases the Court has recognized that while racial classifications deserve the highest level of scrutiny, the government has the right to take actions that are not racially neutral in order to overcome decades of discrimination.

Inconsistent Rulings

But the recent rulings of the Supreme Court regarding affirmative action have not been consistent. For example, last February in *U.S.* v. *Paradise*, the court ruled that the use of a racial quota system to promote blacks in the Alabama state trooper force to remedy past discriminatory acts was constitutional. And, last March in *Johnson* v. *Transportation Agency*, the body maintained that public and private employers may voluntarily implement affirmative action plans to correct sex and race discrimination. Just four years ago, however, in *Firefighter* v. *Stotts* the Supreme Court ruled that an affirmative action plan could not be given priority over a seniority system in the event of massive layoffs. The decision has even more serious implications today given the number of major corporations that are downsizing. And since blacks are often among the last round of employees hired by these companies, they will be the first to be fired when top management makes staff cuts.

The Court has been even more chary in other areas that can impact on the economic well-being of black Americans. It has refused to recognize as "suspect" under the Fourteenth Amendment distinctions based on economic status, though it has attempted to ensure that the poor receive some level of due process. Due to such thinking, efforts to ensure decent housing and health care may fare better in the legislature.

Traditionally, education has been a major factor in overturning generational poverty, and many scholars believe that the court should establish a constitutional right to education. In fact, the Supreme Court has noted that an informed electorate is essential to the survival of democracy. In *Brown* v. *Board of Education*, the court questioned whether "any child may reasonably be expected to succeed in life if he is denied the opportunity of an education." But thus far the body has refused to declare that education is a fundamental right that deserves a heightened level of judicial scrutiny.

In a 1973 case, *San Antonio School District* v. *Rodriguez*, the court refused to rule that a plan by the state of Texas to fund school districts based on property taxes was unconstitutional because it put poorer districts at a disadvantage. The majority of the justices concluded that the disadvantaged students still received an adequate education. And the court recently refused to hear a case involving the Norfolk, Va., school board's decision to eliminate crosstown busing of elementary school children. As a result, approximately 5,000 black children out of the city's total school population of 20,000 will now attend virtually all-black schools.

Although the court has stated that children of illegal aliens should not be deprived of a quality education, it has yet to declare that every citizen has a right to a minimal education. Philip Kurland, professor of constitutional law at the University of Chicago, recently argued that an adequate and appropriate education is essential to the "privileges and immunities" of citizenship as guaranteed by the Fourteenth Amendment. And Charles Black suggests that the right to an adequate education may be derived from the little-used Ninth Amendment, which protects those unenumerated rights "retained by the people."

Future Interpretations

Under Chief Justice William Rehnquist, the Supreme Court can be expected to chart a generally conservative course. But even though the Court's conservative wing has been buoyed recently by the addition of Justice Antonin Scalia, its moderate middle, consisting of Justice Byron White, Lewis Powell, Jr., Sandra Day O'Connor, Harry Blackmun and John Paul Stevens, remains intact.* Justices Brennan and Marshall, while still the body's most liberal members, are also its oldest. However, if President Reagan has the opportunity to appoint another justice, or if another Republican wins the presidency in 1988, the court will probably lose its balance and shift to the right.

But all constitutional issues will not be determined solely by the judicial branch of government. The Constitution binds all levels of government; the Congress must continue to develop legislation, while the executive branch must enforce the laws of the land. In recent years, civil rights activists, led by Jesse Jackson, have been seeking the vigorous enforcement of the 1965 Voting Rights Act. Although such discriminatory tactics as poll taxes, property taxes and literacy tests were abolished more than 20 years ago by the Supreme Court, scores of minorities still remain disenfranchised. During his 1984 presidential campaign, Jackson asserted that "political parity can only be gained if gerrymander-

*Lewis Powell, Jr., left the Court in the summer of 1987.

ing, dual registration requirements, harassment and other practices that discourage voter participation are eliminated." Black political and civil rights leaders will carry this debate into the 1988 presidential and congressional elections.

How the Constitution will evolve in the future depends both on how it is interpreted by the Supreme Court and on the actions of the President and the Congress. Government is supposed to reflect the will of the people. In coming years black Americans must continue to voice their concerns and participate in reinforcing the egalitarian principles that are boldly declared in the Constitution.

WHY BLACKS, WOMEN & JEWS ARE NOT MENTIONED IN THE CONSTITUTION[3]

The bicentennial we celebrate this year honors the Constitution written in 1787, that is, the original, unamended Constitution. Some well-meaning citizens have denounced celebrating or even praising that Constitution. They contend that its many severe defects should be considered a matter of national shame. For example, lacking the Thirteenth Amendment, the original Constitution permitted slavery to continue; lacking the Nineteenth Amendment, it did not secure the right of women to vote; and, lacking the First Amendment, it provided no protection for religious freedom, not to mention other rights. Why, they ask, should we celebrate a constitution that treated blacks as less than human, that left women out, and that did not combat religious intolerance?

These charges would be distressing if true, but fortunately they are false. They stem from a misreading of the document, a misreading that comes from not appreciating the importance of knowing how to read the original Constitution on subjects it does not mention.

Why bother with subjects not mentioned? Because, as a matter of fact, we have no choice. The list of unusually important

[3]Reprint of an article by Robert A. Goldwin, director of constitutional studies at the American Enterprise Institute. *Commentary.* 83:28-33. My. '87. Copyright © 1987 by Robert A. Goldwin.

subjects the Constitution does not mention is very long. The fact that they have not been mentioned has not prevented cases and controversies from arising, nor has it relieved courts and legislatures of the duty of determining what is constitutional with regard to them. The words "education" and "school," for example, do not occur in the Constitution, but even so the courts have been busy for decades deciding school controversies. There is no mention of labor unions, corporations, political parties, the air force, radio and television broadcasting, telecommunications, and so on, but the courts deliberate constitutional controversies on these subjects all the time. The list of subjects not mentioned in the text of the Constitution also includes words like "abortion," "contraceptives," and "sodomy," and phrases like "right to privacy," "substantive due process," and the "high wall separating church and state"—all matters on which the Supreme Court has pronounced.

The inescapable fact is that many subjects not mentioned in the Constitution must be interpreted, unavoidably, by anyone for whom the meaning of the Constitution is important. My argument is that there are valuable lessons to be learned about how we are constituted as a nation, and what in the original Constitution is worth celebrating, by devoting serious attention to subjects not mentioned in it. For that purpose, I propose close attention to three such subjects—blacks, women, and Jews.

Blacks

What to do about black slavery was a major concern in the Constitutional Convention; it was discussed at length in the debates, with frequent direct reference to both slavery and race. But neither term was mentioned when it came to the writing. No words indicating race or color, black or white, occur in the text of the Constitution, and neither do the words "slave" or "slavery." Circumlocutions are used in the text to avoid the use of any form of the word "slave"; for example, "person held to service or labor," and "such persons as any of the States now existing shall think proper to admit."

In fact, the word "slavery" entered the Constitution for the first time, after the Civil War, in the Thirteenth Amendment, which thereafter prohibited slavery anywhere in the United States. The words "race" and "color" were first used in the Fifteenth Amendment for the purpose of securing the right of all citizens to vote. The words "black" and "white" have never been part of the Constitution.

What difference does it make, one may well ask, that the words were not used, if the ugly fact is that black slavery existed and was given constitutional status? Consider, for example, perhaps the most notorious and, I would contend, the most misunderstood constitutional provision relating to black slavery, the famous "three-fifths clause."

As Benjamin Hooks, executive director of the National Association for the Advancement of Colored People, put it recently in criticism of the original Constitution: "Article I, section 2, clause 3 of the Constitution starts off with a quota: three-fifths. That is what black folks were in that original Constitution." Hooks is not alone in this view. The historian John Hope Franklin has written of this same clause that the Founders "degraded the human spirit by equating five black men with three white men"; and the constitutional-law professor Lino Graglia contends that the provision "that a slave was to be counted as three-fifths of a free person for purposes of representation" shows "how little the Constitution had to do with aspirations for brotherhood or human dignity."

These three agree in expressing the widely-held view of this clause that, for the Founders, blacks were less than human, somehow or other only a fraction of a human being. The constitutional clause they are referring to reads as follows:

Representatives and direct taxes shall be apportioned among the several States . . . according to their respective numbers, which shall be determined by adding to the whole number of free persons, including those bound to service for a term of years, and excluding Indians not taxed, three-fifths of all other persons.

In short, count all of the free persons and indentured servants, do not count the Indians, and then add three-fifths of the slaves. The question is, what, if anything, does that provision tell us about what the Founders thought about slavery and about blacks as blacks and as human beings?

James Madison said, in the convention, that slavery was the central problem. Southern delegates emphasized that there was no chance of union including the South without accepting the long-established existence of slavery in the slave-holding states. But slavery was a flat contradiction of the principles of the Declaration of Independence, the principles that are the bedrock foundation of the Constitution—the primacy of the rights of individuals, their equality with respect to their rights, and the consequence that the consent of the governed is the only legitimate source of political power. Almost all the delegates were fully aware that slavery profoundly contradicted these principles and therefore had no proper place in the Constitution.

If, on the one hand, the continuation of slavery was unavoidable, and, on the other hand, it was a contradiction of the most fundamental principles of the Constitution the delegates wanted and thought necessary, what could principled anti-slavery delegates do? One effective and consistent thing they could do was try to make the political base of slavery as weak as possible, to diminish its influence and improve the chances of eradicating it sometime in the future.

The struggle that took place in the convention was between Southern delegates trying to strengthen the constitutional supports for slavery and Northern delegates trying to weaken them. That issue—the initial and subsequent political strength of slavery—was in contention on the question of representation in the House of Representatives. It was agreed that every state, regardless of size, would have two Senators. But the number of representatives from any state would be apportioned according to its population, and that raised the question of whom to include in the count.

Slave-state delegates were in favor of including every slave, just as they would any other inhabitant. Madison's notes indicate that the delegates from South Carolina "insisted that blacks be included in the rule of representation, equally with the Whites."

On the other side, delegates from the non-slave states were opposed to counting the slaves, because it would give the South more votes and because it made a mockery of the principle of representation to count persons who had no influence whatsoever on the lawmaking process and who therefore were not "represented" in the legislature in any meaningful sense of the word. Counting the slaves for purposes of representation would also give the slave states an incentive to increase their slave population instead of decreasing it. In short, considering the chief purpose of this clause in the Constitution, it is obvious that an anti-slavery delegate would not want to count the slaves at all.

In the end, two things were done. First, it was agreed to use the census for two opposed purposes: representation and direct taxation. As the count of persons went up in any state, seats in Congress and direct taxes to be paid went up as well; as the count of persons went down, both the number of Congressmen and the direct taxes to be paid went down. Combining these two, and thereby establishing opposing incentives, seems clearly intended to provide a restraint on a state's either getting too much representation or avoiding paying a fair share of direct taxes. The additional compromise was that three-fifths of the slaves would be included in the population count, as the alternative to including all or none.

If none of the slaves had been included, as Northern delegates wanted, the slave states would have had only 41 percent of seats in the House. If all of the slaves had been included, as Southerners wanted, the slave states would have had 50 percent of the seats. By agreeing to include three-fifths, the slave states ended up with 47 percent—not negligible, but still a minority likely to be outvoted on slavery issues.

However the slavery provisions look to us today, they had to be explained to concerned citizens in the South as well as the North. Charles Pinckney reported to the South Carolina ratifying convention that he thought they had "made the best terms for the security of [slavery] it was in our power to make. We would have made better if we could, but on the whole, I do not think them bad." Northern delegates were, at the same time, saying the opposite in a very similar fashion. James Wilson reported to the Pennsylvania ratifying convention that he thought they had succeeded in "laying the foundation for banishing slavery out of this country," but he regretted that "the period is more distant than I could wish."

In brief, both North and South, in trying to weaken or strengthen slavery, had sought more and gotten less than each had wanted, but for the sake of union had accepted a result that was "not bad."

The struggle between pro-slavery and anti-slavery forces for control of Congress, begun in the Constitutional Convention and continued relentlessly for more than seventy years thereafter, was the major cause of the Civil War, and persisted long after that war and the constitutional amendments that followed it had ended slavery.

But to understand what the original Constitution had to say about blacks, the point is that the "three-fifths clause" had nothing at all to do with measuring the human worth of blacks. *Northern* delegates did not want black slaves included, not because they thought them unworthy of being counted, but because they wanted to weaken the slaveholding power in Congress. *Southern* delegates wanted every slave to count "equally with the Whites," not because they wanted to proclaim that black slaves were human beings on an equal footing with free white persons, but because they wanted to increase the pro-slavery voting power in Congress. The humanity of blacks was not the subject of the three-fifths clause; voting power in Congress was the subject.

Thus, the three-fifths clause is irrelevant to the question of what the Founders thought of the slaves as human beings. What is relevant are two indisputable facts: in the original Constitution there is no mention of color, race, or slavery, and nowhere in it are slaves called anything but "persons."

There is nothing particularly new in the point that the original Constitution does not mention slavery. Luther Martin, a Maryland delegate to the Constitutional Convention who opposed ratification, explained to the Maryland legislature in 1787 that the authors of the Constitution did not use the word slave because they "anxiously sought to avoid the admission of expressions which might be odious in the ears of Americans." And Frederick Douglass, the great black leader and orator, commented on this silence in 1852, arguing against the "slander" on the memory of the Founders that the original Constitution was pro-slavery. "In that instrument," he said, "I hold there is neither warrant, license, nor sanction of the hateful thing." And a major element of his evidence is that "neither *slavery, slaveholding*, nor *slave* can anywhere be found in it." "Now, take the Constitution," he concluded, "according to its plain reading, and I defy the presentation of a single pro-slavery clause in it."

These two very different speakers, Luther Martin and Frederick Douglass, knew this fact about the silence of the Constitution about slavery, and so did many, many others. But apparently it needed to be pointed out in their times, and it needs to be pointed out today. And especially when we recall that there is an equal silence about race, do we see the importance of reminding ourselves about this point that seems to have been persistently forgotten by most Americans, even by unusually knowledgeable ones like Benjamin Hooks and John Hope Franklin.

Despite the existence of slavery and the persistence of it for seventy-five years more, the Founders left us with a constitutional document that has accommodated a very different order of things with regard to the place in our society of the descendants of former slaves. I do not contend that delegates foresaw the present-day consequences of emancipation, that the descendants of black slaves would become voting citizens and officeholders throughout the nation. But it is true that the Founders left in their text no obstacles to the profound improvements that have come about. In what remained in the text after the addition of the amendments abolishing slavery, there is no residue of racism, however much of it may remain in the society itself.

Therefore when the time came to terminate official segregation, we had to purge the racial provisions from federal regulations like those segregating the armed forces, and from state constitutions and state and local laws—but not from the Constitution of the United States. In fact, lawyers and judges were able to argue for profound changes by asserting that they were in accord with and demanded by the Constitution. We did not have to change it to fit new circumstances and times. Instead, the argument could be made, and was made, that conditions had to be changed to fit the Constitution. In that historic national effort, it spelled a very great difference that there was no racism in the original Constitution.

We must acknowledge that there was indeed strong and widespread racism among many Americans that helped to sustain for so long the vicious system of black slavery and its century-long aftermath of racial segregation, discrimination, persecution, and hatred. How best can we understand the meaning of the disjunction between the racism widespread in the society, and the absence of it in the written Constitution?

If a written constitution is not in close accord with the way the society itself is in fact constituted, it will be irrelevant to the everyday life of the people. But it must be more than an accurate depiction of how the society is constituted. A constitution will be a failure if it is no more than a beautiful portrait of an ugly society. A good constitution provides guidance and structure for the improvement of the society. A good constitution is designed to make the political society better than it is, and the citizens better persons. It must be close enough to the institutions and the people as they are to be relevant to the working of the society in its everyday activities, but it should also have what might be called formative features, a capacity to make us better if we live according to its provisions and adhere to its institutional arrangements. The constitutional goal for Americans would be to develop a nation of self-governing, liberty-loving citizens in a new kind of political society where the fundamental rights of all would be secure—and that would mean a society where slavery would have no place.

In that formative way of thinking about the task of constitution-writing, it seems entirely possible that the most foresighted and skillful of the Founders sought to make a constitution that— while accepting and even protecting slavery for a time, as an unavoidable evil, the price to pay for union—tried to make provisions for its ultimate extinction, and even gave thought to the constitutional preparations for a better society that would eventually be free of it. In that respect the original Constitution was better than the political society it constituted.

We would face a very different situation in our own time if there had been in the original Constitution any evidence of the kind of thinking ascribed to the Founders by Chief Justice Taney in the *Dred Scott* case. Taney said that the Founders thought that blacks were not included in the declaration that "all men are created equal," and that blacks were "so far inferior, that they had no rights which the white man was bound to respect." But Taney was wrong; there is no such racism to be found in the Constitution, then or now, not a word of it. Those who wrongly now assert, however laudable their motives, that the "three-fifths clause" was racist, that it somehow denied the humanity of blacks, do a disservice to the truth, first of all, and also to the Constitution, to the nation, and to the cause of justice and equality for black Americans.

Women

The fact that blacks are not mentioned in the original Constitution requires some explanation because there are several provisions obviously concerning black slavery. But no such explanation is required in the case of women. Not only are women not mentioned in the original Constitution, there is no provision anywhere that applies to women as a distinct group. To the best of my knowledge, there is no evidence that the subject of women was ever mentioned in the Constitutional Convention.

This has led to the charge, heard frequently during the prolonged debate over the proposed Equal Rights Amendment, that "women were left out of the Constitution." The fact is, however, that women were not left out; they have always been included in all of the constitutional protections provided to all persons, fully and equally, without any basis in the text for discrimination on the basis of sex. How were they included without being mentioned?

The place to start is that famous provision we considered previously, Article I, section 2, clause 3, describing who will be counted for purposes of representation in the House of Representatives. The phrase "the whole number of free persons" is chiefly where the women are, but they are also among "those bound to service for a term of years," and even among taxed Indians and "all other persons." It is quite remarkable that they are not excluded from any one of these groups because, in 1787, women did not vote or hold office anywhere in the United States and were excluded from every level of government. What would be unremarkable, and typical of the time, would be a clear exclusion of women.

For example, in the Northwest Ordinance we encounter provisions of this sort:

So soon as there shall be five thousand free *male* inhabitants, of full age, in the district . . . they shall receive authority . . . to elect representatives . . . to represent them in the general assembly. . . . Provided also, that a freehold in fifty acres of land . . . shall be necessary to qualify *a man* as an elector of a representative. [Emphasis added]

Under the terms of this famous ordinance, written in the same year as the Constitution and reaffirmed by the first Congress, which included James Madison and many other delegates to the Constitutional Convention, those who are counted for purposes of representation are men only, and voters are spoken of directly as men. That was, for the time, not at all exceptional. What is exceptional is the provision in the Constitution that everyone shall be counted. "The whole number of free persons" includes males and females. In the original Constitution, unlike the Northwest Ordinance, the words "man" or "male" do not occur, nor does any other noun or adjective denoting sex. By not mentioning women or men, speaking instead only of persons, the Constitution must mean that every right, privilege, and protection afforded to persons in the Constitution is afforded to female persons as well as male persons, equally.

The terms used throughout the original Constitution are consistently what are now called non-sexist: for example, "electors," "citizens," "members," "inhabitants," "officers," "representatives," "persons." There are pronouns—"he," "his," and "himself"—but in the entire text of the original Constitution, there is not a single noun or adjective that denotes sex.

There are some who think that because of these pronouns, all masculine, the Founders meant that only men were to hold national office, and most certainly the Presidency. But it can be shown that the text itself presents no obstacle whatever to having a woman in the office of President or any other national office, because these pronouns can clearly be read as generic or neuter or genderless—or whatever we call a pronoun capable of denoting either sex.

The Constitution says of the President that "*He* shall hold *his* office during the term of four years" (the emphases here and throughout this section are all added). It says that when a bill passed by Congress is presented to the President, "if *he* approves *he* shall sign it, but if not *he* shall return it," etc. There are similar usages of the pronoun for the Vice President and for members of Congress, and the question is, are those pronouns exclusively masculine and therefore a definite indication that these offices are to be held by men only, or could they be genderless pronouns, leaving open the possibility that the antecedent is meant to be either a man or a woman? If the latter is the case, as is my contention, then there is no obstacle in the Constitution, and there never has been, to women occupying any office under the Constitution of the United States, including the Presidency, and every protection and every right extended to men by the Constitution is extended equally to women.

My argument rests on several provisions where the masculine pronouns must certainly be read as referring to women as well as men. Consider Article IV, section 2, clause 2, providing for the return of fugitives from justice. "A person" charged with a crime who flees from justice and is found in another state shall be delivered up on demand of the governor "of the State from which *he* fled. . . . " If the "he" in this clause is assumed to mean men only, and not women, we get the absurd result that male fugitives from justice must be returned to face criminal charges, but not female fugitives.

We find similar examples in the amendments. The Fifth Amendment provides that "no person . . . shall be compelled in any criminal case to be a witness against *himself.*" The Sixth Amendment provides that "in all criminal prosecutions, the accused shall enjoy the right . . . to be confronted with the witnesses against *him*; to have compulsory process for obtaining witnesses in *his* favor, and to have the assistance of counsel for *his* defense. Will anyone seriously contend, just because the masculine pronouns are used here, that these protections were extended only to males accused in criminal prosecutions, and that the Constitution means that accused women cannot claim the same rights to confront their accusers, to compel the presence of witnesses, to be represented by a defense lawyer, and to be protected against self-incrimination?

All these examples demonstrate the absurdity of interpreting the masculine pronouns as applying to men only. And if the masculine pronouns in these provisions are genderless, then it is at least plausible that the same pronouns are genderless when used elsewhere in the same text. And if they are, and since, in fact, there is not one noun or adjective in the Constitution as ratified that in any way refers to sex, we must conclude that women are included in the Constitution, on an equal footing with men, as persons, citizens, electors, etc.—and always have been.

We are speaking, of course, of a written document, the text of the original Constitution, which is not the same as asserting that women enjoyed political equality in practice in 1787, or for a long time thereafter. Women's suffrage in the United States seems to have begun in 1838, when women in Kentucky voted in school elections. Women voted on an equal basis with men for the first time anywhere in the United States in 1869, in the Wyoming Territory. But as late as 1914, only ten more states, in addition to the state of Wyoming, had accorded women the right to vote. It was not until the Nineteenth Amendment was ratified in 1920 that the right to vote was made secure for women. That amendment provides that:

The right of citizens of the United States to vote shall not be denied or abridged by the United States or by any State on account of sex.

First we must observe that this article was an addition to the Constitution, but it amended nothing and was intended to amend nothing in the Constitution of the United States. No provision in the text had to be changed or deleted, because there was never any provision in the Constitution limiting or denying the right of women to vote. The barriers to voting by women had always been in the state constitutions or laws.

It may very well be that the Founders never contemplated the possibility of a woman as President, or even women voting on an equal basis with men. Nevertheless, the text they adopted and the American people ratified presents no obstacle whatsoever to the changes that have occurred.

Jews

The significance of not being mentioned in the Constitution becomes clearest when we consider the last of the three unmentioned subjects—Jews. Most of us, when we think of the Constitution and freedom of religion, think of the double security provided by the First Amendment, against "an establishment of religion" and for the "free exercise thereof." These protections were not, of course, part of the original Constitution. The original Constitution mentions religion just once, but that one provision is remarkable. Article VI, section 3, says simply that "no religious test shall ever be required as a qualification to any office or public trust under the United States."

Jews had suffered persecution almost everywhere in the world for millennia. Universally despised, they had been beaten, tortured, murdered, and hounded from country to country and even continent to continent. The best they enjoyed, here and there, now and then, was a kind of safeguarded second-class status, where by one sort of decree or another they were permitted to engage in certain professions or businesses, or to live unmolested behind walls and gates in one or another section of a city. But these occasionally favorable arrangements were always precarious and often short-lived, never theirs by right but only by indulgence, not because they were entitled to decent treatment as citizens or subjects but because someone in authority had reason to protect them. Never did they have the security of political rights, not to mention the political power that comes with voting and holding office.

The question of religious tests was an old one in America and had been deliberated in every state from the moment of independence, and even before. At the time of the founding, almost every state had some form of religious test, but Jews were not the only target or even the main one. The chief concern was to bar Catholics in predominantly Protestant states, to bar some sects of Protestants in other states, and incidentally to exclude the very small numbers of "Jews, Turks, and infidels," as the saying went.

There were religious tests in the constitutions of at least eleven states, but the tests varied. Delaware required state officers to swear a Trinitarian oath; Georgia required that they be of the Protestant religion; Maryland demanded belief "in the Christian religion"—thus including Catholics as well as Protestants, but excluding Jews and nonbelievers; and New York discriminated against Catholics but was the only state in which Jews could hold office.

Against this background we see the history-making significance of the provision prohibiting religious tests in the Constitution. Religious toleration was amazingly prevalent in America, given the intensity of religious conviction observable everywhere, but political equality for members of different religious groups was rare. That is, provisions for the free exercise of religion were common in the state constitutions, but political equality was a different story. The free exercise of religion happened in church or synagogue; it did not assure the right to vote or hold office. Nevertheless, for whatever reasons, in a nation that had almost universal religious testing for state offices, the delegates proposed and the states ratified a constitution barring religious tests for holding national office.

Add to this one other fact, less easily discernible. That fact is that Jews are not mentioned in the Constitution. As we view things now, that Jews are not mentioned is no more remarkable than that Baptists or Roman Catholics or Muslims or any others are also not mentioned. But Jews had never been treated simply as "persons," let alone "citizens," anywhere in the world for more than 1500 years. By not mentioning them, that is, by not singling them out, the Constitution made Jews full citizens of a nation for the first time in all Diaspora history. By this silence, coupled with the prohibition of religious tests, the Founders "opened a door" to Jews and to all other sects as well.

The Constitution of the United States is unusual, and perhaps unique, among the constitutions of the world in the way that it protects the rights of the people. The unspoken principles—at least unspoken in the Constitution—are that rights are inherent in individuals, not in the groups they belong to; that we are all equal as human beings in the sense that no matter what our color, sex, national origin, or religion, we are equal in the possession of the rights that governments are instituted to protect; and, finally, that as a consequence, the only source of legitimate political power is the consent of the governed. Because these principles, all stemming from the primacy of individual rights, are the unmentioned foundation of the Constitution, it is not only unnecessary to mention race, sex, or religion, it is inconsistent and harmful.

In short, the reason no group of any sort included in the nation it founded is mentioned in the Constitution—originally and now—is that the Founders designed a better way to make sure that no one was left out, and that everyone was in on a basis of equality.

To anyone who asks why we should celebrate the bicentennial of this Constitution, let that be the answer.

THE CONSTITUTION AND THE 14TH AMENDMENT[4]

What is a constitution? At one extreme, an analyst might conceive of a constitution as hortatory rhetoric prescribing a set of ideals which a polity admires but to which its public officials, or even its citizens, are not committed in any binding sense. Since the American constitutional document of 1787 proclaims itself to be "the supreme law of the land" and requires public officials to take an oath to support it, such a purely hortatory view seems irrelevant to the situation in the United States. To some extent, those who claim a constitution's terms are infinitely malleable—and so advocate free interpretation, whether by judges, other public officials, or the people—take such a view. For if a constitution has no essential meaning, it can hardly bind either a commu-

[4]McCormick Professor of Jurisprudence (at Princeton University) Walter F. Murphy's "The Constitution and the 14th Amendment," *The Center Magazine*, Vol. 20, No. 4, pp. 9-30. Reprinted by permission of the Robert Maynard Hutchins Center for the Study of Democratic Institutions.

nity or its officials. Moreover, there is not only a venerable set of practices by American presidents but also a set of justifications for the claims by venerable Americans that, at least on some important issues such as national security, the Constitution does not bind. In *Federalist No. 41*, James Madison wrote:

"It is in vain to oppose constitutional barriers to the impulse of self-preservation. It is worse than in vain; because it plants in the Constitution itself necessary usurpations of power, every precedent of which is a germ of unnecessary and multiplied repetitions."

Alexander Hamilton was even more blunt. In *Federalist No. 23*, he wrote:

"These powers ought to exist without limitation, *because it is impossible to foresee or define the extent and variety of the means which may be necessary to satisfy them.* . . .

"The circumstances that endanger the safety of nations are infinite, and for this reason no constitutional shackles can wisely be imposed on the power to which the care of it is committed. This power ought to be co-extensive with all the possible combinations of such circumstances; and ought to be under the direction of the same councils which are appointed to preside over the common defense."

Despite Thomas Jefferson's opposition to the Alien and Sedition Acts, his general views on emergency powers were rather close to those of Hamilton. Because of his insistence on "strict construction" of the Constitution, Jefferson did not advocate taking a broad view of governmental powers to cope with emergencies, but argued that obligation to the Constitution was subject to a higher law. In a letter to J. B. Colvin (September 20, 1810), Jefferson wrote:

"A strict observance of the written laws is doubtless *one* of the high duties of a good citizen, but it is not *the highest*. The laws of necessity, of self-preservation, of saving our country when in danger, are of higher obligation."

Abraham Lincoln was equally candid in justifying his use of courts-martial to try civilians. In a letter to A. G. Hodges (April 4, 1864), Lincoln wrote:

"Was it possible to lose the nation, and yet preserve the Constitution? By general law, life *and* limb must be protected; yet often a limb must be amputated to save a life; but a life is never wisely given to save a limb. I felt that measures, otherwise unconstitutional, might become lawful, by becoming indispensable to the preservation of the Constitution, through the preservation of the nation."

A defender of Madison and Hamilton could argue that they were explaining why the clauses regarding national defense were so open-ended, although that explanation has its own problems. A defender of Jefferson and Lincoln could argue that they were using structural and even more prudential modes of interpretation: To preserve the Constitution's viability, they were willing to sanction temporary violations of some of the document's specific terms. A critic might reply that, at least in this context, Jefferson and Lincoln were implicitly asserting that the Constitution "constitutes" the nation as a people only in good times and thus, given human propensity to view one's own problems as very serious, is a trivial element in public life.

Less dramatic, but perhaps no less illustrative than these incidents, has been the fate of such clauses as Art. I, Sec. 9, cl. 7, requiring Congress to publish "a regular statement and account of the receipts and expenditures of all public money from time to time." The Supreme Court has ruled that individual citizens do not have standing to use the courts to challenge putative violations of either clause. There are other ways of enforcing Sec. 6, cl. 2, including opponents' appeals to the electorate. It is difficult, however, to see how one can enforce Sec. 9, cl. 7 in any fashion at all, including a court order. A judge might hold the Comptroller General or the Secretary of Treasury in contempt for failing to provide an accounting, but no judicial writ could force Congress to make such data available to any official. Given the long practice of secret appropriations, it seems plain that the supposed requirement of Sec. 9, cl. 7 can at best be no more than a wish and has become a vain wish.

At the other end of the spectrum of authority is the view that a constitution controls every action of government, regardless of the nature of the crisis, and, further, that its meaning is immutable except by formal amendment. As Justice David Davis put it for the Court in *Ex Parte Milligan* (1868):

"The Constitution of the United States is a law for rulers and people, equally in war and in peace, and covers with the shield of its protection all classes of men, at all times, and under all circumstances. No doctrine, involving more pernicious consequences, was ever invented by the wit of man than that any of its provisions can be suspended during any of the great exigencies of government."

In *Home Building and Loan Association* v. *Blaisdell* (1934), Justice George Sutherland summed up the parallel assertion that a constitution is essentially changeless in meaning:

"A provision of the Constitution, it is hardly necessary to say, does not admit of two distinctly opposite interpretations. It does not mean one thing at one time and an entirely different thing at another time. . . .

"The provisions of the federal Constitution, undoubtedly, are pliable in the sense that in appropriate cases they have the capacity of bringing within their grasp every new condition which falls within their meaning. But, their *meaning* is changeless; it is only their application which is extensible. . . .

"The whole aim of construction, as applied to a provision of the Constitution, is to discover the meaning, to ascertain and give effect to the intent of the framers and the people who adopted it. . . . As nearly as possible we should place ourselves in the condition of those who framed and adopted it."

There is, of course, a broad range of positions between these two extremes that can hold, in varying degrees, that a constitution does bind, that its general principles are immutable, but the meanings of particular terms may well evolve as experience helps ideas develop. As Earl Warren said, in *Trop* v. *Dulles* (1958), about the "cruel and unusual punishments" clause of the Eighth Amendment: it "must draw its meaning from the evolving standards of decency that mark the progress of a maturing society."

Perhaps the clearest statement of such a middle position can be found in Ronald Dworkin's distinction between constitutional concepts and constitutional conceptions. The former refers to more abstract meaning, the latter to specific views that an individual may have in mind on the subject. "The difference," he explains, "is not just in the *detail* of the instructions given but in the *kind* of instructions given." In *Taking Rights Seriously*, Dworkin wrote: "When I appeal to the concept of fairness I appeal to what fairness means, and I give my own views on that issue no special standing. When I lay down a conception of fairness, I lay down what I mean by fairness, and my view is therefore the heart of the matter."

Much language in constitutional documents—and certainly in the American constitutional document(s)—is phrased in concepts. The due process and equal protection clauses, for instance, express concepts about fairness. But much constitutional language also expresses conceptions, as Articles I and II do about representation in prescribing two-year terms for members of the House, six for senators, four for presidents. The specific meanings of concepts can and do develop over time, though that fact does not mean they are so malleable as to establish no binding standards.

From one point of view, a constitution might function as a set of political fig leaves. Certainly the "constitutions" of the Soviet Union, the People's Republic of China, or of Chile since 1980 serve only as propaganda, although, as hypocrisy, they may function as evidence of the pressure that even absolutist regimes feel to pretend to follow legal rules. More subtly, some of what the Legal Realists wrote in an earlier generation and what members of the Critical Legal Studies Movement are currently writing hint that the entire American legal system is little more than a charade to conceal economic and political exploitation.

Looked at more narrowly, a constitution forms a charter for government. It sets out rules for the ways in which a government will operate; who its officials are; how they are to be chosen and for what terms; how power is to be divided among them; and what rights, if any, are reserved to citizens. To some extent, all constitutions—insofar as they are not shams—fulfill this role, though they may do so more or less well. That is, their capacity to control reality will depend in large part on their authority.

But constitutions may perform other, broader functions as well. One might also look on a constitution as containing a storehouse of substantive values in addition to structuring governmental process. Defenders of this view need not deny that much of the body of the document of 1787 and some amendments deal with governmental structure, but they can make several additional points.

First, distinctions between procedure and substance are easily exaggerated. Structures and procedures seldom represent merely arbitrary choices; they typically embody, indeed often try to advance, certain substantive values. They attempt to lead society toward particular goals—in the American case, toward limited government, individual liberty, and a form of representative democracy. In "Judicial Review and the Rights and Laws of Nature" (the *Supreme Court Review*, 1982) Walter Berns wrote: "The process—or as I should prefer to say, the structure of the governing process—was designed with a view to a particular substantive end. It was designed to secure the rights with which all men are naturally endowed."

Second, some provisions—in the American case, one might cite the Preamble, the First Amendment, the Fourth Amendment, the Ninth Amendment, and the equal protection clause of the Fourteenth Amendment—are blatantly substantive in content. These sorts of provisions reinforce the notion that a constitution's functions include protection of certain basic (natural) rights within a framework of (natural) law.

Third, and perhaps most fundamental, some commentators directly—and some judges less directly—argue that any constitution embodies either a political theory or set of political theories. To understand the specific terms of a constitutional document and/or whatever other elements form "the" constitution, one must understand the theory, or theories.

Related to this view, but perhaps more broadly, one may see a constitution functioning as an authoritative and binding statement of a people's aspirations for themselves and their nation. According to the usual definitions, "to constitute" means to compose or make up; and a thing's "constitution" refers to the way in which it is composed or made up. Thus a constitution purporting to speak in the name of a people could define the sort of people its subjects/authors would like to become, and define, too, not only their governmental structures and procedures but also their goals, ideals, and the moral standards by which they want to judge their own community and others to judge it. In sum, a constitution may guide and shape as well as express a people's hope for themselves as a society.

A constitution—I would argue in support of this wider view—is an ongoing institution; it interacts with its people. The ideals it enshrines, the processes it prescribes, and the actions it legitimizes must either help to change its citizenry or, at minimum, reflect their current values. If a constitution does not articulate, at least in general terms, the ideals that form or will reform its people and express the political character they have or are willing to assume, it will soon be replaced or atrophy. Constitutions—like their people—can fail.

In the American case, the evidence supporting such a view is strong. In *On What the Constitution Means* (1984), Sotirios A. Barber wrote: "The aspirational tone of the Constitution is unmistakable in the Preamble." That preface sets out the republic's purposes, not only to achieve a more perfect union, national defense, the general welfare, and domestic tranquility but also to "establish justice" and "secure the blessings of liberty to ourselves and our posterity." One can view both the concepts and conceptions that follow as efforts to prescribe how those ends can best be achieved. In a symposium at Georgetown University in October 1985 ("The Constitution of the United States: Contemporary Ratification"), Justice William J. Brennan, Jr., said the Constitution "embodies the aspiration to social justice, brotherhood, and human dignity that brought this nation into being. . . . Our amended Constitution is the lodestar for our aspirations."

Australia, India, Japan, and most industrial nations of the western world have written constitutions, but that fact does not settle the question whether "the constitution" is coextensive with the constitutional document. What a constitution includes is a problem, not a datum. "It is an admissibly narrow conception of American constitutional law," Felix Frankfurter asserted in the Steel Seizure Case (1952), "to confine it to the words of the Constitution and to disregard the gloss which life has written upon them." But where and how do we find that gloss? Is there more than gloss that has a constitutional status? What about subtexts that control the text? What documents have constitutional status? What about political theories that underpin the text?

The most obvious candidate for the constitutional canon is the text, the whole text, and nothing but the text. Hugo Black took that position on the American Constitution, and so does Attorney General Edwin Meese III. In "The Law of the Constitution: A Bicentennial Lecture" (Tulane University, October 21, 1986), Meese said the Constitution "begins with 'We the People of the United States . . .' and ends up, some six thousand words later, with the Twenty-sixth Amendment." Such people stress the "writtenness" of the American Constitution, although, as literary critics and biblical commentators might have warned, writtenness raises as well as solves problems of meaning.

At the most general level, every constitutional document formed in a free society is likely to contain a bundle of compromises. These may be necessary to obtain approval among the drafters and/or ratifiers, but they may also pose serious problems for the constitution's operations in that they may not always be compatible with each other. Indeed, they may contradict one another. The Constitutional Court of West Germany has squarely faced this problem. In *The Southwest Case* (1951), one solution was reconciliation through structural analysis:

"An individual constitutional provision cannot be considered as an isolated clause and interpreted alone. A constitution has an inner unity, and the meaning of any one part is linked to that of other provisions. Taken as a unit, a constitution reflects certain overarching principles and fundamental decisions to which individual provisions are subordinate."

The final sentence in this quotation looks less to reconciliation than to invalidation, and the Court went on to make it clear that that option was open:

"That a constitutional provision itself may be null and void is not conceptually impossible just because it is part of the Constitution. There are constitutional principles that are so fundamental and to such an extent an expression of a law that precedes even the Constitution that they also bind the framer of the Constitution, and other constitutional provisions that do not rank so high may be null and void, because they contravene these principles."

It is tempting to dismiss these statements as typical German indulgence in abstract theorizing. One might, however, keep in mind not only that the Supreme Court of India has invalidated a constitutional amendment but also that—despite John Marshall's claim in *Marbury* v. *Madison* (1803) that no "clause in the Constitution is intended to be without effect"—some judges, presidents, legislators, and commentators have tried to exclude portions of the text from the constitutional canon. We all have our favorite example, whether it is *Slaughter-House*'s (1873) pretty much expunging the "privileges or immunities" clause from the Fourteenth Amendment; or, in *United States* v. *Darby Lumber Co.* (1941), Justice Harlan F. Stone's holding that the Tenth Amendment "states but a truism that all is retained which has not been surrendered"; or Justice Hugo L. Black's consistent refusal to accept the Ninth Amendment; or the common omission of the Preamble.

As the German Constitutional Court indicated, recognizing and reconciling tension—even conflict—among different parts of a constitution is a frequent problem in constitutional interpretation. In the American case, reconciling the competing demands of freedom *for* religion and freedom *from* religious establishment is among the more troublesome of such problems. Other difficult problems are maintaining a free press at the same time as conducting fair trials, and providing for affirmative action for groups discriminated against in the past while protecting the rights of others in the present who may have had nothing to do with that discrimination and who themselves have a right not to be discriminated against.

One might argue that the Constitution can only be understood in light of certain "understandings" and "intentions" that the framers neglected to put before the ratifiers in the constitutional document of 1787 and its later amendments. And, indeed, both Black and Meese quickly include more than the text by arguing that we can only understand what the American constitutional text means by referring to other documents—other texts, such as Madison's incomplete notes on the Constitutional Convention or debates in Congress on the Fourteenth Amendment—to discover the intent of the framers, whomever that term might include. Thus such documents take on constitutional—or even superconstitutional—status, for they determine what the constitutional text means.

A third set of candidates might well be other documents. In systems like that of Great Britain, where no one can reasonably claim that "the constitution" is encapsulated in a single text, debate over what is in the constitutional canon is not likely to be resolved. But even in states with "written" constitutions, such as West Germany, the basic constitutional document may specifically incorporate part of another document. In the United States the strongest contender for inclusion is the second paragraph of the Declaration of Independence:

"We hold these truths to be self-evident, that all men are created equal; that they are endowed by their Creator with certain unalienable Rights, that among these are Life, Liberty and the pursuit of Happiness. That to secure these rights, Governments are instituted among men, deriving their just powers from the consent of the governed. That whenever any Form of Government becomes destructive of these ends, it is the Right of the People to alter or abolish it. . . . "

The Declaration is the founding document of the American nation. It explicitly commits the new republic to notions of natural freedom, natural rights, and equality. It implicitly commits the republic to a political theory that we have come to call constitutionalism and, to a lesser extent, to democracy. John Adams somewhat jealously dismissed the Declaration as not containing a single idea "but what had been hackneyed in Congress for two years before." And Jefferson acknowledged he had set out "not to find new principles, or new arguments . . . but to place before mankind the common sense of the subject. . . . " But commonplace or no in the colonies, such a claim was radical in the larger world of 1776. And it was precisely its radicalness in the world and its commonness in the colonies that attest to the distinctiveness of the special political character the American people stamped on their republic.

Given the existence of the common law's doctrine of prescription, long and unchallenged practice may seem at first glance a more viable candidate for canonical status. As the Supreme Court noted in *The Pocket Veto Case* (1929): "Long settled and established practice is a consideration of great weight in a proper interpretation of constitutional provisions. . . . " In *Youngstown Sheet & Tube Co.* v. *Sawyer* (1952), Justice Felix Frankfurter claimed:

"The Constitution is a framework for government. Therefore, the way the framework has consistently operated fairly establishes that it has operated according to its true nature. A systematic, unbroken, executive practice, long pursued in the knowledge of the Congress and never before questioned, engaged in by Presidents who have also sworn to uphold the Constitution, making, as it were, such exercise of power part of the structure of our government, may be treated as a gloss of 'executive Power' vested in the President by Section 1 of Art. II [of the Constitution]."

Despite the melodious way in which Frankfurter's sentences roll, practice presents its share of problems. First, how long is long, whose practice counts, and what constitutes an invalidating or unsettling challenge? Must that challenge be successful? If so, would long usage become a mere tautology? To take a specific case, what about presidential power to commit, without congressional authorization, armed forces to combat in peace time? Does the fact that presidents since George Washington have often done so transform such a power into authority? How does enactment into law of the War Powers Resolution affect an answer here? What effect does the Resolution's apparent ineffectiveness have?

Second, and more fundamentally, can practice per se—even if long followed and never before successfully or even seriously challenged—be a valid criterion for determining constitutionality? One who answers yes might point to senatorial courtesy and executive privilege (or perhaps even judicial review) as evidence. On the other hand, what about discrimination on the basis of race, ethnicity, sex, alienage, or legitimacy? Each has had— perhaps continues to have—long periods of being public policy.

The underlying point is that a sharp distinction exists between practice and tradition. The latter, as a normative concept, refers to a practice, not necessarily unbroken, that fits within a set of ideals—in this context the ideals of the Constitution (whatever that is and whatever they may be). Proponents of a constitutional status for a particular practice must confront this issue. It seems to be difficult to assert that a practice has become part of the constitutional canon if it is not at least congruent with those broader ideals. One might plausibly argue, however, that long practice carries much heavier weight in determining the legitimacy of interdepartmental and intergovernmental relations than in relations between individual citizens and their government(s).

Closely related to practices are interpretations of "the" Constitution. Critics as politically distant as Edwin Meese, III, and Sotirios A. Barber, and presidents from Jefferson through Jackson, Lincoln, Franklin D. Roosevelt, and, by implication, Ronald Reagan, have argued that the American Constitution is not the same as what the Supreme Court says it means. The justices themselves have frequently agreed by overruling constitutional interpretations made by their former selves. Justice William O. Douglas, echoing Andrew Jackson, summed it up in 1949: A judge "remembers above all else that it is the Constitution which he swore to support and defend, not the gloss which his predecessors may have put on it."

Yet, with this much said, it would strain credulity to think that some interpretations have not become part of the Constitution. It is difficult, for instance, to imagine the American system without judicial review, as asserted in *Marbury* and earlier cases; or a broad scope for congressional power as Marshall read out of (or into) the Constitution in *McCulloch* v. *Maryland* (1819) and *Gibbons*

v. *Ogden* (1824); or without at least a loose version of "one person, one vote"; although the last was such a controversial doctrine when the Warren Court first announced it that opponents came close both to pushing Congress to propose a constitutional amendment to modify it and also getting enough state legislatures to petition Congress to call a constitutional convention for the purpose.

As indicated above, in the Western World, the concept of "constitution" has a particular history and, as Karl Lowenstein once remarked, every state may have a constitution, but only some states are constitutional.

At the time of the American Revolution, the colonists protested that the British were: (1) governing (more specifically, taxing) them without granting them representation; and (2) violating certain of their rights, which all governments, representative or not, had to respect. A successful revolution could have cured the first defect without affecting the second. The second paragraph of the Declaration of Independence made clear, however, that the two were linked, though it more clearly affirmed the second than the first, for citizens might consent to any form of government. In any event, this paragraph plainly states the essence of constitutionalism: Citizens bring rights with them into society. Neither society, the state, nor government grants fundamental rights to citizens; rather, public authority has the duty to protect these preexisting rights.

Democratic theory is less concerned with substance than with process, though, again, this distinction is not always either clear or even real. Still, democratic theory tends to recognize, as Hans Linde said in "Due Process of Lawmaking" (*Nebraska Law Review*, 1976), "the primacy of process over product in a free society" and thus legitimizes governmental action largely according to procedural, participational criteria: A law is binding because it was enacted by the people's representatives, chosen in free and open elections. The people are sovereign; therefore their representatives partake of that sovereignty. Democratic theory thus tends toward legal positivism.

There is no assumption here that individuals or the citizenry as a whole will never make mistakes or that all people have equal capacities to understand and choose among the options open to them. Michael Walzer has said that the "claim is most persuasively put, not in terms of what the people know, but in terms of who they are. They are the subjects of the law, and if the law is to bind them as free men and women, they must also be its makers."

The basic assumption, therefore, need only be that all sane adults can cope with political problems to the extent of being able to recognize their own self interests, join with others who share those interests, and choose among candidates. "At its core," Professor Joseph Tussman wrote in *Government and the Mind* (1977) about democratic theory, "is the significance it gives to universal (normal adult) participation in the political process, and the faith that men can, if encouraged and given the opportunity, develop the arts, the skills and habits necessary for a life of responsible deliberation and decision-making. Democracy seeks to universalize the parliamentary state of mind."

The chief check that democratic theory posits against tyranny is that the people will not tyrannize themselves. Therefore they will vote out of office officials who try to enact oppressive measures. Democratic theories agree with the Jefferson who claimed that the "mass of citizens" is "the safest depository for their own rights." Foreknowledge of the likelihood of defeat for reelection will keep most officials from infringing civil rights.

Many theorists find an effective second check in what they perceive to be the way in which democratic politics operates. Echoing Madison in *Federalist No. 10*, they argue that, in a large and diverse nation, the population will seldom be divided between those who fervently favor a given policy and those who adamantly oppose it. More typically, coalitions of minority groups form and re-form as different issues arise. On a particular matter, some group or groups will care very deeply, while others will be more or less indifferent but willing to trade their support for backing on different issues they deem critical.

These theorists stress the claim that political cleavages are seldom cumulative. That is, alliances of groups form and dissolve as issues change; the same interests do not always find themselves in coalition with, and in opposition to, the same other groups. On this view, democratic politics is characterized by shifting coalitions of minorities rather than by a more or less constant division between an equally passionate majority and minority.

Further, open political processes make it very difficult for one set of groups to coalesce without alerting others with conflicting interests to form an opposing alliance. As a result, public officials who wish to be reelected will be forced, or, at the very least strongly pushed, to act as brokers who negotiate compromises rather than adjudicate winner-take-all struggles.

Some theorists add a third check: In a representative democracy, professional politicians develop and internalize a political subculture that constrains them from trying to tyrannize their constituents. Fear of being voted out of office is not a trivial restraint, nor are crosspressures from competing alliances, actual and latent; but they do not always operate effectively. Electorates may have very short memories, and astute politicians can often play groups off against one another. In sum, public officials frequently transform their own, rather than their constituents', wishes into public policy. But, supposedly, the culture of the professional politician puts real limits on official freedom. Acceptance of rules of the political game means that "some things are not done."

Some proponents of democracy add a limitation that links with constitutionalism: to be legitimate, the popular will must will generally, that is, valid laws may not merely reflect prejudices against minorities by imposing burdens only or mainly on minorities. Such a limiting principle flows from the premise that the people *as a whole* are sovereign. But, because "the people" and their representatives are typically divided on public issues of any significance, and because all systems must have procedures for decision-making (in most instances, democracy has to resort to some form of majority rule), any institutional arrangement to police this limitation threatens the people's right to govern themselves. And hence the myriad of problems that American constitutional interpretation lumps under the rubric of "equal protection."

Still, theories of representative democracy and constitutionalism coexist in tension and sometimes in conflict. Constitutionalism, while not denigrating process, determines legitimacy according to a set of values that focus on substantive rights of the individual. Its basic premise is that there are some rights government may not trample on, even if an overwhelming proportion of citizens, after open debate and free elections, conclude such action is both necessary and just.

In addition, the two differ on how best to protect individual rights. Democratic theory esteems the right to political participation as the preeminent civil liberty "because preservative of all rights" (*Yick Wo* v. *Hopkins* 1886). The people, as both governed and governors, will see their interests in oppressing outweighed by their interests in not being oppressed.

Again, constitutionalism does not deny the importance of a right to participate, but it puts far less faith in such checks. Indeed, it sees popular government as posing a serious threat to liberty. It agrees with the Jefferson who wrote, in *Notes on the State of Virginia* (1784): "One hundred and seventy-three despots would surely be as oppressive as one. . . . An elective despotism was not the government we fought for. . . . " In a letter to Jefferson (October 17, 1788), Madison amplified the point:

"In our Governments, the real power lies in the majority of the Community, and the invasion of private rights is chiefly to be apprehended, not from acts of Government contrary to the sense of its constituents, but from acts in which Government is the mere instrument of the major number of its constituents."

Constitutionalism—according to Madison in *Federalist No. 51*—insists on "auxiliary precautions," such as judicial review, to rein in popularly elected officials and to hamper the formation of majorities, separate governmental institutions sharing authority and responsible to different groups, thus pitting ambition against ambition and power against power.

Constitutional democracy—the framers would have preferred "free government"—represents an effort to create a polity that will be morally legitimate because it is based on popular consent and because it both protects and respects the inalienable rights that people have because of their humanity. As Madison noted—in "Vices of the Political System of the United States" (1787)—before the Constitutional Convention met (and later repeated in *Federalist No. 51*): "The great desideratum in Government is such a modification of the sovereignty as will render it sufficiently neutral between the different interests and factions, to control one part of society from invading the rights of another, and at the same time sufficiently controlled itself, from setting up an interest adverse to that of the whole Society."

One might look on usage, interpretation, and formal amendment as forming a hierarchy of legitimate constitutional change. Each, of course, is a process rather than a single event, and each normally involves increasingly conscious efforts at change and increasingly wider areas in which the processes occur. Still, each is inherently creative, and it can be very difficult to tell, except in the most mechanical and least meaningful sense, when we move from one of these processes to the other. Those who begin or continue a usage may well have thought out the implications of their actions in constitutional terms—that is, interpreted the Constitution—just as those who continue an interpretation may unthinkingly accept it as a usage. And there can be little doubt that some congressional, presidential, and judicial interpretations have affected the polity far more fundamentally than have some constitutional amendments.

A practical difficulty does not, however, remove whatever theoretical justification the hierarchy might have. And it is certainly defensible to argue that some changes Congress and the states might effect via the amending processes are not validly open either to judges, to presidents, to representatives and senators, to state officials, or to the electorate acting solely within their own institutional setting. As an example, one might cite the Court's draining the "privileges or immunities" clause of significance in *The Slaughter-House Cases* (1873). Such a drastic amendment of the constitutional text, one might plausibly assert, cried out for revision by re-amendment, assuming the deed were to be done at all.

Inevitably, this discussion leads to the more general question of limitations on any form of constitutional change. Whatever the limitations on change by usage or interpretation, can citizens and/or governmental officials, assuming they follow the procedures set forth in the constitution itself, amend a constitution in any way they see fit? If the answer is yes, then Americans could amend their Constitution to eliminate the equal protection clause and remove any trace of an "equal protection component" from the due process clauses of the Fifth Amendment and Fourteenth Amendment. Indeed, the United States could repeal the Thirteenth Amendment and legalize slavery, repeal the First Amendment and legitimize a state religion and political censorship. In sum, using the procedures of their current Constitution, Americans could progress or regress to any sort of society they wished.

Wendell Wilkie argued for such latitude in *Schneiderman* v. *United States* (1943), where he defended a man threatened with denaturalization because, as a member of the Communist party, he "had not behaved as a person attached to the principles of the Constitution" for the five years prior to his naturalization. Wilkie claimed that the preeminent principle of the Constitution was Article V's provision for amendment. That is, as long as one was willing to use those procedures for peaceful change, one could be "attached" to the Constitution and hold any substantive views on politics whatsoever. Prudently, the Court ducked the issue: "We need not consider the validity of this extreme position for if the Government's construction [of the statute] is accepted, it has not carried its burden of proof even under its own test."

A test of political belief seems offensive. But it is not self-evident that even democratic theory can take a neutral stance toward substantive ends and look only at process. Michael Walzer, for example, argues that a democracy cannot validly decide to give up democracy, for the people cannot alienate their sovereignty. Certainly constitutionalism cannot, consistently with its principles, be indifferent to substantive results. Whether a constitutionalist regime should punish individual citizens for disagreeing with constitutionalism, certainly constitutionalism could accept the legitimacy of a change in the constitution that destroyed one of the fundamental principles of constitutionalism only if it were compelled by the "grinding necessity" of being a lesser evil.

Thus, there are theoretical limits on constitutional change, vague but real nevertheless. Moreover, some constitutional documents contain supposedly unamendable clauses. In the American case, no amendment can deprive a state of its equal representation in the Senate without its consent. And we came close to having an amendment—with what now seems like wonderful irony, it would have been the Thirteenth—that would have barred further amendments that might have given Congress authority to abolish slavery within the states. For structural, more than substantive reasons, William F. Harris II has argued—in "Reconstitutive Words: Are There Limits on the Amending Power?" which he delivered at the Annual Meeting of the American Political Science Association in 1983—that such an "entrenching" amendment "would itself be unconstitutional." For reasons I spell out later, I agree that this particular amendment would have been unconstitutional. But the thesis of this paper is that some parts of constitutional documents may not be amended to subtract from the protection they offer. Harris himself concedes that a constitutional provision might be fundamental and thus unamendable "in terms of some articulated political theory that makes sense of the whole Constitution." My position is that provisions of constitutional documents differ markedly in fundamentality. Some represent more or less arbitrary arrangements, some reflect basic principles of political theory. And, as preceding pages show, I believe it possible to sketch at least the outlines of such a theory, or set of theories, that makes sense of the document of 1787 as amended.

The right to even-handed treatment by government, at least to the extent it is currently guaranteed in the basic American constitutional document, is not repealable, nor is it amendable so as to weaken its guarantee, though it would be constitutionally permissible to strengthen those guarantees.

I do not contend the nation is bound by any particular doctrine of equal protection or any particular interpretive methodology such as "two-tiered" or "three-tiered" analysis, continua, rationality, or "rationality with bite." Furthermore, American history makes it obvious that one can interpret equal protection so as to turn it into a meaningless platitude, to be sneered at as "the usual last resort in constitutional argument," as Justice Oliver W. Holmes said in *Buck* v. *Bell* (1927). I would claim such interpretations would not only be wrong but unconstitutional. As Sotirios A. Barber states in his book *On What the Constitution Means*: "To those who take 'constitutional law' to refer to whatever judges and lawyers say about the Constitution, one can only respond that constitutional law is not always constitutional."

My argument is simpler than it seems, but it does require elaboration. It is based on the content of the Constitution and its functions, on the notion of what "to amend" means, and on the theories that underpin and infuse the document(s) and the larger Constitution with coherent and consistent meaning.

I have mentioned several candidates for inclusion in the Constitution. I deliberately omitted discussion of something akin to what H. L. A. Hart, in *The Concept of Law*, calls the "rules of recognition" for inclusion in the constitutional canon. I have not formulated a complete set of such rules, but certainly one would have to be the candidate's performing a foundational function. That is, it would have to: (a) provide a process by which government shall operate; or (b) serve as a deposit for or expositor of some of the polity's fundamental values; or (c) play a significant role in forming or re-forming a people into a nation. A second, alternative, standard would be that the candidate would have to provide a lens without which the basic constitutional document(s) could not be intelligibly read, or, to repeat the language of the previous paragraph, infuses the document(s) with coherent and consistent meaning.

By the first standard, the Declaration of Independence must be included in the canon. It is the founding document of the American republic. It committed the new nation to a radical political philosophy, to a set of ideals. It established, as Lincoln said in his Speech at Springfield, June 26, 1857, "a standard maxim for free society, which should be familiar to all, and revered by all; constantly looked to, constantly labored for, and even though never perfectly attained, constantly approximated, and thereby constantly spreading and deepening its influence. . . . "

Whether the constitutional document of 1787 and the ensuing Bill of Rights omitted the Declaration's ringing defense of equality because, as Arthur J. Goldberg has claimed in his article "Equality and Governmental Action" in *The New York University Law Review* (1964), the founding generation took it for granted, because of a change of mind after the democratic excesses of state legislatures during Confederation, because of the dark issue of slavery, or some combination of these and other reasons is irrelevant. The Declaration formed us as a people committed to a particular view of the human person and the purposes of government; to escape such clear, radical, and general philosophic principles the country would need explicitly to reject them. As Carl Lotus Becker phrased it in *The Declaration of Independence* (1958): "In the Declaration, the foundation of the United States is indissolubly associated with a theory of politics, a philosophy of human rights which is valid, if at all, not for Americans only, but for all men." Justice William J. Brennan, Jr., at the Text and Teaching Symposium at Georgetown University in 1985, has echoed this theme: "The Declaration of Independence, the Constitution and the Bill of Rights solemnly committed the United States to be a country where the dignity and rights of all persons were equal before all authority."

Proving the existence of a political creed is often difficult, and the methodological problems in proving the efficacy of such a creed may make that task impossible. Still, it is hardly a novel observation that the second paragraph of the Declaration, along with the less-read constitutional document of 1787 as amended, forms the basis of a civil religion. "The Declaration and the Constitution," Samuel P. Huntington asserts in *American Politics: The Promise of Disharmony*, "constitute the holy scripture of the American civil religion." The United States, G. K. Chesterton wrote in *What I Saw in America*, "has a creed . . . set forth with dogmatic and theological lucidity in the Declaration of Independence; perhaps the only piece of practical politics that is also theoretical politics and also great literature. It enunciates that all men are equal in their claim to justice, that governments exist to give them that justice, and that their authority is for that reason just. . . . The point is that there is a creed, if not about divine, at least about human things."

Equality of human dignity and worth; natural rights of individuals that morally, if not factually, pre-exist the state and even society and the purpose of government to protect these rights; the necessity of government by consent; and the right of the people to revolution if government fails in its duty—these are all basic blocks of a coherent if not completely internally consistent political theory. And the course of American constitutional development has run toward greater acceptance of the notion of equal dignity and worth, as the Thirteenth Amendment and the Fourteenth Amendment emphatically attest, and the Fifteenth Amendment, Nineteenth Amendment, Twenty-third Amendment, and Twenty-fourth Amendment repeat. Recognizing the Thirteenth Amendment and the equal protection and privileges or immunities clauses of the Fourteenth Amendment as writing the second paragraph of the Declaration into positive law against state governments is, I believe, the best reading of the American "Constitution."

By the second standard, theories of representational democracy and constitutionalism also form part of the larger Constitution. Without variants of these theories, the American constitutional document of 1787, as amended, would be a political version of a seed catalog, a mere listing of authorities and rights, informed by no general concepts, organized by no architectonic scheme, linked only by consecutively numbered articles and clauses. It would, in sum, be intellectually incoherent, and its claim to be "the supreme law of the land" would be a farce.

Without a serious theory of representative democracy, one could not read the document(s) as an effort to establish a polity based not only on consent but also on representation of the peo-

ple through elected officials. That American political arrangements fall far short of ordaining a "pure" representative
democracy is patent. Nevertheless, not even the most avid defender of any other political theory—and I confess I am more a
constitutionalist than a democrat—could sensibly deny that the
document of 1787 carried out a large, though tempered, element
of democratic theory and that amendments have more fully embodied democratic theory.

The same argument holds for constitutionalism. It was present in the document of 1787 and the Bill of Rights in even larger
doses than was democratic theory; and, while some specific devices the framers foresaw as limiting government have weakened
or vanished, the power of constitutionalism itself has increased.

Despite important differences, both theories start from similar beliefs about human equality. Although neither postulates
that all persons are equal in intelligence, virtue, ambition, or
strength, both are grounded in notions of individual dignity and
equal moral worth. The most significant difference between the
two lies in their view of what government can do to achieve this
general value. Equality, as Giovanni Sartori says in *Democratic
Theory* (1965), "calls for the denaturalization of the political
order." To maintain equal opportunity, much less equality of result, requires constant and sometimes stringent governmental
intervention. Providing that enough popular support was forth-
coming, democratic theory would justify far greater restrictions
on individual liberty than would constitutionalism. Thus, in a
constitutional democracy, affirmative action is likely to be theo-
retically, as well as practically, problematic.

A second, nontrivial difference between the two theories lies
in allocation of authority to decide such questions as whether government has infringed on minority rights and what it may do to
right past wrongs. I have dealt with this issue elsewhere and repeat here only that even some democratic theorists evidence deep
concern about winners in the electoral process being the ultimate
judges of the losers' civil rights.

Despite these differences, the two parts of the Constitution
agree on a basic argument: Government must respect the equal
dignity and worth of its citizens. It must, as Justice John Paul Stevens said in *Fullilove* v. *Klutznick* (1980), "govern impartially."

The American constitutional document of 1787 as amended not only establishes specific governmental processes but also, along with the Declaration, "constitutes" us as a people. The Preamble states the polity's aims, and these, while more mundanely phrased than those of the Declaration, include promoting the general welfare, insuring domestic tranquility, securing the blessings of liberty as well as establishing justice. It makes most sense of the document to take these words at face value and to read the clauses that follow not only as efforts to set out processes of government but also to protect the fundamental values the Preamble lists. These make the American republic, as it would have pleased John Winthrop to note, "a city upon a Hill." And, however short American practice has fallen of these ideals, they have remained vital parts of the nation's culture. As the acerbic Irish writer Malachi Martin, in *Three Popes and the Cardinal* (1972), described the United States during its time of troubles over the war in Vietnam:

"We see in America as a society not merely disturbances, disputes, doubts, and differences. We see the end of all these recognized categories of the human dimension. . . . There is . . . an almost frightening and certainly unprecedented proposition in America today: to make no judgment regarding a man's rights and duties solely on the basis of his skin pigmentation. . . . For the truth is that South African apartheid . . . is strictly traditional and in keeping with all past human history. . . .

"What Americans are attempting today is, historically speaking, anomalous, humanly speaking, unprecedented; and according to the standards entertained in modern France, Italy, Germany, Switzerland, the Soviet Union, and mainland China, repulsive and certainly not to be considered for their individual societies. None of the major human religions (Christianity, Judaism, Buddhism, Islam) ever proposed this or encouraged it of their own accord. It is unheard of. Yet it is the public proposition of American society."

"To amend" means to modify or rephrase, so as to add or subtract. Its root runs to the Latin *emendare*, to correct. My argument here is that the plain words of Article V provide substantive, not merely procedural, limitations on constitutional change, for it speaks of "Amendments," not of creations of a new constitution. Given the commitment of the American Constitution—broadly defined as including the document of 1787 as amended, plus the Declaration, as well as democratic and constitutional theory—my argument is that removing or severely weakening the constitutional command for even-handed governance would be a change so fundamental as to constitute a remaking rather than a rephrasing, modification, or correction. Such a change would mean that the United States had become a different polity, its people would be reconstituted. As I explain below, I do not deny the possibility or even the potential validity of such a transformation, only that—to use William Harris's terminology in his "Reconstitutive Words: Are There Limits to the Amending Power?"—the "Constitution" does not authorize it from "the inside."

Thus Article V establishes procedures for modifications. For legitimation of wholesale revision, we have to look elsewhere.

My argument is that a constitution may include more than the document so labeled. And the American "Constitution" includes, at least, the second paragraph of the Declaration of Independence and democratic and constitutional theory. A constitution can—and the American Constitution does—perform functions other than to establish governmental processes. Among those functions in the American case is to set out the nation's goal, to specify the kind of people we are and want to become. A requirement of even-handed governance is deeply entrenched in the American "Constitution." Moreover, there are limits to changes that a system can effect through amendment under this or any other "real" constitution. A change so fundamental as to destroy what has become a central value of the amended document of 1787, and what has always been part of the larger "Constitution" as well, would be a systemic change. It would be a radical change in the true sense of the word, going to the root of the nation's reason for being, and make the United States a different nation.

Any normative theory that would attempt to bind a nation in perpetuity would be worthy of King Canute. Thus, I do not deny that a nation can escape from even the most fundamental tenets of its constitution; I do deny that it can do so within the terms of its constitution (assuming that its constitution is not a sham). This is not to claim that a constitution, defined narrowly or broadly, may not run for only a set span of years, merely that as long as it is in force, neither its public officials nor its people can validly violate its fundamental principles.

What about radical change then? Is it possible for a people to abandon constitutional democracy or one of its essential elements? The answer, of course, must be yes. As a matter of sheer power, a people may re-form themselves. If one believes in government by consent, one must believe the people may also do so as a matter of right. And while I would argue that some form of constitutional democracy is most likely to secure justice, I would not claim either that there is no room for debate on this issue or that specific circumstances might not occur that would modify my reasoning. My sole point is that one may not validly use a constitution to justify radical changes in that constitution's basic values and underlying principles. Even if the new framers did not admit their attempt to form a new people—to create a new polity—their authority would derive from the people's acceptance of their new work, not from the old constitution.

In the United States, the engine for such a change could be a constitutional convention called by Congress under Article V. But insofar as such a convention asserted authority under Article V, its authority to try to re-form the American people would be severely limited. Its product—even if ratified by conventions chosen in the states—would not be morally or legally binding either on governmental agencies, including but not restricted to courts, or on private citizens. Only by renouncing its authority under Article V could its product—assuming it were accepted—be morally and legally binding. A convention called by state governments, without congressional participation, would not have to dissociate itself from Article V, for it would plainly be extra-constitutional from the start.

I speak of authority here, not power. Backed by governmental force, an amendment could effect radical changes and receive popular acceptance. I would argue, however, that if such an amendment does become operational, the people have to that extent reformed themselves. I think there was one such occurrence in the United States since 1787–88: the Civil War and the Fourteenth Amendment.

Without the violence that broke the nation apart, the Fourteenth Amendment would have been invalid. (It would have been invalid, not because it imposed a duty of equal protection on the states, but because it so radically changed the structure of the American republic.) Southern appeal to arms and early victories on the battlefield tore the nation apart; Northern appeal to arms and final victory on the battlefield re-formed the American people. The Radical Republicans implicitly recognized these changes in status by requiring ex-Confederate states to re-form themselves as subpolities as a condition for readmission to the Union. More explicitly, but still not completely explicitly, the Thirteenth Amendment and the Fourteenth Amendment also recognized these changes. Procedural regularities aside—and these are serious—I do not believe one can justify the Fourteenth Amendment as part of the "Constitution" in any other way.

By the Civil War and the new "amendments," Americans constituted themselves a different people than what they were before the war. Not only did important structural changes occur, but the "Constitution" became much more coherent. The Thirteenth Amendment eliminated the polity's most glaring internal contradiction, the constitutional document's unconstitutional acceptance of slavery. More positively, both the Thirteenth Amendment and the Fourteenth Amendment carried forward the Declaration's commitment to freedom, equality, and basic rights. They advanced, without completing, the demands of the Declaration as well as both democratic and constitutional theory, at least as far as a demand for impartial governance is concerned.

If what I have argued is mostly valid, it follows that the American system cannot, without re-forming its people, relax its requirements that government treat its people equally. The system can, however, tighten those requirements. Yet there again that tightening is not without limits, for equality of treatment is a very complex problem and may raise questions of more than one person's or group's rights. Chief Justice William Rehnquist, in *Trimble* v. *Fordon* (1977), has described the equal protection clause as both "one of the majestic generalities of the Constitution" and "a classic paradox." The generality is obvious. The paradox is that the plain words forbid states to discriminate; but, by their nature, almost all laws of any significance must make distinctions—discriminations—among people. Thus, according equal protection often requires unequal treatment. Affirmative action presents the critical case for constitutional democracy; for democratic and constitutional theories differ on how far government can go in reducing some people's rights to achieve equality for others.

What practical course is open to governmental agencies and private citizens if such a radical change as elimination or severe reduction of government's duty to govern impartially became operational?

First, if the change was effected legitimately—that is, on its own merits as a radical re-forming of the people—then it would open the whole question of consent. Certainly by the theories underlying the old constitution, individuals would have the moral and legal right to exist, though the new regime, depending on how authoritarian it was, might deny such a right.

What about the states? William Harris argues that the new constitution should be valid, as Article VII specifies, only among these states that ratify. For two reasons, I am less sure: (1) invoking Article VII implies that the radical change derives some legitimacy from the old constitution, and that I deny; (2) I am not certain—I am not prepared to deny or affirm it—that gradual changes over the last two centuries—most important, the implications of the Fourteenth Amendment itself—have not deprived states of the status they held in 1787 as primary political entities.

Second, if the change was effected illegitimately—that is, under the guise of a mere amendment rather than a re-formation—then individual citizens would face the age-old dilemma of what to do about unjust laws. Silent acquiescence might be the most prudent course, though the gallant might well fight to restore the old order, either peacefully or even through revolution. The less quietistic and less gallant might choose to exit.

Public officials would face similar difficulties. And democracy and constitutionalism might pull in different directions. If the new system accepted political freedom—that is, allowed free and open debate, campaigns, and elections, and did not take away participational rights even from minorities whom it might otherwise oppress—democratic theory would face a severe crisis. If the people govern because of who they are rather than what they know, as Walzer claims, then the obligation to obey is strong. Still, the value Walzer and many other democratic theorists share with constitutionalists—that even the people must govern impartially—would indicate something less than full acceptance of the new system, even if it was the people's choice.

Constitutionalism would be less ambivalent. Although prudence might dictate extreme caution, constitutional theory would not easily admit a moral or legal obligation to obey any system that violated constitutionalism's norms. Thus it would most probably justify a public official's refusing to enforce the new order.

Would such resistance be effective? There can be no abstract answer beyond: "It depends." If an official or set of officials in a

respected institution—the president or the Supreme Court, for
instance—declared the "amendment" unconstitutional and refused to enforce it, we might see change. Public officials can act
as republican schoolmasters. They can also whistle in the dark.

HOW HARD IT IS TO CHANGE[5]

I worked hard for many years to change the United States
Constitution—and I failed. Like so many others, I wanted the
Constitution to assert the principle of equal rights without regard
to gender. I had high hopes for the equal rights amendment, but
I knew from the beginning that a constitutional amendment is
difficult to obtain. So I was not surprised when the measure
failed.

I was disappointed at the defeat but no less glad that the Constitution is so hard to change. I appreciate even more deeply now
the obstacles the framers of the Constitution put in the way of the
amendment process. The reason is simple: even though my efforts were unsuccessful, and there is no E.R.A. in the Constitution, there is also no official school prayer amendment or anti-
abortion amendment.

Article V of the Constitution—the amending article—plays
no favorites. It disciplines even the most ardent proponents to its
commands and occasionally turns opponents into allies. There is
an irony of sorts, for instance, that Phyllis Schlafly, who did so
much to stop the E.R.A., and I now find ourselves in agreement
in opposing a constitutional convention that has lately been proposed to consider a balanced budget amendment. I'll get to our
unlikely alliance a little later.

The makers of the Constitution wanted to create a firm basis
for the exercise of governmental power. However, they were wise
enough to know that if they made their document too rigid, if
they wrote it so that it could not be revised to suit future times
and events, they were inviting future revolution. They would be
creating a situation in which the only methods to effect change

[5]Reprint of an article by Mary Frances Berry, Geraldine R. Segal Professor of American Thought at the University of Pennsylvania. *New York Times Magazine.* p. 93+. S. 13, '87. Copyright © 1987 by The New York Times Company. Reprinted by permission.

would be to cast aside the Constitution itself. As George Mason noted at the 1787 convention, changes would be necessary, and it would be "better to provide for them in an easy, regular and constitutional way than to trust to chance and violence."

So they made it open to change—but not open to change without great effort. James Madison was among those who warned against making things too easy. It was important, he said, to guard "against that extreme facility which would render the Constitution too mutable." For if it could be altered easily, the Constitution would be mere temporary law, not a document for the ages.

The great idea in Article V is that change requires two elements: consensus and necessity. There must be substantive national agreement, as well as agreement in most of the states, that an urgent problem exists that cannot be remedied by the courts, legislatures or Congress, and which can be solved only if the Constitution is changed.

The public expression of consensus and necessity that Article V requires can come to light in two ways. In the first, an amendment may be proposed by a two-thirds vote in each house of Congress. The approved amendment then must be ratified by majority votes in the legislatures or conventions of three-fourths of the states before it can become part of the Constitution. The second way is that, if two-thirds of the states ask for a constitutional convention to consider amendments, Congress should be obliged to call one. Any changes such a convention passes must then be ratified by three-fourths of the states. This second path has, so far, gone untried in United States history: no constitutional convention, since the first one in 1787, has ever been called.

Meanwhile, the first route to constitutional amendments has been well traveled. Almost 10,000 of them have been proposed in the Congress since Article V became law. Only 26 have been ratified. Of these, the Bill of Rights, the 13th, 14th and 15th Amendments resulting from the Civil War, and the 19th, permitting women to vote, remedied major defects in the original document. Most of the others smoothed out procedural difficulties. One, Prohibition, was the result of an artificial consensus and was soon repealed.

Six other amendments have been approved by Congress but not ratified by the states. These include the E.R.A., an amendment to prohibit child labor and an amendment that would have given the District of Columbia a voting member of the House and two Senators.

It is easy to see why so many amendments have been proposed in Congress. For politicians, advocating solution by amendment is a convenient response to hot political problems. For instance, whenever the Supreme Court makes a widely publicized decision on a controversial issue, there are Congressional proposals to limit the power of the Justices. The legislator can thereby show concerned voters back home that action, however ineffectual, has been taken, something has been done.

It is clear that a strong effort to gain an amendment can influence government even when it fails. It acts as a brooding omnipresence in the sky, signaling to politicians that they must act. Some proposals that fail as amendments result in legislation. Proposed amendments reflecting public opposition to busing for desegregation purposes led to a 1972 education law restricting Federal involvement in busing. More recently, official school prayer amendment proposals led to the passage of the Equal Access Act of 1984, which provides that religious activities may not be excluded from among any extracurricular activities allowed on a public school's premises. Instead of passing an amendment requiring the balancing of the Federal budget, Congress in 1985 tried the expedient of enacting the Gramm-Rudman-Hollings Act to achieve a balanced budget in stages. In each of these cases, the stringent requirements for ratification of an amendment have prevented changing the Constitution. But politicians who needed to do so could show constituents that they were responding to their concerns.

In the case of an amendment calling for a balanced budget, however, apprehensions about the Federal deficit have created a feeling of necessity that may not be satisfied by legislation. The issue may well bring about the first constitutional convention since 1787. Already, 32 states (only two fewer than required) have called for a convention to consider a budget-balancing amendment, and President Reagan supports the idea. Proponents of the convention say it would be a fast, easy assembly that would simply meet, adopt an amendment, send it to the states to ratify, and then go home.

Those who oppose the convention, including myself, are not sure. Ordinarily disparate forces such as Phyllis Schlafly's Eagle

Forum, the National Organization for Women, the American Civil Liberties Union and the John Birch Society are all opposed, because they fear the convention has the potential of putting the Constitution at risk.

The fact is, nothing in the language of Article V limits the subjects to be considered at a constitutional convention, nothing establishes rules of procedure to be followed or precludes scrapping the entire Constitution. The sole convention we have had, in 1787, was called only for the purpose of amending our first constitution, the Articles of Confederation. But the Founding Fathers discarded the Articles altogether and drafted a new document. They even modified the ratification procedure to insure success. That could happen again.

The purpose of Article V's convention provision is to make it possible for amendments to be proposed that Congress does not want proposed, and it would be illogical indeed to assume that Congress could bind a convention's agenda. Even if the Congress decided to call a convention for the sole purpose of proposing amendments to balance the budget, and even if the convention agreed to this overall goal, the gathering would still have great freedom. The participants might decide that Congressional budgetary authority should be limited to support for the national defense. They could delete support for the general welfare from the Constitution, thus precluding such items as Social Security, Medicaid and Medicare. They could decide to amend Congressional power to regulate commerce, which now allows for such activities as environmental regulation, labor regulation and antitrust enforcement. This would, after all, abolish a whole series of Federal agencies and decrease the budget.

But if the participants decided to ignore any instructions controlling their agenda—and who could stop them—they could decide to ban abortion and void the First Amendment, require the government to provide jobs, housing and education for all Americans, or any other proposal that gained approval by whatever majority they decided to require. Any proposals that gained ratification by three-fourths of the states would become part of the nation's fundamental law. However, the convention might decide, as the original convention did, to change the mode of ratification, perhaps to require only a simple majority of the states. Given this very real possibility for wide-ranging action and unprecedented mischief, the pertinent question is not whether we want a constitutional convention to require a balanced budget, but whether we want to risk a convention at all.

I am tempted by the argument that believers in pure democracy and majoritarian rule ought to favor a convention in order to let the people reign and make whatever decisions they choose. However, the Founding Fathers created not pure democracy, but a republican form of government in which the people govern through their representatives and with checks and balances, including a check on the majority's impulses.

I am reminded in my service on the United States Commission on Civil Rights, whenever issues such as voting rights or affirmative action come before us, of how dangerous it would be to define civil rights by the will of an administration elected by a political majority. In our system of government, the rights of all, liberals and conservatives, people of all races and both sexes, the majority and minority groups, are accorded constitutional protection.

The amendment process set up in Article V allows our government to adapt itself to social change. At the same time, it gives us a check against beliefs that may be strongly held but are not widely approved. Because our Constitution can be amended, we can repair tears in our social fabric and try different strategies and tactics to resolve problems. Because our Constitution cannot be amended easily, we can preserve the stability and continuity that lasting republican government requires.

SHOULD THE U.S. CONSTITUTION BE AMENDED TO PERMIT SCHOOL PRAYER?—PRO[6]

This is a momentous occasion. Today we begin consideration of Senate Joint Resolution 73, the voluntary school prayer constitutional amendment, which I, along with some other Senators, introduced at the request of the President on March 24, 1983. This

[6]Remarks by Senator Strom Thurmond, Republican of South Carolina and Chairman of the Senate Committee on the Judiciary. From the debate of March 5, 1984, on the floor of the U.S. Senate during consideration of Senate Joint Resolution 73. Reprinted from *Congressional Digest.* 63:138+. My. '84.

amendment to the Constitution, as President Reagan has repeatedly emphasized, is of vital importance to the well-being of our Nation. It would restore to our youth their right to pray in the public schools—a right which was freely exercised under our Constitution until the Supreme Court removed prayer from the classroom over two decades ago.

In 1962, the Supreme Court abruptly ended over 170 years of religious exercise in the schools of this Nation. Until the Engel and Abington School District decisions, the establishment clause of the first amendment was generally understood only to prohibit the national government from officially approving, or holding in special favor, any particular religious faith or denomination, as was the practice in European countries when our Nation was founded. Justice Story clearly states this understanding in his nearly contemporaneous "Commentaries on the Constitution": "The real object of the first amendment," he said, "was . . . to prevent any national ecclesiastical establishment which would give to an hierarchy the exclusive patronage of the National Government."

In writing the establishment clause of the first amendment, our Founding Fathers wanted to prevent what had originally caused many colonial Americans to emigrate to this country—an official, state religion. At the same time, they sought, through the free exercise clause, to guarantee to all Americans the freedom to worship God without Government interference or restraint.

The unfortunate constitutional interpretation which has banned voluntary prayer in our public schools runs contrary to this dual intent of the framers. They understood, as I think we all do, that the general welfare of our Republic depends to a large degree on the spiritual and moral fiber of the citizenry. That fiber is, in turn, dependent upon the guidance given our young people. A ban on school prayer is, therefore, contrary to the best interests of our Nation as a whole.

Justice Douglas once stated an obvious truth when he observed on behalf of the Supreme Court: "We are a religious people whose institutions presuppose a Supreme Being." Nearly every President since George Washington has proclaimed a day of public prayer to acknowledge the many blessings that Almighty God has bestowed upon this Nation. Moreover, we, as a Nation, continue to recognize the Deity and His Guidance in our Pledge of Allegiance by affirming that we are a Nation "under

God." The coins in our pockets are inscribed with the motto, "In God We Trust."

In this body, we begin our workday with the comfort and stimulus of voluntary group prayer. Recently, such a practice has been constitutionally blessed by the Supreme Court. It is patently absurd, in my judgment, that the opportunity for the same beneficial experience is denied to the boys and girls who attend public schools. The average pupil spends over 7 hours in school each day. During this time, he receives both an intellectual and athletic education, but is denied the opportunity to acknowledge his God even briefly. This situation simply does not comport with the intentions of the framers of the Constitution and is, in fact, antithetical to the rights of our youngest citizens to freely exercise their respective religions. It simply must be changed, without further delay.

Let there be no doubt about the constituency involved here. The movement to restore prayer to public schools and other institutions is not an attempt by a small minority to impose their views upon an apathetic majority. Public opinion polls show strong support for a constitutional amendment like Senate Joint Resolution 73 on the part of the vast majority of Americans—over three-quarters of our population.

I believe the latest poll showed around 80 percent of our people favored prayers in public schools. These are not religious zealots, but average Americans who want their children and grandchildren to enjoy the same simple privilege that they had as public school students. The change which we propose here today is not revolutionary—it is merely a return to the status quo which began with our forefathers and ended on questionable constitutional grounds only a few years ago.

If ratified by the States, Senate Joint Resolution 73 would amend the Constitution to clarify that it does not prohibit vocal, voluntary prayer in the public school and other public institutions. It emphatically states that no person may be required to participate in any prayer. When I introduced this resolution 1 year ago, I strongly urged my colleagues to come together in support of the concept of restoring school prayer and to give me their ideas on how the measure could be improved. Based on the input which was received, I offered an amendment in committee to add a third sentence which would preclude any government from drafting prayers to be said in public schools.

As it reads today, I believe that we have a well-crafted amendment which meets with the approval of the overwhelming majority of Americans.

I strongly urge my colleagues to champion religious liberty in this country by joining President Reagan, myself, and others in this body in support of Senate Joint Resolution 73.

It is clear that this is purely voluntary prayer—not formulated by school officials, not formulated by State officials, not formulated by Federal officials—purely voluntary prayer that the students themselves may originate.

When I came along in school, we had what was called "chapel" every morning. Every morning we sang. We sang patriotic songs, and we had prayer. I do not know if anybody was ever hurt by those prayers. I never heard of anybody ever being hurt in that school or any other school in the United States because of prayer.

However, this amendment does not require any attendance and does not permit, as I said, any school official, State official, or Federal official, to inaugurate a prayer or compose a prayer that would have to be used.

It is really inconsistent to say we cannot have prayer in the schools. After all, the people look to Washington for guidance. They look to Washington to be a model somewhat. And it ought to be. Every morning that this Senate meets, as President pro tempore of the Senate, I walk up those steps and walk up to the desk where the President pro tempore sits. Before I sit down, the first thing I do is rap for order. The next thing I do is call upon the Chaplain of the U.S. Senate to lead us in prayer.

If the U.S. Senate can open its day with prayer, why cannot the schools of this Nation open their day with prayer if they care to do it?

I happen to be a member of a group called the "Prayer Group" that has been meeting here ever since I have been in the Senate, right down here in the Vandenberg Room, S. 139. Every Wednesday morning we meet there and we have prayer. We have a discussion by one of the Senators. Outsiders are not allowed to lead in the discussions. One of the Senators leads the discussion, and we hold hands and pray.

If the U.S. Capitol can be used for prayer by Senators, why cannot the school children use a public building for prayer if they so desire? I think it is nothing but fair, it is nothing but just, and it sounds to me unreasonable to deny the school children of this Nation the right to pray voluntarily if they wish to do so.

SHOULD THE U.S. CONSTITUTION BE AMENDED
TO PERMIT SCHOOL PRAYER?—CON[7]

The central question in this debate as I see it is simply:

How can we adequately protect the right of our people to be free from having an alien religious practice forced upon their children by governmental action, but at the same time allow them to freely exercise their own religion without government hostility. In my view, Senate Joint Resolution 73 fails to measure up to this crucial standard.

Objections to the pending prayer amendment that I wish to comment on:

First, I think if you look at the pending prayer amendment you will find that amendment looks to the State, to the teacher, and to the school board to initiate, orchestrate, structure, and organize prayer or religious activity in our public schools.

Second, the pending prayer amendment fundamentally alters the careful balance in the first amendment between the free exercise clause and the prohibition against the establishment of religion. When our Constitution was established, no other nation provided so carefully to prevent the combination of the power of religion with the power of the national government.

Where government sponsors, initiates, and dominates in matters of religion there is stagnation, monolithic church institutions and little creativity. Where government stays neutral and benevolently accommodates the religious expressions of all, religion flourishes and a vitality is evident in the healthy diversity of religious practices. In my view, there is nothing wrong with the first amendment as it is presently written.

Third, the pending prayer amendment violates another central premise of the first amendment, and that is that government should be prohibited from favoring certain religions at the expense of others.

[7]Remarks by Senator Mark O. Hatfield, Republican of Oregon. From the debate of March 8, 1984, on the floor of the U.S. Senate during consideration of Senate Joint Resolution 73. Reprinted from *Congressional Digest.* 63:139+. My. '84.

The primary thrust of these objections to Senate Joint Resolution 73 applies as well to other constitutional amendments that are being floated around as potential compromises. Let me reiterate again. There is nothing wrong with the first amendment in its present form. It has served us well. While we may individually disagree on various Supreme Court decisions from time to time let us pause carefully before we fundamentally alter the balance that already exists. In my view, there is no overwhelming defect that demands a constitutional remedy.

What is really behind the school prayer controversy, we might legitimately ask.

In the 1962 landmark decision of Engel against Vitale, the U.S. Supreme Court ruled that the recitation of prescribed non-denominational prayer by government officials violated the first amendment's protection against the establishment of religion.

In language that echoed the warnings of Madison, Justice Black noted that the first amendment "rested on the belief that a union of government and religion tends to destroy government and to degrade religion."

Since that decision, the Supreme Court's ruling has been claimed for the deteriorating quality of public education, for the breakdown of the American family, for the decay in moral principles, and abdication of governmental institutions to the norm of secular humanism.

In his 1964 dissent in Abington against Schempp, Justice Stewart noted that the total absence of religious exercises in public schools places religion at a state created disadvantage. It is viewed not as state neutrality, "but rather as the establishment of a religion of secularism."

Proponents reject the very notion of "value-free education." When strict separationists seek to confine all religious expression to the church and to the home enormous tension is created in our political process and in our schools.

There is an alternative. The first amendment to the U.S. Constitution sets limits on the ability of government to promote, establish, and inculcate religious beliefs in public school students—but it sets no limit on student-initiated prayer or religious discussion during noninstructional time periods. Instead of concentrating upon a school prayer amendment, I urge my colleagues to devote their energies to rooting out ridiculous barriers that have been erected to forbid voluntary meetings of students who seek to meet and pray in nondisruptive ways.

A growing number of Federal courts have expanded the prohibitions on the sponsorship by the state of religious activity in
public schools to encompass equal access policies adopted by
school boards as well as student requests to meet on their own
time before or after school hours for prayer, devotional reading
or religious discussions. These prohibitions are hostile to the
rights of religious expression and, in my view, violate the free
speech rights of students.

In the Lubbock School Board case, 23 Senators joined with
me in filing a friend of the court brief asking the Supreme Court
to grant a hearing and reverse the decision. In that brief, we argued that:

"Neither legislation nor a constitutional amendment is required to permit a school to open its facilities for all appropriate
student-initiated and student-managed activities including, if the
students wish, religious activities. The Constitution already so
provides. The Establishment, Free Exercise and Free Speech
clauses of the First Amendment require treatment of such activities in a neutral manner. Consequently, public schools properly
may allow students equal access to school facilities for voluntary,
extra-curricular, religious speech and assembly."

As the original sponsor of equal access legislation that was introduced on September 17, 1982, I want the Senate to know that
I am adamantly opposed to the idea of including equal access language in a constitutional amendment for it undercuts the very
heart of my legislation. A student's right to gather together with
others for prayer and religious discussion is inherent in the first
amendment right now. It comes under the protections of free
speech and the freedom of association when an open forum is established by the school. Including this language in a constitutional amendment will significantly reverse the progress that has been
made in pending litigation and puts a stamp of approval behind
the logic of Brandon and Lubbock opinions. Instead of ill-
conceived constitutional amendments, let us proceed to a simple
statute that provides a judicial remedy to aggrieved high school
students.

Some 26 Senators have joined me in offering Senate bill 815
which would make clear that secondary school students have the
right to meet voluntarily during noninstructional time periods
for prayer or devotional reading. S. 815 has united a number of
Senators who differ on constitutional amendments that permit

school sponsored prayer or statutory approaches which deny jurisdiction to Federal courts to decide school prayer cases. But the sponsors of S. 815 agree that the constitution does not allow our public schools to be hostile to religion.

S. 815 also has the support of religious groups that have opposed school prayer amendments. S. 815 can pass this Congress and provide a reasonable solution to the school prayer controversy.

The focus of S. 815 is on student-initiated religious activities instead of the government inculcation of religious belief. Given the strong bipartisan support that this bill has received in the Senate, I urge the Senate to approve S. 815.

The thing that concerns me at this point in time is that—not that I own a bill that I introduce; I recognize it becomes the property of the Senate—I have not had any consultation with those who have taken the initiative to add this to the constitutional amendment.

Now, notwithstanding that—and I cannot hang any major objection to that action being taken on the basis that I had not been consulted—let me say that I refrained from raising this bill or the content of this bill at this time because I felt that the Senate ought to have an opportunity to deal with the issue of a constitutional amendment procedure. It was also felt that it might undermine the possibility of that constitutional amendment being passed by raising this other issue on equal access.

I accommodated that request. I refrained from offering that. Then I awaken to the fact that that has been offered and combined, fused, linked to the constitutional amendment.

I think it raises confusion on what has been clarified as it relates to public universities and colleges. Le me explain.

We have had a case that went to the Supreme Court in which students who had asked to use public university facilities for religious purposes had been denied the right to use such facilities. That case was taken to the U.S. Supreme Court, and the U.S. Supreme Court ruled in the Widmar case that once a public university or a college had established the right of students to voluntarily organize and use public facilities for student associations of camera clubs, drama clubs, music clubs, or whatever else, that the same university that established the right of forum could not dictate the content of the forum and, therefore, students would be denied their constitutional right to use those same facilities for religious purposes that they could use for every other purpose. Now the Court has ruled on that.

What I attempted to do in S. 815 was merely to apply that same constitutional right that has been extended to university students in public institutions to students at the secondary level.

Now, all of a sudden along comes this constitutional amendment that wants to set up a prayer program for the secondary-elementary school students and S. 815, which deals with the Widmar case, is now being added to the constitutional amendment. It could do nothing but create question and raise confusion.

So those who think they are promoting religious activity, those who think they are promoting the possibility of spiritual renewal by some kind of civil religion in our public schools, ought to realize that they are also raising some serious questions and confusion among those activities that are now in place and functioning without question in our public universities.

So I oppose the constitutional amendments—all of them—that relate to school prayer, whether it is silent meditation or anything else. It is all part of our civil religion, not spiritual, Biblical faith.

MOVE OVER, JAMES MADISON[8]

If you could add one amendment to the Constitution, what would it be? We posed this question to a variety of distinguished people and extended a general invitation to our distinguished readership. Here are some of the more interesting responses, edited for length and to avoid repetitions. The most common repeat suggestions involved limiting congressional tenure or (paradoxically) repealing the limit on presidential tenure; restricting campaign contributions; and forbidding the designated-hitter rule.

Article V, providing that two-thirds of the state legislatures can call a constitutional convention, is a constitutional crisis waiting to happen. Fearful of those wild-eyed folk in the states, Congress

[8]Reprint of an article. *The New Republic.* 196:19-21. Je. 29, '87. Copyright © 1987 by *The New Republic.*

has never clarified how and when states can use their authority to initiate a constitutional convention. If Congress won't act, the states should petition for a convention with the sole purpose of amending Article V. The mere threat might force Congress to adopt legislation stipulating how and when states can use their right to originate amendments—a concession that all wisdom does not reside in Washington. The last time that happened, the states ganged up on Congress to force the direct election of U.S. senators. Would any genuine federalist today argue against that result?

BRUCE BABBITT
Phoenix, Arizona

Abolish the Electoral College? Get rid of the separation of powers? Eliminate those frustrating checks and balances? No, thanks. Like James Madison, and out of a similar concern for the rights of all, I am opposed to any effort to make the Constitution a more efficient instrument of unrestrained popular majorities. I would, therefore, add an amendment forbidding future amendments.

WALTER BERNS
Washington, D.C.

"No person shall be prosecuted under any law if it can be shown that that law is not consistently and uniformly enforced for all persons."

GUY BLACK
Fairfax, Virginia

Hayek was correct when he wrote that the progressive income tax is "the chief source of irresponsibility of democratic action . . . and the crucial issue on which the whole character of future society will depend." Accordingly, the Hayek-Buckley amendment would forbid unequal treatment of income by the law.

WILLIAM F. BUCKLEY
New York, New York

"The designated-hitter rule shall not be allowed in professional baseball at any level in the United States."

ROBERT L. COHEN
Brooklyn, New York

"Supreme Court Justices shall serve a single, non-renewable term of nine years."

WILLIAM E. COOPER
Iowa City, Iowa

"No person shall be eligible to vote in an election for the U.S. Congress, nor for the office of President or Vice President, who has not fulfilled a term of National Service. The term of National Service includes, but need not be limited to, military service, and shall be for a duration of one to three years. Congress shall, by law, specify the term and nature of the National Service."

There is a built-in bias, in thorough-going democratic government, toward satisfying the demands of the electorate regardless of whether or not these demands are prudent. Representatives will reflect the views of the voters whom they represent. Rather than trying to limit the discretion of the representatives by means such as a balanced budget amendment, the approach here is to apply a filter. Those who don't wish to devote a few years to the country shouldn't have a say in what the country does.

JOHN CUGINI
Walkersville, Maryland

The Constitution should be amended to provide for a limitation of congressional service. Senators should be restricted to two terms (12 years) and Representatives to 12 years of service or six terms. Such a change would force Congress to elect representative leadership and reduce the paralyzing effect of parochial politics as practiced by all senior members of Congress.

KIM GORDON DAVIS
New York, New York

"1. In any general election for federal office, there shall be a choice on the ballot labeled 'Reject' after all the candidates.
"2. If no candidate receives more votes than 'Reject' did, then a new election with different candidates shall be held."

STEVEN DEN BESTE
Arlington, Massachusetts

If the question had been put to me 15 years ago, I would have proclaimed, "The ERA." But no longer. Here's why. First, the Supreme Court, in a string of cases, has used the 14th Amendment to strike down nearly all the laws and practices Congress aimed to eliminate when it passed the ERA in 1972. Second, in the absence of anything approaching a consensus on whether, for example, women should be drafted and no longer exempt even from combat, there is little chance for ratification. Third, the decade-long struggle over the ERA demonstrates that once an amendment becomes a bitterly contested partisan question, the amending process is ill-suited to generate a working majority on substantive issues. Why? Because vital concerns left unanswered by the amendment will be thrown directly into the lap of the Supreme Court, the least democratic of our governing institutions. This makes people wary, as it should.

JEAN BETHKE ELSHTAIN
Amherst, Massachusetts

Riders should be added to the First Amendment explicitly protecting the right of smokers to assemble in public, and to the Seventh Amendment explicitly declaring bans on smoking to be cruel and unusual punishment.

HENRY FAIRLIE
Washington, D.C.

I propose an amendment to overturn the *Buckley* v. *Valeo* decision of 1976. In that case, the Supreme Court said, in effect, that campaign contributions were a form of free speech and therefore protected by the First Amendment. My new amendment would say: "Congress may regulate the amount of personal funds a candidate can spend in his/her own election." Without this amendment the House of Representatives may well evolve into a House of Lords as heirs and CEOs increasingly purchase congressional seats as they might stock exchange seats (except stock exchange seats are cheaper).

MARK GREEN
New York, New York

"The Congress shall not authorize any expenditure of public funds in excess of the funds that exist in the Treasury of the United States, or that exceeds the revenues to be collected during the term of the authorized expenditure, unless it simultaneously enacts a tax to provide the required funds."

CHARLES W. HAIR
Baton Rouge, Louisiana

"Every working-age person in the United States shall be guaranteed a right to a job at a wage equal to at least 50 percent of the median wage in the society."

MICHAEL HARRINGTON
New York, New York

It is time (morally and sensibly, if not politically) to ratify a constitutional amendment guaranteeing subsistence—that is, sufficient food, clothing, and shelter—for all Americans. One in every four children growing up in this country is so poor that either hunger or homelessness is inevitable. We are wasting a generation of children, for whom poverty renders all other constitutional rights meaningless. Wild-eyed idealists may still think we live in an 18th-century era of rugged individualism. The caretakers of the Republic's third century must be harder-headed.

ROBERT HAYES
New York, New York

I would propose Thomas Jefferson's unadopted version of the First Amendment, which reads: "The people shall not be deprived of the right to speak, to write, or otherwise publish anything but false facts affecting injuriously the life, liberty, or reputation of others, or affecting the peace of the confederacy with other nations."

REED IRVINE
Washington, D.C.

The single amendment I would tack on to the Constitution would delete from the Fifth Amendment the following words: "No person shall be compelled in any criminal case to be a witness against himself." In recent years, men such as Klaus Fuchs, DeLorean, the Butcher Brothers, Poindexter, North, and miscellaneous mobsters have tied our judicial system in knots. It is time that conservatives and liberals alike revisit this amendment and look at its need in today's advanced society.

EUGENE L. JOYCE
Oak Ridge, Tennessee

"No court of the United States shall issue any opinion exceeding eight (8) pages in length." To prevent cheating, the amendment might specify margin dimensions and type sizes, the way most court rules do in wisely limiting the pages in lawyers' briefs.

JOHN G. KESTER
Washington, D.C.

I would remove the provision of Article V allowing amendments to the Constitution to be proposed by calling a constitutional convention.

NORMAN LEAR
Los Angeles, California

"The right of the people to engage in private, consensual sexual activity shall not be infringed."

PAUL LERNER
New York, New York

A provision, in the interest of achieving real "arms control," that mandates that we match Soviet percentage growth in defense spending, thereby eliminating any incentive they might have for trying to outspend us militarily.

Steve Lenzner
Maple Glen, Pennsylvania

"The subordination of women to men is hereby abolished." Or, similarly interpreted, Alice Paul's original 1923 Equal Rights Amendment: "Men and women shall have equal rights . . . " This would help counter sex-based de facto job segregation, feminized poverty, and sexist violation in which government now colludes, such as domestic battery, sexual abuse of children, rape, pornography, and prostitution. These conditions now exclude women from meaningful constitutional rights and meaningful lives.

CATHARINE MACKINNON
Palo Alto, California

I would repeal the 25th Amendment, on presidential succession, and abolish the office of Vice President. The possibilities of mischief and confusion inherent in this amendment are almost beyond imagination. The application of the amendment might well establish something like the "Great Schism" of the 14th century, when one pope held out in Rome and another in Avignon. Abolishing the vice presidency has several advantages. First, the presence of a vice presidential candidate confuses politics. The concept of a balanced ticket is unsound since it implies that by putting two candidates on the ticket, each unbalanced in some way, a balance in the presidential office is achieved. Also, a good man or woman can be wasted for four or eight years. A good man or woman can have a political career, even character, seriously and negatively affected by service as Vice President. Finally, the office puts in line for the presidency persons who may not have qualifications for the presidency, and who would not be candidates without the vice presidency as a launching base.

EUGENE J. McCARTHY
Washington, D.C.

I would repeal the 22nd Amendment, which restricts a President's service to two terms. The Founding Fathers demonstrated their faith in democracy by permitting the voters to determine each President's length of service. An election every four years provides ample opportunity to remove an unsatisfactory President. The power of impeachment permits the removal of a President at any time for improper conduct.

GEORGE McGOVERN
Washington, D.C.

"In any national, state, or local election, the Victor shall be determined by calculating the highest numerical ratio obtained by dividing the number of votes cast in favor of any candidate by the sum of all dollars spent by any Person, real or corporate, on any bona fide advertising or other activity designed or intended to influence the Electorate to vote for the Candidate."

JONATHAN T. McPHEE
Chicago, Illinois

"Capital punishment shall be unconstitutional."

VICTOR NAVASKY
New York, New York

I think I will beg off. My reason is twofold. First, so little in fact is known about the operation of government that it is hard to be confident that any change in the system (a six-year presidency, or whatever) would be an improvement. Second, it is almost impossible to find a form of words that the courts couldn't and wouldn't twist into unrecognizable shape.

RICHARD A. POSNER
Chicago, Illinois

I propose that a new sentence be added to the Ninth Amendment, so that it would read as follows: "The enumeration in the Constitution of certain rights shall not be construed to deny or disparage others retained by the people. *And we really mean it.*" The Ninth Amendment makes it clear that there was an "original intent" that individual rights be construed broadly, not in the miserly fashion advocated by the Rehnquists and Meeses of the world.

GLENN HARLAN REYNOLDS
Washington, D.C.

In my heart I love the Constitution and believe it is a splendid document as is. However, given the low regard for human life of both the elderly and the unborn, it may be necessary to add an amendment guaranteeing as inviolate the life of all people.

PAT ROBERTSON
Virginia Beach, Virginia

I am ardently and vocally pro-choice, but even my two-month tenure in law school was more than enough to demonstrate that the Supreme Court's *Roe* v. *Wade* decision is seriously flawed, threatening to self-destruct under its own logic. I think it is time to pass a constitutional amendment clearly guaranteeing to women their right to abortion as a fundamental and basic human right of reproductive freedom.

JOHN SCHACTER
Arlington, Virginia

The Constitution presupposes that those who participate in the American polity will be informed, not ignorant. Unfortunately, the progressive extension of the franchise hasn't been matched by a concomitant rise in cultural literacy. Fortunately, there is a

simple solution. To wit: we should limit the vote to those who pass
a cultural literacy test.

ARNON D. SIEGAL
New Haven, Connecticut

My amendment would change the system we use to nominate
presidential candidates: "The parties in the House of Representatives will nominate the candidates for President and Vice President and the field will be limited to the party's Governors and
Senators."

ERIC STEEL
Oakland, California

"The Leadership of the opposition party in the Congress, or their
designees, shall have the right to question the President or any
member of the Administration before a joint session of the Congress at least one time per week whenever the Congress is in
session."

MARK STERN
Orlando, Florida

Abolish the Electoral College, and in its place establish a system
under which the President and the Vice President would be elected by direct popular vote.

RICHARD A. STIFEL
Washington, D.C.

The District of Columbia should become our 51st state. Creation
of the state of New Columbia would reduce municipal corruption
by putting it on the state level where it belongs.

RICHARD A. STIFEL
& CARL A. LICHVARCIK
Washington, D.C.

Ideally, amend the Constitution to change to the parliamentary
system. Realistically, an amendment to require that treaty ratification can take effect with the approving vote of a constitutional
majority of both houses, rather than the two-thirds approval of
the Senate.

RICHARD L. STROUT
Washington, D.C.

I would like something aimed at reducing the corrupting influence of private campaign spending and counteracting Congress's unwillingness to take unpopular short-term actions for the long-term public welfare. The trick is how to do this without making things worse. Electing all members of Congress to four-year terms at the same time as the President might help, along with limiting private campaign spending.

STUART TAYLOR JR.
Washington, D.C.

I would restore federalism, one of our most basic constitutional principles, with a Federalism Amendment that would put back into the Constitution what activist judges have taken away—a *reasonable* amount of state sovereignty. It should clearly state that the Bill of Rights, intended originally to restrain *federal* power, is not legitimately incorporated in the 14th Amendment as a bar against *state* power, and that the federal judiciary, through its remedial powers, may not intrude into and manage the domestic affairs of the states.

PAUL M. WEYRICH
Washington, D.C.

Twenty-seventh Amendment: "Because this Constitution is an instrument of government designed only to assure the democratic disposition of power, the First Amendment of this Constitution is hereby amended by insertion of the words 'explicitly political' between the phrase 'abridging freedom of' and the word 'speech.' Furthermore, the First Amendment shall not be interpreted to restrict the right of the states to compensate persons who have been libeled and to punish the defendant with unrestricted punitive damages, notwithstanding the absence of a showing of actual malice."

GEORGE WILL
Washington, D.C.

Make voting mandatory.

GARRY WILLS
Chicago, Illinois

I would propose reviving James Madison's original plan to make representation in the upper house of Congress proportional to population. Madison dropped the idea when the small states threatened to leave the Convention. Now that the small states no longer pose a threat, we should return to Madison's initial, more equitable formulation.

ROSEMARIE ZAGARRI
Washington, D.C.

EDITOR'S INTRODUCTION

The proper way to interpret a canonized text has been a matter of debate in the Western world for at least two millennia. The scholars whose teachings are recorded in the Talmud discerned four levels of meaning in Scripture; the Protestant fundamentalists of our own day discern one level, the literal. A similar disagreement exists between those who view the Constitution as strictly "the sum of its words," which have been given specific meanings by their authors, and those who see the Constitution as animated by principles that supersede the particular words in which they are expressed. As Judge Joseph Story said in 1845, "How easily men satisfy themselves that the Constitution is exactly what they wish it to be."

The case for sticking to the intent of the Framers was restated in a series of speeches given by Attorney General Edwin Meese in the fall of 1985. One of these is reprinted as the first selection in this section. The second selection presents a rebuttal to this view by William J. Brennan, Jr., an associate justice of the U.S. Supreme Court since 1956.

The exchange of accusations between Meese and Brennan on the eve of the Constitution's bicentennial touched off a sharp debate among legal scholars, historians, and government officials over the role of the judiciary and the willingness of some judges to take an active role in setting public policy. The third and fourth selections, "How the Constitution Disappeared" by Lino A. Graglia and "The Constitution and Original Intent" by Henry Steele Commager, attack the Brennan and Meese views, respectively. The Commager piece includes the transcript of a dialogue on the subject in which ten scholars and an assistant attorney general participated.

The "jurisprudence of original intent" advocated by Attorney General Meese depends entirely on the ability of modern Americans to determine the beliefs of the delegates who stitched together the Constitution—a patchwork of compromises and best guesses—during the Constitutional Convention. Interestingly, the precise language of the Constitution—language that has had a fateful effect on the lives of millions of people—was decided by the Committee of Style, a five-member panel that met at the close of the convention to revise and rearrange the articles approved by the delegates. The famed introductory phrase "We the People of the United States" is their substitution for the original "We the undersigned delegates of the States of. . . ." In the last selection, "Mr. Meese, Meet Mr. Madison," Jack N. Rakove, in an article from *The Atlantic Monthly*, analyzes what we can and cannot know about the intentions of the prescient elite that gathered in Philadelphia to reform the Union.

INTERPRETING THE CONSTITUTION[1]

A large part of American history has been the history of constitutional debate. From the Federalists and the Anti-Federalists, to Webster and Calhoun, to Lincoln and Douglas, we find many examples. Now, as we approach the bicentennial of the framing of the Constitution, we are witnessing another debate concerning our fundamental law. It is not simply a ceremonial debate, but one that promises to have a profound effect on the future of our Republic.

The current debate is a sign of a healthy nation. Unlike people of many other countries, we are free both to discover the defects of our laws and our government through open discussion and to correct them through our political system.

This debate on the Constitution involves great and fundamental issues. It invites the participation of the best minds the bar, academia, and the bench have to offer. Recently, there have been important new contributions to this debate from some of the most distinguished scholars and jurists in the land. Representatives of the three branches of the Federal government have entered the debate, as have journalistic commentators.

[1]Reprint of an article by Edwin Meese, Attorney General of the United States. Based on an address to the Washington, D.C., chapter of the Federalist Society Lawyers Division, on November 15, 1985. Reprinted from USA TODAY MAGAZINE, Sept. 1986. Copyright © 1986 by the Society for the Advancement of Education.

A great deal has already been said, much of it of merit and on point, but occasionally there has been confusion and in some cases even distortion. Caricatures and straw men, as one customarily finds even in the greatest debates, have made appearances. I've been surprised at some of the hysterical shrillness that we've seen in editorials and other commentary. Perhaps this response is explained by the fact that what we've said defies liberal dogma. Still, whatever the differences, most participants are agreed about the same high objective—fidelity to our fundamental law.

In this article, I would like to discuss further the meaning of constitutional fidelity. In particular, I would like to describe in more detail this Administration's approach. Before doing so, I would like to make a few commonplace observations about the original document itself.

It is easy to forget what a young country America really is. The bicentennial of our independence was just a few years ago, that of the Constitution still two years off.

The period surrounding the creation of the Constitution is not a dark and mythical realm. The young America of the 1780's and 1790's was a vibrant place, alive with pamphlets, newspapers, and books chronicling and commenting upon the great issues of the day. We know how the Founding Fathers lived, and much of what they read, thought, and believed. The disputes and compromises of the Constitutional Convention were carefully recorded. The minutes of the Convention are a matter of public record. Several of the most important participants—including James Madison, the "father" of the Constitution—wrote comprehensive accounts of the Convention. Others, Federalists and Anti-Federalists alike, committed their arguments for and against ratification, as well as their understandings of the Constitution, to paper, so that their ideas and conclusions could be widely circulated, read, and understood.

In short, the Constitution is not buried in the mists of time. We know a tremendous amount of the history of its genesis. The bicentennial is encouraging even more scholarship about its origins. We know who did what, when, and many times why. One can talk intelligently about a "founding generation."

With these thoughts in mind, I would like to discuss the Administration's approach to constitutional interpretation which has been led by Pres. Reagan and which we at the Department of Justice and my colleagues in other agencies have advanced. To begin, it may be useful to say what it is not.

Our approach does not view the Constitution as some kind of super municipal code, designed to address merely the problems of a particular era—whether those of 1787, 1789, or 1868. There is no question that the Constitutional Convention grew out of widespread dissatisfaction with the Articles of Confederation. However, the delegates at Philadelphia moved beyond the job of patching that document to write a *Constitution*. Their intention was to write a document not just for their times, but for posterity.

The language they employed clearly reflects this. For example, they addressed *commerce*, not simply shipping or barter. Later, the Bill of Rights spoke, through the Fourth Amendment, of "unreasonable searches and seizures," not merely the regulation of specific law enforcement practices of 1789. Still later, the framers of the 14th Amendment were concerned not simply about the rights of black citizens to personal security, but also about the equal protection of the law for all persons within the states.

The Constitution is not a legislative code bound to the time in which it was written. Neither, however, is it a mirror that simply reflects the thoughts and ideas of those who stand before it.

A Written Document

Our approach to constitutional interpretation begins with the document itself. The plain fact is, it exists. It is something that has been written down. Walter Berns of the American Enterprise Institute has noted that the central object of American constitutionalism was "the effort" of the Founders "to express fundamental governmental arrangements in a legal document—to 'get it in writing.'"

Indeed, judicial review has been grounded in the fact that the Constitution is a written, as opposed to an unwritten, document. In *Marbury* v. *Madison*, Supreme Court Chief Justice John Marshall rested his rationale for judicial review on the fact that we have a written Constitution with meaning that is binding upon judges. "[I]t is apparent," he wrote, "that the framers of the constitution contemplated that instrument as a rule for the government of *courts*, as well as of the legislature. Why otherwise does it direct the judges to take an oath to support it?"

The presumption of a written document is that it conveys meaning. As Thomas Grey of the Stanford Law School has said, it makes "relatively definite and explicit what otherwise would be relatively indefinite and tacit."

We know that those who framed the Constitution chose their words carefully. They debated at great length the most minute points. The language they chose meant something. They proposed, substituted, edited, and carefully revised. Their words were studied with equal care by the state ratifying conventions.

This is not to suggest that there was unanimity among the framers and ratifiers on all points. The Constitution and the Bill of Rights, and some of the subsequent amendments, emerged after protracted debate. Nobody got everything he wanted. What is more, the framers were not clairvoyants—they could not foresee every issue that would be submitted for judicial review. Nor could they predict how all foreseeable disputes would be resolved under the Constitution. The point is, however, that the meaning of the Constitution can be known.

What does this written Constitution mean? In places, it is exactingly specific. Where it says that Presidents of the United States must be at least 35 years of age, it means exactly that. (I have not heard of any claim that 35 means 30 or 25 or 20.) Where it specifies how the House and Senate are to be organized, it means what it says.

The Constitution, including its 26 amendments, also expresses particular principles. One is the right to be free of an unreasonable search or seizure. Another concerns religious liberty. Another is the right to equal protection of the laws. Those who framed these principles meant something by them, and the meanings can be found, understood, and applied.

The Constitution itself is also an expression of certain general principles. These principles reflect the deepest purpose of the Constitution—that of establishing a political system through which Americans can best govern themselves consistent with the goal of securing liberty.

The text and structure of the Constitution are instructive. It contains very little in the way of specific political solutions. It speaks volumes on how problems should be approached, and by *whom.* For example, the first three articles set out clearly the scope and limits of three distinct branches of national government, the powers of each being carefully and specifically enumerated. In this scheme, it is no accident to find the legislative branch described first, as the framers had fought and sacrificed to secure the right of democratic self-governance. Naturally, this faith in republicanism was not unbounded, as the next two articles make clear.

Yet, the Constitution remains a document of powers and principles. Its undergirding premise remains that democratic self-government is subject only to the limits of certain constitutional principles. This respect for the political process was made explicit early on. When John Marshall upheld the act of Congress chartering a national bank in *McCulloch* v. *Maryland*, he wrote: "The Constitution [was] intended to endure for ages to come, and, consequently, to be adapted to the various crises of human affairs." However, to use *McCulloch*, as some have tried, as support for the idea that the Constitution is a protean, changeable thing is to stand history on its head. Marshall was keeping faith with the original intention that Congress be free to elaborate and apply constitutional powers and principles. He was not saying that the Court must invent some new constitutional value in order to keep pace with the times. In Walter Berns' words, "Marshall's meaning is not that the Constitution may be adapted to the 'various crises of human affairs,' but that the legislative powers granted by the Constitution are adaptable to meet these crises."

The approach this Administration advocates is rooted in the text of the Constitution as illuminated by those who drafted, proposed, and ratified it. In his famous "Commentary on the Constitution of the United States," Justice Joseph Story explained that, "The first and fundamental rule in the interpretation of all instruments is, to construe them according to the sense of the terms, and the intention of the parties."

Our approach understands the significance of a written document and seeks to discern the particular and general principles it expresses. It recognizes that there may be debate at times over the application of these principles, but it does not mean these principles can not be identified.

Constitutional adjudication is obviously not a mechanical process. It requires an appeal to reason and discretion. The text and intention of the Constitution must be understood to constitute the banks within which constitutional interpretation must flow. As James Madison said, if "the sense in which the Constitution was accepted and ratified by the nation . . . be not the guide in expounding it, there can be no security for a consistent and stable, more than for a faithful exercise of its powers."

Thomas Jefferson, so often cited incorrectly as a framer of the Constitution, in fact shared Madison's view: "Our peculiar security is in the possession of a written Constitution. Let us not make it a blank paper by construction." Jefferson was even more explicit in his personal correspondence:

On every question of construction [we should] carry ourselves back to the time, when the constitution was adapted; recollect the spirit manifested in the debates; and instead of trying [to find], what meaning may be squeezed out of the text, or invented against it, conform to the probable one, in which it was passed.

In the main, a jurisprudence that seeks to be faithful to our Constitution—a jurisprudence of original intention, as I have called it—is not difficult to describe. Where the language of the Constitution is specific, it must be obeyed. Where there is a demonstrable consensus among the framers and ratifiers as to a principle stated or implied by the Constitution, it should be followed. Where there is ambiguity as to the precise meaning or reach of a constitutional provision, it should be interpreted and applied in a manner so as to at least not contradict the text of the Constitution itself.

The Misuse of History

Sadly, while almost everyone participating in the current constitutional debate would give assent to these propositions, the techniques and conclusions of some of the debaters do violence to them. What is the source of this violence? In large part, I believe that it is the misuse of history stemming from the neglect of the idea of a written constitution.

There is a frank proclamation by some judges and commentators that what matters most about the Constitution is not its words, but its so-called "spirit." These individuals focus less on the language of specific provisions than on what they describe as the "vision" or "concepts of human dignity" they find embodied in the Constitution. This approach to jurisprudence has led to some remarkable and tragic conclusions.

In the 1850's, the Supreme Court under Chief Justice Roger B. Taney, read blacks out of the Constitution in order to invalidate Congress' attempt to limit the spread of slavery. The *Dred Scott* decision, famously described as a judicial "self-inflicted wound," helped bring on Civil War. There is a lesson in such history. There is danger in seeing the Constitution as an empty vessel into which each generation may pour its passion and prejudice.

Our own time has its own fashions and passions. In recent decades, many have come to view the Constitution—more accurately, part of the Constitution, provisions of the Bill of Rights, and the Fourteenth Amendment—as a charter for judicial activism on behalf of various constituencies. Those who hold this view often have lacked demonstrable textual or historical support for their conclusions. Instead, they have "grounded" their rulings in appeals to social theories, to moral philosophies or personal notions of human dignity, or to "penumbras," somehow emanating ghostlike from various provisions—identified and not identified—in the Bill of Rights. The problem with this approach, as John Hart Ely, Dean of the Stanford Law School, has observed with respect to one such decision, is not that it is bad constitutional law, but that it is not constitutional law in any meaningful sense at all.

Despite this fact, the perceived popularity of some results in particular cases has encouraged some observers to believe that any critique of the methodology of those decisions in an attack on the results. This perception is sufficiently widespread that it deserves an answer. My answer is to look at history.

When the Supreme Court, in *Brown* v. *Board of Education of Topeka*, sounded the death knell for official segregation in this nation, it earned all the plaudits it received. However, the Supreme Court in that case was not giving new life to old words, or adapting a "living," "flexible" Constitution to new reality; it was restoring the original principle of the Constitution to constitutional law. The *Brown* Court was correcting the damage done 50 years earlier, when, in *Plessy* v. *Ferguson*, an earlier Supreme Court had disregarded the clear intent of the framers of the Civil War amendments to eliminate the legal degradation of blacks, and had contrived a theory of the Constitution to support the charade of "separate but equal" discrimination.

It is amazing how so much of what passes for social and political progress is really the undoing of old judicial mistakes. Mistakes occur when the principles of specific constitutional provisions—such as those contained in the Bill of Rights—are taken by some as invitations to read into the Constitution values that contradict the clear language of other provisions.

Acceptances to this illusory invitation have proliferated in recent decades. One Supreme Court Justice identified the proper judicial standard as asking "what's best for this country?" Another said it is important to "keep the Court out in front" of the general society. Various academic commentators have poured rhetorical gasoline on this judicial fire, suggesting that constitutional interpretation appropriately be guided by such standards as whether a public policy "personifies justice," or "comports with the notion of moral evolution," or confers "an identity" upon our society, or was consistent with "natural ethical law," or was consistent with some "right of equal citizenship." These amorphous concepts, as opposed to the written Constitution, form a very poor base for judicial interpretation.

Unfortunately, as I've noted, navigation by such lodestars has in the past given us questionable economics, governmental disorder, and racism—all in the guise of constitutional law. Recently, one of the distinguished judges of one of our Federal appeals courts got it about right when he wrote: "The truth is that the judge who looks outside the Constitution always looks inside himself and nowhere else." Or, as we recently put it before the Supreme Court in an important brief, "The further afield interpretation travels from its point of departure in the text, the greater the danger that constitutional adjudication will be like a picnic to which the framers bring the words and the judges the meaning."

In the *Osborne* v. *Bank of United States* decision 21 years after *Marbury*, Chief Justice Marshall further elaborated his view of the relationship between the judge and the law, be it statutory or constitutional:

Judicial power, as contradistinguished from the power of the laws, has no existence. Courts are the mere instruments of the law, and can will nothing. Wehn they are said to exercise a discretion, it is a mere legal discretion, a discretion to be exercised in discerning the course prescribed by law; and, when that is discerned, it is the duty of the Court to follow it.

Any true approach to constitutional interpretation must respect the document in all its parts and be faithful to the Constitution in its entirety.

What must be remembered in the current debate is that interpretation does not imply results. The framers were not trying to anticipate every answer. They were trying to create a tripartite national government, within a federal system, that would have the flexibility to adapt to face new exigencies—as it did, for example, in chartering a national bank. Their great interest was in the distribution of power and responsibility in order to secure the great goal of liberty for all.

A jurisprudence that seeks fidelity to the Constitution—a jurisprudence of original intention—is not a jurisprudence of political results. It is very much concerned with process, and it is a jurisprudence that in our day seeks to depoliticize the law. The great genius of the constitutional blueprint is found in its creation and respect for spheres of authority and the limits it place on governmental power. In this scheme, the framers did not see the courts as the exclusive custodians of the Constitution. Indeed, because the document posits so few conclusions, it leaves to the more political branches the matter of adapting and vivifying its principles in each generation. It also leaves to the people of the states, in the Tenth Amendment, those responsibilities and rights not committed to Federal care. The power to declare acts of Congress and laws of the states null and void is truly awesome. This power must be used when the Constitution clearly speaks. It should not be used when the Constitution does not.

In *Marbury* v. *Madision*, as the same time he vindicated the concept of judicial review, Marshall wrote that the "principles" of the Constitution "are deemed fundamental and permanent" and, except for formal amendment, "unchangeable." If we want a change in our Constitution or in our laws, we must seek it through the formal mechanisms presented in that organizing document of our government.

What Is at Issue

In summary, I would emphasize that what is at issue here is not an agenda of issues or a menu of results. At issue is a way of government. A jurisprudence based on first principles is neither conservative nor liberal, neither right nor left. It is a jurisprudence that cares about committing and limiting to each organ of government the proper ambit of its responsibilities. It is a jurisprudence faithful to our Constitution.

By the same token, an activist jurisprudence, one which anchors the Constitution only in the consciences of jurists, is a chameleon jurisprudence, changing color and form in each era. The same activism hailed today may threaten the capacity for decision through democratic consensus tomorrow, as it has in many yesterdays. Ultimately, as the early democrats wrote into the Massachusetts state constitution, the best defense of our liberties is a government of laws and not men.

On this point, it is helpful to recall the words of the late Justice Felix Frankfurter:

[t]here is not under our Constitution a judicial remedy for every political mischief, for every undesirable exercise of legislative power. The Framers carefully and with deliberate forethought refused so to enthrone the judiciary. In this situation, as in others of like nature, appeal for relief does not belong here. Appeal must be to an informed, civically militant electorate.

I close, unsurprisingly, by returning a last time to the period of the Constitution's birth. As students of the Constitution are aware, the struggle for ratification was protracted and bitter. Essential to the success of the campaign was the outcome of the debate in the two most significant states, Virginia and New York. In New York, the battle between Federalist and Anti-Federalist forces was particularly hard. Both sides eagerly awaited the outcome in Virginia, which was sure to have a profound effect on the struggle in the Empire State. When news that Virginia had voted to ratify came, it was a particularly bitter blow to the Anti-Federalist side. Yet, on the evening the message reached New York, an event took place that speaks volumes about the character of early America. The losing side, instead of grousing, feted the Federalist leaders in the taverns and inns of the city. There followed a night of good fellowship and mutual toasting. When the effects of the good cheer wore off, the two sides returned to their inkwells and presses, and the debate resumed.

There is a great temptation among those who view this debate from the outside to see in it a clash of personalities, a bitter exchange, but you and I, and I hope the other participants in this dialogue, know better. We and our distinguished opponents carry on the old tradition of free, uninhibited, and vigorous debate. Out of such arguments come no losers, only truth. It's the American way, and the Founding Fathers wouldn't want it any other way.

THE CONSTITUTION OF THE UNITED STATES: CONTEMPORARY RATIFICATION[2]

I am deeply grateful for the invitation to participate in the "Text and Teaching" symposium. This rare opportunity to explore classic texts with participants of such wisdom, acumen and insight as those who have preceded and will follow me to this podium is indeed exhilarating. But it is also humbling. Even to approximate the standards of excellence of these vigorous and graceful intellects is a daunting task. I am honored that you have afforded me this opportunity to try.

It will perhaps not surprise you that the text I have chosen for exploration is the amended Constitution of the United States, which, of course, entrenches the Bill of Rights and the Civil War amendments, and draws sustenance from the bedrock principles of another great text, the Magna Carta. So fashioned, the Constitution embodies the aspiration to social justice, brotherhood, and human dignity that brought this nation into being. The Declaration of Independence, the Constitution and the Bill of Rights solemnly committed the United States to be a country where the dignity and rights of all persons were equal before all authority. In all candor we must concede that part of this egalitarianism in America has been more pretension than realized fact. But we are an aspiring people, a people with faith in progress. Our amended Constitution is the lodestar for our aspirations. Like every text worth reading, it is not crystalline. The phrasing is broad and the limitations of its provisions are not clearly marked. Its majestic generalities and ennobling pronouncements are both luminous and obscure. This ambiguity of course calls forth interpretation, the interaction of reader and text. The encounter with the Constitutional text has been, in many senses, my life's work.

My approach to this text may differ from the approach of other participants in this symposium to their texts. Yet such differences may themselves stimulate reflection about what it is we do when we "interpret" a text. Thus I will attempt to elucidate my approach to the text as well as my substantive interpretation.

[2]Reprint of an address by William J. Brennan, Jr., Associate Justice of the U.S. Supreme Court, at Georgetown University on October 12, 1985. *University of California, Davis, Law Review*, Vol. 19, pp. 2-14, 1985.

Perhaps the foremost difference is the fact that my encounters with the constitutional text are not purely or even primarily introspective; the Constitution cannot be for me simply a contemplative haven for private moral reflection. My relation to this great text is inescapably public. That is not to say that my reading of the text is not a personal reading, only that the personal reading perforce occurs in a public context, and is open to critical scrutiny from all quarters.

The Constitution is fundamentally a public text—the monumental charter of a government and a people—and a Justice of the Supreme Court must apply it to resolve public controversies. For, from our beginnings, a most important consequence of the constitutionally created separation of powers has been the American habit, extraordinary to other democracies, of casting social, economic, philosophical and political questions in the form of lawsuits, in an attempt to secure ultimate resolution by the Supreme Court. In this way, important aspects of the most fundamental issues confronting our democracy may finally arrive in the Supreme Court for judicial determination. Not infrequently, these are the issues upon which contemporary society is most deeply divided. They arouse our deepest emotions. The main burden of my twenty-nine Terms on the Supreme Court has thus been to wrestle with the Constitution in this heightened public context, to draw meaning from the text in order to resolve public controversies.

Two other aspects of my relation to this text warrant mention. First, constitutional interpretation for a federal judge is, for the most part, obligatory. When litigants approach the bar of court to adjudicate a constitutional dispute, they may justifiably demand an answer. Judges cannot avoid a definitive interpretation because they feel unable to, or would prefer not to, penetrate to the full meaning of the Constitution's provisions. Unlike literary critics, judges cannot merely savor the tensions or revel in the ambiguities inhering in the text—judges must resolve them.

Second, consequences flow from a Justice's interpretation in a direct and immediate way. A judicial decision respecting the incompatibility of Jim Crow with a constitutional guarantee of equality is not simply a contemplative exercise in defining the shape of a just society. It is an order—supported by the full coercive power of the State—that the present society change in a fundamental aspect. Under such circumstances the process of deciding can be a lonely, troubling experience for fallible human beings conscious that their best may not be adequate to the challenge. We Justices are certainly aware that we are not final because we are infallible; we know that we are infallible only because we are final. One does not forget how much may depend on the decision. More than the litigants may be affected. The course of vital social, economic and political currents may be directed.

These three defining characteristics of my relation to the constitutional text—its public nature, obligatory character, and consequentialist aspect—cannot help but influence the way I read that text. When Justices interpret the Constitution they speak for their community, not for themselves alone. The act of interpretation must be undertaken with full consciousness that it is, in a very real sense, the community's interpretation that is sought. Justices are not platonic guardians appointed to wield authority according to their personal moral predilections. Precisely because coercive force must attend any judicial decision to countermand the will of a contemporary majority, the Justices must render constitutional interpretations that are received as legitimate. The source of legitimacy is, of course, a wellspring of controversy in legal and political circles. At the core of the debate is what the late Yale Law School professor Alexander Bickel labeled "the counter-majoritarian difficulty." Our commitment to self-governance in a representative democracy must be reconciled with vesting in electorally unaccountable Justices the power to invalidate the expressed desires of representative bodies on the ground of inconsistency with higher law. Because judicial power resides in the authority to give meaning to the Constitution, the debate is really a debate about how to read the text, about constraints on what is legitimate interpretation.

There are those who find legitimacy in fidelity to what they call "the intentions of the Framers." In its most doctrinaire incarnation, this view demands that Justices discern exactly what the Framers thought about the question under consideration and simply follow that intention in resolving the case before them. It is a view that feigns self-effacing deference to the specific judgments of those who forged our original social compact. But in truth it is little more than arrogance cloaked as humility. It is arrogant to pretend that from our vantage we can gauge accurately the intent of the Framers on application of principle to specific, contemporary questions. All too often, sources of potential enlightenment such as records of the ratification debates provide sparse or ambiguous evidence of the original intention. Typically, all that can be gleaned is that the Framers themselves did not agree about the application or meaning of particular constitutional provisions, and hid their differences in cloaks of generality. Indeed, it is far from clear whose intention is relevant—that of the drafters, the congressional disputants, or the ratifiers in the states?—or even whether the idea of an original intention is a coherent way of thinking about a jointly drafted document drawing its authority from a general assent of the states. And apart from the problematic nature of the sources, our distance of two centuries cannot but work as a prism refracting all we perceive. One cannot help but speculate that the chorus of lamentations calling for interpretation faithful to "original intention"—and proposing nullification of interpretations that fail this quick litmus test—must inevitably come from persons who have no familiarity with the historical record.

Perhaps most importantly, while proponents of this facile historicism justify it as a depoliticization of the judiciary, the political underpinnings of such a choice should not escape notice. A position that upholds constitutional claims only if they were within the specific contemplation of the Framers in effect establishes a presumption of resolving textual ambiguities against the claim of constitutional right. It is far from clear what justifies such a presumption against claims of right. Nothing intrinsic in the nature of interpretation—if there is such a thing as the "nature" of interpretation—commands such a passive approach to ambiguity. This is a choice no less political than any other; it expresses antipathy to claims of the minority to rights against the majority. Those who would restrict claims of right to the values of 1789 specifically articulated in the Constitution turn a blind eye to social progress and eschew adaptation of overarching principles to changes of social circumstances.

Another, perhaps more sophisticated, response to the potential power of judicial interpretation stresses democratic theory: because ours is a government of the people's elected representatives, substantive value choices should by and large be left to them. This view emphasizes not the transcendent historical authority of the framers but the predominant contemporary authority of the elected branches of government. Yet it has similar consequences for the nature of proper judicial interpretation. Faith in the majoritarian process counsels restraint. Even under more expansive formulations of this approach, judicial review is appropriate only to the extent of ensuring that our democratic process functions smoothly. Thus, for example, we would protect freedom of speech merely to ensure that the people are heard by their representatives, rather than as a separate, substantive value. When, by contrast, society tosses up to the Supreme Court a dispute that would require invalidation of a legislature's substantive policy choice, the Court generally would stay its hand because the Constitution was meant as a plan of government and not as an embodiment of fundamental substantive values.

The view that all matters of substantive policy should be resolved through the majoritarian process has appeal under some circumstances, but I think it ultimately will not do. Unabashed enshrinement of majority will would permit the imposition of a social caste system or wholesale confiscation of property so long as a majority of the authorized legislative body, fairly elected, approved. Our Constitution could not abide such a situation. It is the very purpose of a Constitution—and particularly of the Bill of Rights—to declare certain values transcendent, beyond the reach of temporary political majorities. The majoritarian process cannot be expected to rectify claims of minority right that arise as a response to the outcomes of that very majoritarian process. As James Madison put it:

The prescriptions in favor of liberty ought to be levelled against that quarter where the greatest danger lies, namely, that which possesses the highest prerogative of power. But this is not found in either the Executive or Legislative departments of Government, but in the body of the people, operating by the majority against the minority.*

Faith in democracy is one thing, blind faith quite another. Those who drafted our Constitution understood the difference. One cannot read the text without admitting that it embodies substantive value choices; it places certain values beyond the power of any legislature. Obvious are the separation of powers; the privilege of the Writ of Habeas Corpus; prohibition of Bills of Attainder and ex post facto laws; prohibition of cruel and unusual punishments; the requirement of just compensation for official taking of property; the prohibition of laws tending to establish re-

*1 Annals of Cong. 437 (J. Gales ed. 1789).

ligion or enjoining the free exercise of religion; and, since the Civil War, the banishment of slavery and official race discrimination. With respect to at least such principles, we simply have not constituted ourselves as strict utilitarians. While the Constitution may be amended, such amendments require an immense effort by the People as a whole.

To remain faithful to the content of the Constitution, therefore, an approach to interpreting the text must account for the existence of these substantive value choices, and must accept the ambiguity inherent in the effort to apply them to modern circumstances. The Framers discerned fundamental principles through struggles against particular malefactions of the Crown; the struggle shapes the particular contours of the articulated principles. But our acceptance of the fundamental principles has not and should not bind us to those precise, at times anachronistic contours. Successive generations of Americans have continued to respect these fundamental choices and adopt them as their own guide to evaluating quite different historical practices. Each generation has the choice to overrule or add to the fundamental principles enunciated by the Framers; the Constitution can be amended or it can be ignored. Yet with respect to its fundamental principles, the text has suffered neither fate. Thus, if I may borrow the words of an esteemed predecessor, Justice Robert Jackson, the burden of judicial interpretation is to translate "the majesty generalities of the Bill of Rights, conceived as part of the pattern of liberal government in the eighteenth century, into concrete restraints on officials dealing with the problems of the twentieth century."*

We current Justices read the Constitution in the only way that we can: as Twentieth Century Americans. We look to the history of the time of framing and to the intervening history of interpretation. But the ultimate question must be, what do the words of the text mean in our time? For the genius of the Constitution rests not in any static meaning it might have had in a world that is dead and gone, but in the adaptability of its great principles to cope with current problems and current needs. What the constitutional fundamentals meant to the wisdom of other times cannot be their measure to the vision of our time. Similarly, what those fundamentals mean for us, our descendants will learn, cannot be their measure to the vision of their time. This realization is not,

*West Virginia Bd. of Educ. v. Barnette, 319 U.S. 624, 639 (1942).

I assure you, a novel one of my own creation. Permit me to quote from one of the opinions of our Court, *Weems* v. *United States*,* written nearly a century ago:

> Time works changes, brings into existence new conditions and purposes. Therefore, a principle to be vital must be capable of wider application than the mischief which gave it birth. This is peculiarly true of constitutions. They are not ephemeral enactments, designed to meet passing occasions. They are, to use the words of Chief Justice John Marshall, "designed to approach immortality as nearly as human institutions can approach it." The future is their care and provision for events of good and bad tendencies of which no prophesy can be made. In the application of a constitution, therefore, our contemplation cannot be only of what has been but of what may be.**

Interpretation must account for the transformative purpose of the text. Our Constitution was not intended to preserve a preexisting society but to make a new one, to put in place new principles that the prior political community had not sufficiently recognized. Thus, for example, when we interpret the Civil War Amendments to the charter—abolishing slavery, guaranteeing blacks equality under law, and guaranteeing blacks the right to vote—we must remember that those who put them in place had no desire to enshrine the status quo. Their goal was to make over their world, to eliminate all vestiges of slave caste.

Having discussed at some length how I, as a Supreme Court Justice, interact with this text, I think it time to turn to the fruits of this discourse. For the Constitution is a sublime oration on the dignity of man, a bold commitment by a people to the ideal of libertarian dignity protected through law. Some reflection is perhaps required before this can be seen.

The Constitution on its face is, in large measure, a structuring text, a blueprint for government. And when the text is not prescribing the form of government it is limiting the powers of that government. The original document, before addition of any of the amendments, does not speak primarily of the rights of man, but of the abilities and disabilities of government. When one reflects upon the text's preoccupation with the scope of government as well as its shape, however, one comes to understand that what this text is about is the relationship of the individual and the state. The text marks the metes and bounds of official authority and individual autonomy. When one studies the boundary that

*217 U.S. 349 (1909).
**Id. at 373.

the text marks out, one gets a sense of the vision of the individual embodied in the Constitution.

As augmented by the Bill of Rights and the Civil War Amendments, this text ia a sparkling vision of the supremacy of the human dignity of every individual. This vision is reflected in the very choice of democratic self-governance; the supreme value of a democracy is the presumed worth of each individual. And this vision manifests itself most dramatically in the specific prohibitions of the Bill of Rights, a term which I henceforth will apply to describe not only the original first eight amendments, but the Civil War amendments as well. It is a vision that has guided us as a people throughout our history, although the precise rules by which we have protected fundamental human dignity have been transformed over time in response to both transformations of social condition and evolution of our concepts of human dignity.

Until the end of the nineteenth century, freedom and dignity in our country found meaningful protection in the institution of real property. In a society still largely agricultural, a piece of land provided men not just with sustenance but with the means of economic independence, a necessary precondition of political independence and expression. Not surprisingly, property relationships formed the heart of litigation and of legal practice, and lawyers and judges tended to think stable property relationships the highest aim of the law.

But the days when common law property relationships dominated litigation and legal practice are past. To a growing extent economic existence now depends on less certain relationships with government—licenses, employment, contracts, subsidies, unemployment benefits, tax exemptions, welfare and the like. Government participation in the economic existence of individuals is pervasive and deep. Administrative matters and other dealings with government are at the epicenter of the exploding law. We turn to government and to the law for controls which would never have been expected or tolerated before this century, when a man's answer to economic oppression or difficulty was to move two hundred miles west. Now hundreds of thousands of Americans live entire lives without any real prospect of the dignity and autonomy that ownership of real property could confer. Protection of the human dignity of such citizens requires a much modified view of the proper relationship of individual and state.

In general, problems of the relationship of the citizen with government have multiplied and thus have engendered some of the most important constitutional issues of the day. As government acts ever more deeply upon those areas of our lives once marked "private," there is an even greater need to see that individual rights are not curtailed or cheapened in the interest of what may temporarily appear to be the "public good." And as government continues in its role of provider for so many of our disadvantaged citizens, there is an even greater need to ensure that government act with integrity and consistency in its dealings with these citizens. To put this another way, the possibilities for collision between government activity and individual rights will increase as the power and authority of government itself expands, and this growth, in turn, heightens the need for constant vigilance at the collision points. If our free society is to endure, those who govern must recognize human dignity and accept the enforcement of constitutional limitations on their power conceived by the Framers to be necessary to preserve that dignity and the air of freedom which is our proudest heritage. Such recognition will not come from a technical understanding of the organs of government, or the new forms of wealth they administer. It requires something different, something deeper—a personal confrontation with the well-springs of our society. Solutions of constitutional questions from that perspective have become the great challenge of the modern era. All the talk in the last half-decade about shrinking the government does not alter this reality or the challenge it imposes. The modern activist state is a concomitant of the complexity of modern society; it is inevitably with us. We must meet the challenge rather than wish it were not before us.

The challenge is essentially, of course, one to the capacity of our constitutional structure to foster and protect the freedom, the dignity, and the rights of all persons within our borders, which it is the great design of the Constitution to secure. During the time of my public service this challenge has largely taken shape within the confines of the interpretive question whether the specific guarantees of the Bill of Rights operate as restraints on the power of State government. We recognize the Bill of Rights as the primary source of express information as to what is meant by constitutional liberty. The safeguards enshrined in it are deeply etched in the foundation of America's freedoms. Each is a protection with centuries of history behind it, often dearly bought with the blood and lives of people determined to prevent oppression by their rulers. The first eight Amendments, however, were added to the Constitution to operate solely against federal power. It was not until the Thirteenth and Fourteenth Amendments were added, in 1865 and 1868, in response to a demand for national protection against abuses of state power, that the Constitution could be interpreted to require application of the first eight amendments to the states.

It was in particular the Fourteenth Amendment's guarantee that no person be deprived of life, liberty or property without due process of law that led us to apply many of the specific guarantees of the Bill of Rights to the States. In my judgment, Justice Cardozo best captured the reasoning that brought us to such decisions when he described what the court has done as a process by which the guarantees "have been taken over from the earlier articles of the federal bill of rights and brought within the Fourteenth Amendment by a process of absorption . . . [that] has had its source in the belief that neither liberty nor justice would exist if [those guarantees] . . . were sacrificed"* But this process of absorption was neither swift nor steady. As late as 1922 only the Fifth Amendent guarantee of just compensation for official taking of property had been given force against the states. Between then and 1956 only the First Amendment guarantees of speech and conscience and the Fourth Amendment ban of unreasonable searches and seizures had been incorporated—the latter, however, without the exclusionary rule to give it force. As late as 1961, I could stand before a distinguished assemblage of the bar at New York University's James Madison Lecture and list the following as guarantees that had not been thought to be sufficiently fundamental to the protection of human dignity so as to be enforced against the states: the prohibition of cruel and unusual punishments, the right against self-incrimination, the right to assistance of counsel in a criminal trial, the right to confront witnesses, the right to compulsory process, the right not to be placed in jeopardy of life or limb more than once upon accusation of a crime, the right not to have illegally obtained evidence introduced at a criminal trial, and the right to a jury of one's peers.

The history of the quarter century following that Madison Lecture need not be told in great detail. Suffice it to say that each

*Palko v. Connecticut, 302 U.S. 319, 326 (1937).

of the guarantees listed above has been recognized as a fundamental aspect of ordered liberty. Of course, the above catalogue encompasses only the rights of the criminally accused, those caught, rightly or wrongly, in the maw of the criminal justice system. But it has been well said that there is no better test of a society than how it treats those accused of transgressing against it. Indeed, it is because we recognize that incarceration strips a man of his dignity that we demand strict adherence to fair procedure and proof of guilt beyond a reasonable doubt before taking such a drastic step. These requirements are, as Justice Harlan once said, "bottomed on a fundamental value determination of our society that it is far worse to convict an innocent man than to let a guilty man go free."* There is no worse injustice than wrongly to strip a man of his dignity. And our adherence to the constitutional vision of human dignity is so strict that even after convicting a person according to these stringent standards, we demand that his dignity be infringed only to the extent appropriate to the crime and never by means of wanton infliction of pain or deprivation. I interpret the Constitution plainly to embody these fundamental values.

Of course the constitutional vision of human dignity has, in this past quarter century, infused far more than our decisions about the criminal process. Recognition of the principle of "one person, one vote" as a constitutional one redeems the promise of self-governance by affirming the essential dignity of every citizen in the right to equal participation in the democratic process. Recognition of so-called "new property" rights in those receiving government entitlements affirms the essential dignity of the least fortunate among us by demanding that government treat with decency, integrity and consistency those dependent on its benefits for their very survival. After all, a legislative majority initially decides to create governmental entitlements; the Constitution's Due Process Clause merely provides protection for entitlements thought necessary by society as a whole. Such due process rights prohibit government from imposing the devil's bargain of bartering away human dignity in exchange for human sustenance. Likewise, recognition of full equality for women—equal protection of the laws—ensures that gender has no bearing on claims to human dignity.

*In re Winship, 397 U.S. 358, 372 (1969).

Recognition of broad and deep rights of expression and of conscience reaffirm the vision of human dignity in many ways. They too redeem the promise of self-governance by facilitating—indeed demanding—robust, uninhibited and wide-open debate on issues of public importance. Such public debate is of course vital to the development and dissemination of political ideas. As importantly, robust public discussion is the crucible in which personal political convictions are forged. In our democracy, such discussion is a political duty; it is the essence of self government. The constitutional vision of human dignity rejects the possibility of political orthodoxy imposed from above; it respects the right of each individual to form and to express political judgments, however far they may deviate from the mainstream and however unsettling they might be to the powerful or the elite. Recognition of these rights of expression and conscience also frees up the private space for both intellectual and spiritual development free of government dominance, either blatant or subtle. Justice Brandeis put it so well sixty years ago when he wrote: "Those who won our independence believed that the final end of the State was to make men free to develop their faculties; and that in its government the deliberative forces should prevail over the arbitrary. They valued liberty both as an end and as a means."*

I do not mean to suggest that we have in the last quarter century achieved a comprehensive definition of the constitutional ideal of human dignity. We are still striving toward that goal, and doubtless it will be an eternal quest. For if the interaction of this Justice and the constitutional text over the years confirms any single proposition, it is that the demands of human dignity will never cease to evolve.

Indeed, I cannot in good conscience refrain from mention of one grave and crucial respect in which we continue, in my judgment, to fall short of the constitutional vision of human dignity. It is in our continued tolerance of State-administered execution as a form of punishment. I make it a practice not to comment on the constitutional issues that come before the Court, but my position on this issue, of course, has been for some time fixed and immutable. I think I can venture some thoughts on this particular subject without transgressing my usual guideline too severely.

*Whitney v. California, 274 U.S. 357, 375 (1927).

As I interpret the Constitution, capital punishment is under all circumstances cruel and unusual punishment prohibited by the Eighth and Fourteenth Amendments. This is a position of which I imagine you are not unaware. Much discussion of the merits of capital punishment has in recent years focused on the potential arbitrariness that attends its administration, and I have no doubt that such arbitrariness is a grave wrong. But for me, the wrong of capital punishment transcends such procedural issues. As I have said in my opinions, I view the Eighth Amendment's prohibition of cruel and unusual punishments as embodying to a unique degree moral principles that substantively restrain the punishments our civilized society may impose on those persons who transgress its laws. Foremost among the moral principles recognized in our cases and inherent in the prohibition is the primary principle that the State, even as it punishes, must treat its citizens in a manner consistent with their intrinsic worth as human beings. A punishment must not be so severe as to be utterly and irreversibly degrading to the very essence of human dignity. Death for whatever crime and under all circumstances is a truly awesome punishment. The calculated killing of a human being by the State involves, by its very nature, an absolute denial of the executed person's humanity. The most vile murder does not, in my view, release the State from constitutional restraints on the destruction of human dignity. Yet an executed person has lost the very right to have rights, now or ever. For me then, the fatal constitutional infirmity of capital punishment is that it treats members of the human race as nonhumans, as objects to be toyed with and discarded. It is, indeed, "cruel and unusual." It is thus inconsistent with the fundamental premise of the Clause that even the most base criminal remains a human being possessed of some potential, at least, for common human dignity.

This is an interpretation to which a majority of my fellow Justices—not to mention, it would seem, a majority of my fellow countrymen—does not subscribe. Perhaps you find my adherence to it, and my recurrent publication of it, simply contrary, tiresome, or quixotic. Or perhaps you see in it a refusal to abide by the judicial principle of *stare decisis*, obedience to precedent. In my judgment, however, the unique interpretive role of the Supreme Court with respect to the Constitution demands some flexibility with respect to the call of *stare decisis*. Because we are the last word on the meaning of the Constitution, our views must be subject to revision over time, or the Constitution falls captive, again, to the anachronistic views of long-gone generations. I mentioned earlier the judge's role in seeking out the community's interpretation of the Constitutional text. Yet, again in my judgment, when a Justice perceives an interpretation of the text to have departed so far from its essential meaning, that Justice is bound, by a larger constitutional duty to the community, to expose the departure and point toward a different path. On this issue, the death penalty, I hope to embody a community striving for human dignity for all, although perhaps not yet arrived.

You have doubtless observed that this description of my personal encounter with the constitutional text has in large portion been a discussion of public developments in constitutional doctrine over the last quarter century. That, as I suggested at the outset, is inevitable because my interpretive career has demanded a public reading of the text. This public encounter with the text, however, has been a profound source of personal inspiration. The vision of human dignity embodied there is deeply moving. It is timeless. It has inspired Americans for two centuries and it will continue to inspire as it continues to evolve. That evolutionary process is inevitable and, indeed, it is the true interpretive genius of the text.

If we are to be as a shining city upon a hill, it will be because of our ceaseless pursuit of the constitutional ideal of human dignity. For the political and legal ideals that form the foundation of much that is best in American institutions—ideals jealously preserved and guarded throughout our history—still form the vital force in creative political thought and activity within the nation today. As we adapt our institutions to the ever-changing conditions of national and international life, those ideals of human dignity—liberty and justice for all individuals—will continue to inspire and guide us because they are entrenched in our Constitution. The Constitution with its Bill of Rights thus has a bright future, as well as a glorious past, for its spirit is inherent in the aspirations of our people.

HOW THE CONSTITUTION DISAPPEARED[3]

Attorney General Edwin Meese's recent statement in a speech
to the American Bar Association that judges should interpret the
Constitution to mean what it was originally intended to mean
probably did not strike most people as controversial. Nevertheless it brought forth immediate denunciation by a sitting Supreme Court Justice as "doctrinaire," "arrogant," and the product
of "facile historicism." "It is a view," Justice William J. Brennan,
Jr. said in a speech at Georgetown University, "that feigns self-
effacing deference to the specific judgments of those who forged
our original social compact," but that "in truth . . . is little more
than arrogance cloaked as humility" because it is not possible to
"gauge accurately the intent of the Framers on application of
principle to specific, contemporary questions." The view is not
only mistaken, but misguided, Justice Brennan continued, because it would require judges to "turn a blind eye to social progress and eschew adaptation of overarching principles to changes
of social circumstance."

To state that judges should interpret the Constitution as intended by those who wrote and ratified it ("the Framers") is only
to state the basic premise of our political-legal system that the
function of judges is to apply, not to make, the law. Indeed, it
would be difficult to say what interpretation of a law means if not
to determine the intent of the lawmaker. Justice Brennan's angry
attack on the obvious as if it were disreputable, soon joined by the
attacks of his colleague Justice John Paul Stevens and a legion of
media commentators, makes evident that much is at stake in this
debate on a seemingly esoteric matter of constitutional interpretation. What is at stake is nothing less than the question of how
the country should be governed in regard to basic issues of social
policy: whether such issues should be decided by elected representatives of the people, largely on a state-by-state basis, or, as has
been the case for the last three decades, primarily by a majority
of the nine Justices of the United States Supreme Court for the
nation as a whole.

[3]Reprint of an article by Lino A. Graglia, professor of constitutional law at the University of Texas Law School.
Commentary. 81:19–27. F. '86. Copyright © 1986 by Lino A. Graglia.

The modern era of constitutional law began with the Supreme Court's 1954 decision in *Brown* v. *Board of Education*, holding compulsory school racial segregation and, it soon appeared, all racial discrimination by government, unconstitutional. The undeniable rightness of the decision as a matter of social policy, in effect ending legally-imposed second-class citizenship for blacks, and its eventual acceptance by the public and ratification by Congress and the President in the 1964 Civil Rights Act, gained for the Court a status and prestige unprecedented in our history. The moral superiority of decision-making by judges to decision-making by mere "politicians" seemed evident. The result was to enable the Court to move from its historic role as a brake on social change to a very different role as the primary engine of such change.

In the years since *Brown*, nearly every fundamental change in domestic social policy has been brought about not by the decentralized democratic (or, more accurately, republican) process contemplated by the Constitution, but simply by the Court's decree. The Court has decided, on a national basis and often in opposition to the wishes of a majority of the American people, issues literally of life and death, as in its decisions invalidating virtually all restrictions on abortion and severely restricting the use of capital punishment. It has decided issues of public security and order, as in its decisions greatly expanding the protection of the criminally accused and limiting state power to control street demonstrations and vagrancy, and issues of public morality, as in the decisions disallowing most state controls of pornography, obscenity, and nudity. The Court has both prohibited the states from making provision for prayer in the schools and disallowed most forms of aid, state or federal, to religious schools. It has required that children be excluded from their neighborhood public schools and bused to more distant schools in order to increase school racial integration; ordered the reapportionment of state and federal legislatures on a "one-man-one-vote" basis; invalidated most of the law of libel and slander; and disallowed nearly all legal distinctions on the basis of sex, illegitimacy, and alienage. The list could easily be extended, but it should be clear that in terms of the issues that determine the nature and quality of life in a society, the Supreme Court has become our most important institution of government.

Since his appointment to the Court by President Eisenhower in 1956, Justice Brennan has participated in all of the Court's major constitutional decisions, has consistently voted in favor of Court intervention in the political process, and often was a leader on the Court in reaching the decision to intervene. Indeed, he has ordinarily differed with the Court only in that he would often go even farther in disallowing political control of some issues; he would, for example, go farther than the Court has in disallowing state regulation of the distribution of pornographic material and he would prohibit capital punishment in all cases. If the Court has been our most important institution of government for the past three decades, Justice Brennan—although his name is probably unknown to the great majority of his fellow citizens—has surely been our most important government official. To argue that the Supreme Court should confine itself or be confined to interpreting the Constitution as written is to undermine the basis of this status and challenge the legitimacy of his life's work.

Constitutional law is as a practical matter the product of the exercise of the power of judicial review, the power of judges, and ultimately of Supreme Court Justices, to invalidate legislation and other acts of other officials and institutions of government as inconsistent with the Constitution. The central question presented by constitutional law—the only question the great variety of matters dealt with under that rubric have in common—is how, if at all, can such a power in the hands of national officials who are unelected and effectively hold office for life be justified in a system of government supposedly republican in form and federalist in organization? The power is not explicitly provided for in the Constitution and had no precedent in English law—where Parliament, not a court, is said to be supreme—which could well be taken as reason enough to assume that no such power had been granted. Alexander Hamilton argued for the power in *Federalist 78*, however, and Chief Justice John Marshall established it in *Marbury* v. *Madison* in 1803 on the ground that it is inherent in a written constitution that declares itself to be supreme law. The argument is hardly unanswerable—other nations have written constitutions without judicial review—but judicial review limited to interpretation of the Constitution in accordance with the Framers' intent does obviate the problem of policy-making by judges.

Constitutional limitations on popular government are undoubtedly undemocratic, even if they were themselves democratically adopted by a super-majority, but the only function of judges in exercising judicial review on the basis of a written constitution with determinate meaning would be the entirely judicial one of enforcing the Constitution as they would any other law. The judges, Hamilton assured the ratifying states, would have neither "force nor will"; able to "take no active resolution whatever" in enforcing the Constitution, their power would be "next to nothing." "Judicial power," Marshall reiterated, "has no existence. Courts are mere instruments of the law, and can will nothing." The notion that a court has "power to overrule or control the action of the people's representatives," Justice Owen Roberts confirmed during the New Deal constitutional crisis, "is a misconception"; the Court's only function in a constitutional case is "to lay the article of the Constitution which is invoked beside the statute which is challenged and to decide whether the latter squares with the former."

Even Justice Brennan purports to recognize what, as he notes, Alexander Bickel called "the counter-majoritarian difficulty" presented by judicial review. "Our commitment to self-governance in a representative democracy must be reconciled," Justice Brennan concedes, "with vesting in electorally unaccountable Justices the power to invalidate the expressed desires of representative bodies on the ground of inconsistency with higher law." Supreme Court Justices, he acknowledges at the beginning of his speech, echoing Judge Learned Hand, "are not platonic guardians appointed to wield authority according to their personal moral predilections." At several points he even seems to offer the standard justification for judicial review, that the judges merely interpret the written Constitution. He states, for example, that the duty of the judge is to "draw meaning from the text" and "remain faithful to the content" of the Constitution and that "the debate is really a debate about how to read the text, about constraints on what is legitimate interpretation." These statements are consistent with the remainder of his speech, however, only if reading or interpreting a document is considered indistinguishable from composing or rewriting it.

Unfortunately, however, the debate is not about how judges should read or interpret the text of the Constitution, but about whether that is what they should in fact confine themselves to doing in deciding constitutional cases. The view that the duty of judges is to read and interpret the Constitution—to attempt to determine what the Framers intended to say—is precisely the view that Justice Brennan seeks to rebut and derides as uninformed and misguided. The whole point of his speech is that judges should not be confined to that task, for so to confine them would be to give them much too limited a role in our system of government and leave us insufficiently protected from the dangers of majority rule.

Justice Brennan is far from alone today in his view of the proper role of judges in exercising judicial review and of the essential irrelevance of the Constitution to constitutional law. It is, indeed, the view taken by most contemporary constitutional-law scholars, who share the political ideology of the modern-era Supreme Court and see it as their professional duty to legitimize the fruits of that ideology. Because it has become increasingly difficult—in fact, impossible—to justify the Court's controversial decisions as the result of constitutional interpretation, the bulk of modern constitutional-law scholarship consists of the invention and elaboration of "non-interpretivist" or "non-originalist" theories of judicial review—justifications for a judicial review that is not confined to constitutional interpretation in any sense that would effectively restrain judicial choice. Because the product of this review is nonetheless always called "constitutional law" and attributed in some way to the Constitution, the result is the paradox of non-interpretivist constitutional interpretation, constitutional law without the Constitution.

That more and more constitutional scholars, and now a Supreme Court Justice, should come to recognize and acknowledge that the Supreme Court's constitutional decisions of recent decades cannot be justified on any other basis—that they are not in fact based on the Constitution—can be taken as a hopeful sign. Although the effort today in an increasing flood of books, articles, and speeches is to justify those decisions nonetheless, the inevitable failure of such efforts must, it would seem, eventually cause the enterprise to be abandoned and the fact that they cannot be justified in a system of self-government to be also generally recognized and acknowledged. Justice Brennan has performed a public service by bringing this extremely important and little understood issue to greater public attention, conveniently summarizing the standard arguments for "non-interpretivist" or "non-originalist" review—i.e., what is popularly referred to as "judicial activism"—and stating his own position with unusual, even if not total, clarity and candor.

Defenders of judicial activism face the dilemma that, on the one hand, judicial policy-making cannot be defended as such in our system—the Justices, even Justice Brennan must concede, are not authorized to enact their "personal moral predilections" into law and must therefore claim that their decisions derive somehow from the Constitution. On the other hand, it happens that the Constitution is most ill-suited as a basis for substantial judicial policy-making by frequent judicial intervention in the political process in the name of protecting individual rights from majority rule. The central difficulty is that although the Constitution does create some individual rights, they are actually rather few, fairly well-defined, and rarely violated. The first task of the defender of judicial activism, therefore, is to dispose of the Constitution as unhelpful, inadequate, or irrelevant to contemporary needs. Reasons must be found why the Constitution cannot be taken to mean what it rather clearly is known to mean—especially when read, as all writings must be, in historical context—or, even better, to have any determinate meaning at all.

After disposing of the Constitution by depriving it of its historic meaning, the next task of defenders of judicial activism is to imagine a much more expansive, elevated, and abstract constitution that, having no specific meaning, can be made to mean anything and serve therefore as simply a mandate for judges to enact their versions of the public good. In response to the objection that the very thinly veiled system of government by judges thus achieved is obviously inconsistent with democracy, the argument is made that the value of democracy is easily overrated and its dangers many. The "very purpose of a Constitution," as Justice Brennan states the standard argument, is to limit democracy by declaring "certain values transcendent, beyond the reach of temporary political majorities." In any event, no real inconsistency with democracy is involved, the argument concludes, because the judges, though unrestrained by the actual text of the Constitution, will continue to be restrained by its principles, the adaptation of which to changing circumstances is the true and indispensable function of judges. Justice Brennan's speech can serve as a textbook illustration of each of these moves.

Justice Brennan's attack on the notion of a constitution with a determinable historic meaning could hardly be more thorough. First of all, he finds that the Court's "sources of potential enlightenment" as to the intended meaning are often "sparse or ambiguous." Even more serious, the search for meaning is likely to be futile in any event because even the Framers, he believes, usually did not know what they meant: "Typically, all that can be gleaned is that the Framers themselves did not agree about the application or meaning of particular constitutional provisions, and hid their differences in cloaks of generality." Then there is the question of "whose intention is relevant—that of the drafters, the congressional disputants, or the ratifiers in the states?" Indeed, there is the most basic question of all, whether the very notion of intent makes sense, "whether the idea of an original intention is a coherent way of thinking about a jointly drafted document drawing its authority from a general assent of the states." It is almost as if the Constitution and its various provisions might have been drafted and adopted with no purpose at all. Finally, there is the problem that "our distance of two centuries cannot but work as a prism refracting all we perceive." For all these reasons, the idea that judicial review is legitimate only if faithful to the intent of the Framers can be held only by "persons who have no familiarity with the historical record."

Justice Brennan has still another, although it would seem unnecessary, nail to put in the coffin of the now demolished Constitution. Should any shred of constitutional meaning somehow survive the many obstacles he sees to finding it, he would accord it little or no value. The world of the Framers is "dead and gone," and it would not do, he believes, to hold the Constitution captive to the "anachronistic views of long-gone generations." "[A]ny static meaning" the Constitution "might have had" in that dead world must, therefore, be of dubious relevance today. In any event, "the genius of the Constitution rests," in his view, not in any such meaning but in "the adaptability of its great principles to cope with current problems and current needs," strange as it may seem that a writing can be great apart from its meaning and solely by reason of its supposed ability to mean anything.

Most of Justice Brennan's objections regarding the difficulties of constitutional interpretation have some basis, but they could also be made in regard to interpretation of almost any law. For example, one can almost always wish for a clearer or more detailed legislative history, and it is always true that legislators cannot foresee and agree on every possible application of a law. If these difficulties made the effort to determine legislative intent futile, a system of written law would hardly be possible. In any event, from the premise of an unknowable or irrelevant Constitution, the conclusion should follow that judges have no basis or justification for declaring laws unconstitutional, not that they are therefore free to invalidate laws on some other basis and still claim to be interpreting the Constitution.

Most important, whatever the difficulties of legal interpretation, they have little or no relevance to actual constitutional decision-making by the Supreme Court because no issue of interpretation, no real dispute about the intended meaning of the Constitution, is ordinarily involved. For example, the Constitution contains no provision mentioning or apparently in any way referring to the authority of the states to regulate the practice of abortion. However one might undertake to defend the Court's abortion decisions, it does not seem possible to argue that they are the result of constitutional interpretation in any non-fanciful sense. As another example, although the Constitution does mention religion, no process that could be called interpretation permits one to go from the Constitution's protection of religious freedom from federal interference to the proposition that the states may not provide for prayer in the schools.

A constitution so devoid of ascertainable meaning or contemporary relevance would seem quite useless as a guide to the solution of any contemporary problem and certainly as a written law enforceable by judges. The judges might as well be told to enforce a document written in an unknown language or, more in keeping with Justice Brennan's view, in disappearing ink. Having effectively eliminated the actual Constitution, however, Justice Brennan proceeds to remedy the loss—judicial activism cannot proceed with no constitution at all—by imagining and substituting a much more impressive, inspiring, and usefully uncertain one.

The constitution of Justice Brennan's vision is undoubtedly a wonderful thing, one of "great" and "overarching" principles and "majestic generalities and ennobling pronouncements [that] are both luminous and obscure." It is nothing less grand than the embodiment of "the aspiration to social justice, brotherhood, and human dignity that brought this nation into being," "a sublime oration on the dignity of man," and "a sparkling vision of the supremacy of the human dignity of every individual." Justice Brennan accurately reflects current constitutional-law scholarship, here as throughout his speech, by seeing the Constitution as simply "the lodestar for our aspirations." It is a source of constant wonderment that scholars and judges of otherwise the most secular and rationalist turn of mind can grow mystical when discussing the Constitution.

The temptation is strong, of course, to dismiss Justice Brennan's rapturous statements as mere flights of poetic fancy or utopian ecstasy, obviously not meant as serious descriptions or explanations of the Constitution. The fact remains, however, that this view of the Constitution is the only justification offered by him, or other contemporary defenders of judicial activism, for the Court's assumption and exercise of enormous government power. Fanciful as it may seem, a constitution that is simply the embodiment of "our," or at least his, aspirations accurately describes the constitution he has been enforcing for nearly three decades to override the will of the people of this country on issue after issue. It cannot be too strongly emphasized, therefore, that the Constitution we actually have bears almost no relation to, and is often clearly irreconcilable with, the constitution of Justice Brennan's vision. No more is necessary to rebut all contemporary defenses of judicial activism than that a copy of the Constitution be kept close at hand to demonstrate that the defenders of judicial activism are invariably relying on something else.

Although it may come as something of a disappointment to some, an "aspiration for social justice, brotherhood, and human dignity" happens not to have been what brought this nation, or at least the government founded on the Constitution, into being. The convention to revise the Articles of Confederation was called and the Constitution was drafted and ratified not to provide additional protections for human rights—on the contrary, the stronger national government created by the Constitution was correctly seen as a potential danger to human rights—but almost entirely for commercial purposes. The primary motivating force for the creation of a stronger national government was the felt need of a central authority to remove state-imposed obstacles to interstate trade. How little the Constitution had to do with aspirations for brotherhood or human dignity is perhaps most clearly seen in its several provisions regarding slavery. It provides, for example, that a slave was to be counted as three-fifths of a free person for purposes of representation and that slaves escaping to free states were nonetheless to be returned to their masters. It is not, as Justice Brennan would explain this, that part of the "egalitarianism in America has been more pretension than realized fact," but that there was at the time the Constitution was adopted very little pretension to egalitarianism, as is illustrated by, for example, the widespread use of property qualifications for voting.

Given the original Constitution's limited and mundane purposes, it is not surprising that it provides judges with little to work with for the purpose of advancing their personal notions of social justice. The Constitution is, first of all, a very short document—easily printed, with all twenty-seven Amendments and repealed matter, on fewer than twenty pages—and apparently quite simple and straightforward, not at all like a recondite tome in which many things may be found with sufficient study. The original Constitution is almost entirely devoted to outlining the structure of the national government and setting forth the sometimes complicated methods of selection, and the responsibilities, of members of the House of Representatives, Senators, the President, and Supreme Court Justices. It contains few provisions protecting individual rights from the national government—federalism, i.e., limited national power and a high degree of local autonomy, was considered the principal protection—and even fewer restrictions on the exercise of state power. As to the national government, criminal trials are to be by jury, treason is narrowly defined, the writ of habeas corpus is protected, and bills of attainder and ex-post-facto laws are prohibited. The prohibition of bills of attainder and ex-post-facto laws is repeated as to the states, which are also prohibited from discriminating against citizens of other states. Finally and by far the most important in terms of actual challenges to state laws, the Framers, nicely illustrating their lack of egalitarian pretension, undertook to protect creditors from debtor-relief legislation by prohibiting the states from impairing contract rights.

The first eight of the first ten Amendments to the Constitution, the Bill of Rights adopted in 1791, provide additional protections of individual rights, but only against the federal gov-

ernment, not the states, and these, too, are fewer than seems to
be generally imagined and certainly fewer than is typical of later
declarations of rights, such as in the United Nations Charter. In
terms of substantive rights, the First Amendment prohibits Congress from establishing or restricting the free exercise of religion—the main purpose of which was to leave matters of religion
to the states—and from abridging the freedom of speech, press,
or assembly. In addition, a clause of the Fifth Amendment prohibits the taking of private property without just compensation;
the Second Amendment, rarely mentioned by rights enthusiasts,
grants a right to bear arms; and the Third Amendment, of little
apparent contemporary significance, protects against the forced
quartering of troops in private homes. The Seventh Amendment,
requiring jury trials in civil cases involving more than twenty dollars, is hard to see today as other than an unnecessary inconve-
nience. The remaining provisions (search and seizure, grand-jury
indictment, double jeopardy, privilege against self-incrimination,
due process, jury trial, right to counsel and to confront adverse
witnesses, and cruel and unusual punishment) are related to criminal procedure.

Additional protections of individual rights are provided by
the post-Civil War Amendments. The Thirteenth Amendment
prohibits slavery and the Fifteenth prohibits denial of the right
to vote on grounds of race. The great bulk of constitutional litigation concerns state law and nearly all of that litigation purports
to be based on a single sentence of the Fourteenth Amendment
and, indeed, on one or the other of two pairs of words, "due
process" and "equal protection." If the Constitution is the embodiment of our aspirations, it must have become so very largely because of those four words. The clear historic purpose of the
Fourteenth Amendment, however, was to provide federal protection against certain state discriminations on the basis of race, historically our uniquely intractable problem, but not otherwise to
change fundamentally the constitutional scheme. Finally, the
Nineteenth Amendment protects the right to vote from denial on
grounds of sex, and the Twenty-seventh from denial on grounds
of age for persons over eighteen.

The Constitution's protections of individual rights are not
only few but also, when read in historical context, fairly clear and
definite. State and federal legislators, all of whom are American
citizens living in America and generally at least as devoted as

judges to American values, have, therefore, little occasion or desire to violate the Constitution. The result is that the enactment of a clearly unconstitutional law is an extremely rare occurrence; the clearest example in our history perhaps is a 1933 Minnesota debtor-relief statute plainly prohibited by the contract clause, although, as it happens, the Supreme Court upheld it by a five-to-four decision. If judicial review were actually confined to enforcing the Constitution as written, it would be a much less potent force than the judicial review argued for and practiced by Justice Brennan.

The Constitution is undoubtedly a great document, the foundation of one of the freest and most prosperous nations in history. It does not detract from that greatness to point out that it is not, however, what Justice Brennan would make of it, a compendium of majestic generalities and ennobling pronouncements luminous and obscure; indeed, its greatness and durability surely derive in large part from the fact that the Framers' aims were much more specific and limited. Far from intending to compose an oration to human dignity, the Framers would have considered that they had failed in their effort to specify and limit the power of the national government if the effect of the Constitution should be to transfer the focus of human-rights concerns from the state to the national level. The Framers' solution to the problem of protecting human freedom and dignity was to preserve as much as possible, consistent with national commerce and defense requirements, a system of decentralized democratic decision-making, with the regulation of social conditions and personal relations left to the states. Justice Brennan's solution, virtually unlimited Supreme Court power to decide basic social issues for the nation as a whole, effectively disenfranchising the people of each state as to those issues, is directly contrary to the constitutional scheme.

Judicial review on the basis of a constitution divorced from historical meaning and viewed, instead, as simply "the lodestar for our aspirations" is obviously a prescription for policy-making by judges. It should therefore be defended, if at all, as such, free of obfuscating references to "interpretation" of the Constitution. The only real question it presents is, why should the American people prefer to have important social-policy issues decided for the whole nation by the Supreme Court—a committee of nine lawyers unelected to and essentially unremovable from office—

rather than by the decentralized democratic process? Justice
Brennan's answer to this question is, in essence, why not? The argument that judicial interpretation of the Constitution in accordance with the Framers' intent is essential for "depoliticization
of the judiciary," he points out, has its own "political
underpinnings"; it "in effect establishes a presumption of resolving textual ambiguities against the claim of constitutional right,"
which involves "a choice no less political than any other."

Justice Brennan is certainly correct that the presumption of
constitutionality accorded to challenged acts of government officials has a political basis, but it is surprising that he should find
"far from clear what justifies such a presumption." What justifies
it is the basic premise of democratic government that public-
policy issues are ordinarily to be decided through the electoral
process, not by unelected judges; that constitutional restrictions
on representative government—even if, unlike judge-made restrictions, they were once democratically adopted—are the exception, not the rule. To refuse to assume the validity of the acts
of the electorally responsible officials and institutions of government is to refuse to assume the validity of representative self-
government. It has, therefore, from the beginning been considered the bedrock of constitutional litigation that one who would
have a court invalidate an act of the political branches must assume the burden of showing its inconsistency with the
Constitution, ordinarily a most difficult task. By reversing the
presumption of constitutionality, Justice Brennan would simply
reject political decision-making as the norm and require elected
representatives to justify their policy choices to the satisfaction of
Supreme Court Justices, presumably by showing that those
choices contribute to the Justices' notion of social progress.

Justice Brennan would justify the judicial supremacy he fa-
vors on the not entirely consistent grounds that, on the one hand,
the Justices are the true voice of the people and, on the other,
that the people are in any event not always to be trusted. "When
Justices interpret the Constitution," Justice Brennan assures us,
"they speak for their community, not for themselves alone" and
"with full consciousness that it is, in a very real sense, the community's interpretation that is sought." Apart from the fact that no
question of constitutional interpretation is in fact involved in
most "constitutional" cases—the judges do not really decide cases
by studying the words "due process" or "equal protection"—the

community is, of course, fully capable of speaking for itself through the representatives it elects and maintains in office for that purpose. Justice Brennan does not explain why he thinks the community needs or wants unelected judges to speak for it instead or why the judges can be expected better to reflect or express the community's views.

The actual effect of most judicial rulings of unconstitutionality is, of course, not to implement, but to frustrate the community's views. For example, Justice Brennan would disallow capital punishment as constitutionally prohibited despite not only the fact that it is repeatedly provided for in the Constitution, but also the fact that it is favored by a large majority of the American people. In some cases, however, he explains, a Justice may perceive the community's "interpretation of the text to have departed so far from its essential meaning" that he "is bound, by a larger constitutional duty to the community, to expose the departure and point toward a different path." On capital punishment, Justice Brennan hopes to "embody a community striving for human dignity for all, although perhaps not yet arrived." Interpreting an aspirational constitution apparently requires prescience as well as a high degree of self-confidence.

The foundation of all defenses of judicial activism, however, is not any fanciful notion that the judges are the true voice of the people, but on the contrary, the conviction that the people, and their elected representatives, should not be permitted to have the last word. Rarely has this conviction, common among our intellectual elite, been expressed with more certainty than in Justice Brennan's speech. Judicial acceptance of the "predominant contemporary authority of the elected branches of government" must be rejected, he argues, for the same reason he rejects judicial acceptance of the "transcendent historical authority of the Framers." That reason, it now appears, is not so much that original intent is unknowable or irrelevant as that its acceptance as authoritative would be inconsistent with his notion of "proper judicial interpretation" of the Constitution because it would leave judges with too little to do. "Faith in the majoritarian process," like fidelity to original intent, is objectionable, he is frank to admit, simply because it "counsels restraint." It would, he points out, lead the Court generally to "stay its hand" where "invalidation of a legislature's substantive policy choice" is involved. Justice Brennan's confidence that his university audience shared his suspicion of democracy and distrust of his fellow citizens was such as to put beyond need of argument the unacceptability of a counsel of restraint by Supreme Court Justices in deciding basic issues of social policy.

Legislative supremacy in policy-making is derided by Justice Brennan as the "unabashed enshrinement of majority will." "Faith in democracy is one thing," he warns, but "blind faith quite another." "The view that all matters of substantive policy should be resolved through the majoritarian process has appeal," he concedes, but only "under some circumstances," and even as so qualified "it ultimately will not do." It will not do because the majority is simply not to be trusted: to accept the mere approval of "a majority of the legislative body, fairly elected," as dispositive of public-policy issues would be to "permit the imposition of a social-caste system or wholesale confiscation of property," a situation "our Constitution could not abide." How a people so bereft of good sense, toleration, and foresight as to adopt such policies could have adopted the Constitution in the first place is not explained. Justice Brennan seems to forget that if the Constitution prohibits such things—indeed, if it is an oration to human dignity, as he maintains—it must be because the American people have made it so and therefore, it would seem, can be trusted. It cannot be Justice Brennan's position that political wisdom died with the Framers and that we are therefore fortunate to have their policy judgments to restrain us; he rejects those judgments as unknowable or irrelevant. Like other defenders of judicial activism, however, he seems to view the Constitution not as an actual document produced by actual people but as a metaphysical entity from an extraterrestrial source of greater authority than the mere wishes of a majority of the American people, which source, fortunately, is in effective communication with Supreme Court Justices.

The social-caste system feared by Justice Brennan would probably be prohibited by the post-Civil War Amendments, without undue stretching, and confiscation of property by the national government—though not by the states—would be prohibited by the just-compensation clause of the Fifth Amendment. (These constitutional provisions, it may be noted in passing, would operate as impediments to such policies, providing grounds for opposing arguments, even if they were not judicially enforceable.) The real protection against such fears, however—and columnist Anthony Lewis's similar fear that without activist judicial review Oregon might establish the Reverend Sun Myung Moon's Unification Church as the official state religion—is simply the good sense of the American people. No extraordinary degree of confidence in that good sense is necessary in order to believe that these and similarly outrageous policies that are invariably offered as providing an unanswerable justification for judicial activism are so unlikely to be adopted as not to be a matter of serious concern. If they should be a matter of concern nonetheless—if, for example, it is truly feared that the people of some state might establish a church and believed that no state should be free to do so—the appropriate response would be the adoption of a constitutional amendment further limiting self-government in the relevant respects. To grant judges an unlimited power to rewrite the Constitution, Justice Brennan's recommended response, would be to avoid largely imaginary dangers of democratic misgovernment by creating a certainty of judicial misgovernment.

Judicial activism is not necessary to protect us from state-established churches, favored by almost no one, but it does operate to deprive the people of each state of the right to decide for themselves such real issues as whether provision should be made for prayer in the public schools. In any event, the issue presented by contemporary judicial activism is not whether majority rule is entirely trustworthy—all government power is obviously dangerous—or even whether certain specific constitutional limitations on majority rule might not be justifiable; the issue is whether freewheeling policy-making by Supreme Court Justices, totally centralized and undemocratic, is more trustworthy than majority rule.

Defenders of judicial activism invariably match their skepticism about democratic policy-making with a firm belief in the possibility and desirability of policy-making on the basis of principle. To free judicial review from the constraint of a constitution with a determinate meaning is not to permit unrestrained judicial policy-making in constitutional cases, it is argued, for the judges will continue to be constrained by the Constitution's principles, which, like the smile of the Cheshire cat, somehow survive the disappearance of the Constitution's text. According to this argument, judicial activism amounts to nothing more than the adaptation and application of these basic principles to changing circumstances, a necessary task if the Constitution is to remain a "living document" and a contributor rather than an obstacle to the national welfare. Thus, judicial activism is necessary in Justice Brennan's view, as already noted, if we are not to "turn a blind eye to social progress and eschew adaptation of overarching principles to changes of social circumstance" and because the genius of the Constitution rests not in what, if anything, the Framers actually intended to provide, but in the "adaptability of its great principles to cope with current problems and current needs."

The argument that judges are constrained by constitutional principles, even though not by the constitutional text, bears no relation to reality. In the first place, it is not possible to formulate useful constitutional principles apart from or beyond the Constitution's actual provisions. The Constitution protects certain interests to a certain extent, from which fact the only principle to be derived is that the Constitution does just that. An even more basic fallacy is the argument's assumption that the solution of social problems lies in the discovery, adaptation, and application of preexisting principles to new situations. Difficult problems of social choice arise, however, not because of some failure to discern or adapt an applicable principle, but only because we have many principles, many interests we regard as legitimate, and they inevitably come into conflict. Some interests have to be sacrificed or compromised if other interests are to be protected—for example, public demonstrations will have to be regulated at some point in the interest of maintaining public order—and there is no authoritatively established principle, rule, or generality that resolves the conflict. If there were such a principle, the conflict would not present a serious problem, but would be a matter that has already been decided or that anyone can decide who can read and reason. Value judgments have to be made to solve real policy issues, and the meaning of self-government is that they are to be made in accordance with the collective judgment of those who will have to live with the results.

There is also very little basis for Justice Brennan's apparent belief that judicial review confined to the Constitution as written would somehow be incompatible with social progress—unless social progress is simply defined as the enactment of his views. The Constitution does contain several provisions that we would probably be better off without, for example, the Seventh Amendment's requirement of a jury trial in federal civil cases involving more than twenty dollars and the Twenty-second Amendment's limitation of Presidents to two terms. Apart from the fact, however, that the Constitution, of course, provides procedures for its amendment—it can be updated if necessary without the Court's help—judicial activism has not generally served to alleviate the undesirable effects of such provisions. In any event, the Constitution's restrictions on self-government are, as already noted, relatively few and rarely such as a legislature might seek to avoid. Rarely if ever will adaptation of the Constitution's overarching principles, if any, be necessary in order to permit a legislature to implement its views of social progress.

Indeed, on the basis of our actual constitutional history—which includes the Supreme Court's disastrous decision that Congress could not prohibit the extension of slavery and, after the Civil War that decision helped bring on, the decision that Congress could not prohibit racial segregation in public places—it is possible to believe that social progress might go more smoothly without the Court's supposed adaptations of principles. If the Constitution can be said to have an overarching principle, the principle of federalism, of decision-making on most social-policy issues at the state level, is surely the best candidate, and that principle is not adapted or updated but violated by the Court's assertion of power to decide such issues. Far from keeping the Constitution a "living document," judicial activism threatens its demise.

Whatever merit Justice Brennan's justifications for judicial activism might have in theory, they do not seem relevant to the judicial activism actually practiced by the Supreme Court for the past three decades. It would be very difficult to justify the Court's major constitutional decisions during this period, and particularly its most controversial decisions, on any of the grounds Justice Brennan suggests. It would not seem possible to argue, for example, that the Justices spoke for the community, not for themselves, in reaching their decisions on abortion, busing, criminal procedure, and prayer in the schools. Nor does it seem that any of those decisions can be justified as providing a needed protection from a possible excess of democracy, as merely delaying effectuation of the aberrational enthusiasms of "temporary political majorities" until they could return to their senses. Judicial review may, as Chief Justice Harlan Fiske Stone put this standard rationalization, provide the people with an opportunity for a "sober second thought," but no amount of thought or experience is likely to change the view of the vast majority of the American people that, for example, their children should not be excluded from their neighborhood public schools because of their race or that no new protections of the criminally accused should be invented with the effect of preventing the conviction and punishment of the clearly guilty.

Finally, the contribution of most of the Court's constitutional decisions of recent decades to social progress—for example, its decision that California may not prohibit the parading of vulgarity in its courthouses or that Oklahoma may not impose a higher minimum drinking age on men than on women—is at best debatable. Very few of these decisions, it seems, could be used to illustrate the adaptation of overarching constitutional principles or transcendent constitutional values to changing circumstances. They could probably more easily be used to illustrate that, rather than helping us to cope with current problems and current needs, the Court's constitutional decisions have often been the cause of those problems and needs.

Whatever the merits of the Supreme Court's constitutional decisions of the past three decades, they have as to the issues decided deprived us of perhaps the most essential element of the human dignity Justice Brennan is concerned to protect, the right of self-government, which necessarily includes the right to make what others might consider mistakes. It is not the critics of judicial activism but the activist judges who can more properly be charged with being doctrinaire and arrogant, for it is they who presume to know the answers to difficult questions of social policy and to believe that they provide a needed protection from government by the misguided or ignorant. An opponent of judicial activism need not claim to know the answer to so difficult a question of social policy as, say, the extent, if any, to which abortion should be restricted to know that it is shameful in a supposedly democratic country that such a question should be answered for all of us by unelected and unaccountable government officials who have no special competence to do so.

THE CONSTITUTION AND ORIGINAL INTENT[4]

Thomas Jefferson, in his First Inaugural Address, said, "Every difference of opinion is not a difference of principle. We have called by different names brethren of the same principle." That was true during George Washington's Administration, it is not true today.

In the summer of 1985, Attorney General Edwin Meese called for a "jurisprudence of original intention." Perhaps a more appropriate wording would be that which Finley Peter Dunne put in the words of his fictional Mister Dooley: "The Constitution was what some dead Englishman thought Thomas Jefferson was going to mean when he wrote the Constitution."

The issue in the debate of how to interpret the inevitably ambiguous words and phrases of the Constitution and who should do the interpreting is much more than simply the difference between broad and narrow interpretations of the Constitution. It is the great and permanent issue, which Jefferson put in the form of a question: "Does the earth belong to the living or the dead?"

Original intention means the intention of those who were living in 1787. Concealed in Mr. Meese's seductive and extraordinary phrase is also the question that Justice Oliver Wendell Holmes raised when he assured us that "the life of the law has not been logic, it has been experience." The felt necessities of the time, the prevalent moral and political theories, intuitions of public policy, even the prejudices that judges share with their fellow men, all have had a good deal more to do than syllogisms in determining the rules by which men should be governed.

Mr. Meese's solution to ambiguity in the Constitution is familiar enough. Over thirty years ago, it was stated with utmost simplicity by Supreme Court Justice Owen J. Roberts in the steel seizure case of *Youngstown Sheet & Tube Co.* v. *Sawyer* (1952): "When an act of Congress is appropriately challenged in the courts as not conforming to the Constitutional mandate, the judicial branch of the government has only one duty: to lay the article of the Constitution which is invoked beside the statute which is

[4]Professor of history (at Amherst College) Henry Steele Commager's "The Constitution and Original Intent," *The Center Magazine*, Vol. 19, No. 6, pp. 4–17. Reprinted by permission of the Robert Maynard Hutchins Center for the Study of Democratic Institutions.

challenged, and to decide whether the latter squares with the former. All the Court does or can do is to announce its considered judgment."

In the same case, Justice Robert H. Jackson wrote: "We may be surprised at the poverty of really useful and unambiguous authority applicable to concrete problems of Executive power as they actually present themselves. Just what our forefathers did envision, or would have envisioned had they foreseen modern conditions, must be divined from the materials almost as enigmatic as the dreams Joseph was called upon to interpret for the Pharaoh. A century and a half of partisan debate and scholarly speculation yields no net result, but only supplies more or less apt quotations from respected sources on each side of any or every question."

Chief Justice Fred M. Vinson, eschewing both the simplicity of Justice Roberts and the metaphors of Justice Jackson, pronounced judicially: "If the President has any power under the Constitution to meet a critical situation in the absence of expressed statutory authorization, there is no basis whatever for criticizing the exercise of such power in his case." I am confident that that is what President Reagan was told by Attorney General Meese when he was planning his private war on Grenada or the mining of the harbors of Nicaragua—that is, there was no reason to challenge his interpretation of the Constitution.

For their writing of the Constitution, the Framers were instructed—in a brief statement from the declining Congress of the Confederacy and authorizations from the states—to take adequate steps "to meet the exigencies of union." The members of the Constitutional Convention were mandated to meet those exigencies, and they did. We, too, must continue to do what is necessary to meet the exigencies of union. The Constitution has always proved adequate to that task because it is a dynamo, not a straightjacket.

The Preamble of the Constitution explains what the Constitution was about and what it was to do. The Constitution was to create a more perfect union, justice, domestic tranquility, common defense, general welfare, and secure the blessings of liberty, not only for the founding generation, but for posterity.

When we look for original intention in the body of the Constitution itself, we do not find confusion, obfuscation, or contradiction. We find clarity and specificity, wherever these are called for, and broad general terms, wherever those are called for. We find the sagacious understanding of the true nature of federalism: the essential distinction between things of a general nature that had to be assigned to the national government and things of a local nature that could be managed by the state and local governments. We also find the realization that these distinctions were not and could never be clear, nor were they, nor could they ever be, fixed and rigid.

The Founding Fathers created the first federal system by not only conforming to reality, but by including language in the Constitution that permitted continuous readjustment to reality, and by creating a system of dual citizenship, dual government, and dual courts, with the national courts as supreme. On questions of jurisdiction, they lodged ultimate authority in the courts.

For all the Constitution's comprehensiveness and clarity, it does, however, contain inevitable ambiguities, some of which were included quite deliberately. When members of the Constitutional Convention could not agree on something, they took refuge in ambiguous words. Even today there is no agreement on certain words in the Preamble: "justice, domestic tranquility, defense, welfare, liberty." The Founding Fathers had the good sense to leave to posterity the task of working out the meanings of many of the key words in the Constitution. The generation of the Founding Fathers always invoked posterity. The word appeared nine times in one of Washington's addresses. Neither John Adams nor Jefferson could write a letter without using the word. Today, we have abandoned the concept of posterity, possibly because we do not believe there will be any.

We seem to know almost at once what is meant by "common defense." But what is meant by "general welfare"? Both terms are inextricably united in the same phrase twice in the Constitution: in the Preamble and in Article I, Section 8. So, logically, Congress can tax anything for general welfare that it can tax for common defense. Both terms have exactly the same Constitutional status.

The Founding Fathers were not afraid of ambiguity. They trusted the courts to work out the meanings of these ambiguous words in the light of history and of the exigencies of the time. Indeed, they even required the courts to interpret the meanings of the phrases of the Constitution in accordance with experience.

This is a job the courts have taken on and largely fulfilled. Furthermore, because the Founding Fathers foresaw the vast changes in the future and had confidence in posterity, and because they knew, as John Marshall said, that the "Constitution was intended to endure for ages to come and be adapted to the various crises of human affairs," they accepted the key word "adapted" as a natural term for interpretation of the Constitution. "Adapted" is still the key word today.

Consider the ambiguities in Article I, Section 7. It says that "all bills for raising money shall originate in the House." What does "orginate" mean? Today all bills for raising money originate in the White House, in the Bureau of the Budget. That was not the intention of the Founding Fathers. Their concept on this point came from the two-hundred-year struggle in England for constitutional independence, for control of the purse, and the supremacy of Parliament. That is why the Founding Fathers said that all money bills shall originate in the House.

That the House of Representatives has largely abrogated its responsibility in this matter is a strong case to suggest Mr. Meese's jurisprudence of original intention, because the Framers' original intent was for the House to originate the budget. How wholesome it would be if, when Secretary of Defense Caspar Weinberger sits in front of the House Committee and tells that committee what must go into the Defense Department's budget and what must not be taken out of it, a committee member would have the backbone to say, "Mister Secretary, our authority comes from the Constitution, your authority comes from us! We can abolish your position, as we can abolish every department, if we chose to do so."

Article I, Section 8 says: "The Congress shall have power to lay and collect taxes, duties, imposts and excises, to pay the debts and provide for the common defence and general welfare of the United States. . . . " We still do not know what is meant by "general welfare," at least the Supreme Court has been unable to decide on its meaning. Debate rages over whether "general welfare" is merely a broad term for whatever other authority Congress may have in legislation, or whether it has an independent status as has common defense.

Article I, Section 9 says: "No money shall be drawn from the treasury," and "a regular statement of receipts and account of the expenditures of all public money shall be published from time to time," which, constitutionally, means at least once a year. I know of no regular statement of revenues and expenditures of the Central Intelligence Agency ever having been made public. When Senator Frank Church's committee tried to get one, the C.I.A. refused to provide it, and President Reagan supported the C.I.A. Shouldn't the public have the right to know how its money is being spent in the activities—secret or otherwise—of the C.I.A.?

Article II concerns Executive power, but does not define that power. It says Executive power is vested in a President. The question is, is Executive power limited to those few powers that are specified in the Constitution, such as appointing and receiving ambassadors and public ministers and so forth? Or should Executive power be recognized as an "open sesame" to almost anything the President thinks is appropriate for the Executive office? Also, Article II states that the President is Commander-in-Chief. Does that mean the President is the Commander-in-Chief of the Army and Navy and so forth? James Madison and Alexander Hamilton differed diametrically on the meaning of both "Executive power" and "Commander-in-Chief." That question has never been resolved, though it is often settled by the President's unilateral action for military purposes if he sees fit.

Article II also states that the President conducts foreign affairs with the "advice and consent of the Senate." "Advice and consent" means what it meant when it was written: Congress, not the Executive, prepares appropriations. Here, again, I agree with the Attorney General: we should go back to the original meaning of "advice and consent," and see to it that the Senate does indeed advise and, if it chooses, consent.

Chief Justice Roger Taney, a man of enormous learning, did not agree with President Abraham Lincoln on the use of Executive power in wartime. A jurisprudence of original intention should have clarified that difference of opinion. Lincoln imposed a blockade of all the southern ports. Taney said that that was unconstitutional, that he had no right to declare a blockade. Fortunately, Lincoln had his way, and Mr. Taney was soon retired. There are a hundred other cases in which constitutional scholars hold diametrically different interpretations of what the Constitution really means.

Consider the statement in Article IV, Section 4: "The United States shall guarantee to every State in this Union a republican form of government." What do "republican form of government" and "guarantee" mean? How does Congress guarantee a republican form of government? If the people choose to create a socialist or a communist government, can Congress do anything about that? Undoubtedly Congress would take action, but as long as the democratic process is observed, one looks in vain in the Constitution for the significance of that guarantee clause.

Article V concerns provisions for amendments. No one quite knows what to do about amendments. Can Congress confine a new constitutional convention to a particular issue, such as balancing the budget or abortion? Congress cannot do that if the principle of the Constitutional Convention means what it originally meant. The only way the American people, in their state or in their nation, can exercise their sovereignty is in a convention that has the power to wipe out all existing government and create a new government.

Presidents and Congresses, Presidents and Supreme Court Justices, Presidents and attorney generals have often differed in their interpretation of what might seem to be simple and elementary features of the Constitution itself. The elementary conclusion is that there is no single, authoritative original intention. Justices Learned Hand, Oliver Wendell Holmes, and Louis Brandeis all disagreed on interpretations of the Constitution. Chief Justice Earl Warren and his associate justices were consistently astigmatic in their reading of the Constitution, whereas ex-Chief Justice Warren Burger and his associate justices always seem to have had twenty-twenty vision in their reading of the Constitution.

The real issue in this debate that Mr. Meese has somewhat recklessly launched is not over the concept or the technique of original intention or any grammatical, rhetorical, or legal issues; the argument concerns political and philosophical issues. Mr. Meese approaches the Constitution not as an erudite scholar searching for the origin and history of each word, but as a politician. He champions jurisprudence of original intention, not out of consummate respect for historical accuracy, but as a weapon in a political contest. Mr. Meese is persuaded that a jurisprudence-of-original-intention interpretation of the Constitution should, might, and probably would sustain states' rights.

Almost the entire conservative camp refuses to recognize the most elementary fact of our Constitutional system: states do not have rights—people have rights. The states, like the nation itself, have only those rights given to them by the people, who are citizens of both state and nation. The people not only made the Constitution the supreme law of the land for the original thirteen states, they called into being, in the overwhelming majority, thirty-seven existing states, no one of which had any claim to be originally independent. In other words, states were creatures of both the United States and the Constitution, both of which are themselves creatures of the people.

Finally, Justice Joseph Story wrote: "No man will pretend to say that the affection of the state governments has been sensibly diminished by the operations of the general government. If the latter has become more deeply an object of regard or reverence, of attachment and pride, it is because it is the parental guardian of all our public and private rights, and the natural ally of all the state governments in the administration of justice and the promotion of the general prosperity. It is beloved, not for its power, but for its beneficence; not for its commands, but because it protects; not because it controls, but because it sustains the common interests and the common liberties and the common rights of the people."

DIALOGUE

Dialogue Participants

W. B. ALLEN, Professor of Government, Harvey Mudd College.

GEORGE ANASTAPLO, Professor of Law, Loyola University, Chicago.

HERMAN BELZ, Professor of History, University of Maryland, College Park.

EDWARD J. ERLER, Professor of Political Science, California State University, San Bernardino.

RICHARD FLACKS, Professor of Sociology, University of California, Santa Barbara.

GERALD GUNTHER, William Nelson Cromwell Professor of Law, Stanford University.

STEPHEN MARKMAN, Assistant Attorney General, U.S. Department of Justice.

PAUL L. MURPHY, Professor of History, University of Minnesota, Minneapolis.

JONATHAN D. VARAT, Professor of Law, University of California, Los Angeles.

THOMAS G. WEST, Professor of Politics, University of Dallas.

DONALD McDONALD, Center Staff.

Herman Belz: The Constitution, in order to be effective and useful, should be suited to the character of a people. The purpose of our fixed Constitution is to be not only suited to the character of the people, but to shape that character in order that we may be a prosperous and free people.

The American character is defined by republican self-government. Certain basic Constitutional principles define the character of our constitutional government: (1) the people as constituent power; (2) the separation of powers—with its checks and balances as the way of having a pluralistic, policymaking, sharing-of-power system within the basic separation structure; (3) federalism—the division of sovereignty; (4) the idea that the Constitution, as text and document, is authoritative and must be consulted.

When political leadership repudiates or rejects these four Constitutional principles, there is a reaction. Separation of powers if the reaction to both excessive Executive power and judicial policymaking. Judicial liberals—whom I call the "anything goes" judicial policymaking activists—have called into question the authoritative character and nature of the Constitution as a document. They would do without the document except as a convenient symbol which they can invoke to legitimize whatever they want to do. For our purposes here in this dialogue, the reaction against the seeming repudiation of these key Constitutional principles has taken the form of Mr. Meese's "jurisprudence of original intention."

Mr. Meese wants the country and the national political leadership to pay attention to the four basic Constitutional principles. He and others object to the "anything goes" judicial policymaking. I also think that judicial policymaking violates the separation-of-powers idea that lawmakers, not the courts, should make policy.

The reaction against the seeming repudiation of these basic Constitutional principles means that the people want a Constitutional realignment, the people want to realign national politics on the basis of original, fundamental Constitutional principles.

Commager: The Constitutional realignment from 1865 to 1868 revolutionized the Constitution. It made the national government, rather than the states, the protector of the liberties of all the people. Indeed, many of the individual states had failed as protectors. That realignment has to be interpreted by someone. Yet no one has been interpreting that realignment but the Supreme Court, which has the authority to do so.

Belz: The Fourteenth Amendment did not get rid of the states. The states continue to be the primary, though not the ultimate, interpreters of that realignment.

Commager: The key word is "ultimate." Of course the states are not the ultimate interpreters—the nation is, the courts are.

Gerald Gunther: The Attorney General suggests that the key and virtually sole content of Constitutional interpretation is the original intent of the Framers. In current American Constitutional debates, this is an extremely unusual position. Of the many scholars writing on the proper criteria of Constitutional interpretation, I know of only one—Raoul Berger—who advocates simply reading the legislative debates of the Constitutional Convention to define what the Framers would have said about all the problems this Constitutional polity has faced over the years. I know nobody who seriously believes you can read the Constitution simply in terms of that kind of originalism. I think Attorney General Meese has made a great mistake by apparently identifying himself with that discredited notion of Constitutional interpretation.

By contrast, Supreme Court Justice William J. Brennan argues that it is hopeless to read—either in principle or in practice—the Constitution solely by original intent. His alternative is extraordinarily open-ended, one that permits judges to read their own agendas into the Constitution.

Many constitutional scholars, including I, believe that neither pure originalism nor complete open-endedness is the true guide to the Constitution. It is something in between these extremes that provides guidance. Permissible guidelines can be found in the text, history, and structure of the Constitution. These are far superior to simply reading political mores or contemporary intellectual views into the Constitution.

W. B. Allen: Perhaps we need to understand the Attorney General's position as something other than the taking of positions in contemporary political debates. Perhaps a broader conversation about Constitutional interpretation is taking place.

It is slightly artificial to oppose Justice Brennan to contemporary scholarship or to Mr. Meese, as it is slightly artificial to seek an authoritative or useful interpretation of Constitutional principles only among scholars, as if Constitutional interpretation can be isolated from the political and Constitutional experience of the country.

Justice Brennan's argument relies on knowing the intent of the Founding Fathers. Yet, in order to accept his open-ended interpretation, we must understand the intent of the Founding Fathers as Brennan understands it. But before we can understand Brennan's open-ended interpretation, he must convince us that he really does understand the intent of the Founding Fathers.

Is it possible to engage the Founding Fathers in a conversation about fundamental questions of Constitutional order and human nature? Attorney General Meese also asks that question. Does anyone deny that it is possible for us to understand the intent of the Founding Fathers that we find in both their drafting and their defense of the Constitution? If we can understand their intent, can we then guide ourselves by that understanding?

Commager: Interestingly, in 1791, Madison and Hamilton disagreed on the reading of the Constitution about whether Congress had the power to incorporate a national bank. That is an example of how two men who probably knew the Constitution best could disagree fundamentally on the meaning of words and phrases that had been agreed upon only four years earlier.

Today the Reagan Administration and the strict interpreters think that the Constitution was made once and for all, that it cannot change, that it means what it meant in 1787, that we should not monkey with government, law, or existing standards and principles.

We should be asking not what did the Framers think or what did they accept or not accept, but how should we think and what is in the best interests in dealing with our great objective: meeting the exigencies of union. We should quarrel not over *explication de texte* or restructuralism in the field of literary criticism, but over the question of the Constitution as an organic and dynamic instrument that changes because circumstances change. We should ask, what kind of constitution do we want? Can we find authority to adjust and adapt the Constitution—as we adjust and adapt similar instruments—to pressing needs?

The question, How far do we go in interpretation? lies between those who prefer a broad interpretation that would adjust the Constitution to current realities and those who prefer a narrow interpretation that would adjust current realities to the Constitution.

Stephen Markman: Attorney General Meese is saying that if the text of the Constitution provides guidance as to what the Founders intended, so be it. When that text is either ambiguous or provides limited direction, we then look at how discrete provisions of the Constitution mesh, and at the overall structure of and the implicit values in the Constitution to discern the original intention of the Founders.

The Attorney General realizes that we cannot always know with certainty what was intended by the Founders. But he also knows that a large body of knowledge has developed as to what the Founders thought. I think his conclusion is that, when we cannot find guidance to the Founders' intentions, the courts are not free to do anything they want to do. In fact, the direction to the courts is that states are permitted to do what they want—consistent with limitations in the Constitution—and that the federal government is not able to do anything it wants, subject to the express grants of authority contained in the Constitution.

There certainly is more guidance in what the Founders thought the Constitution meant than there is in the vague standards of some of today's law professors. One professor thinks that natural law is the standard to which the courts ought to look. Another says that the role of the courts is to determine what the values of the citizenry are. Another talks about fundamental organic rights. Another talks about the basic values inherent in the welfare state. All those standards provide some guidance to some people, but I think it is the Attorney General's view that the idea of what the Founders intended is a much better index of what the Constitution means than are the vague standards of certain law professors.

If interpretivism, or original intent, is not the appropriate standard by which we interpret the Constitution, the Attorney General wants to know what the alternative standard is. What is the value of a written Constitution in the absence of that particular standard?

Commager: We can know what the Framers meant by reading their writings. Madison kept a record of the debates. He wrote considerably on constitutional interpretation. In addition, we should trust what was said by those who debated in the Constitutional Convention. And we have *The Federalist*, which is still unequaled as an interpretation of the Constitution.

It is not enough to know only what the Founding Fathers might have thought they meant, or might have meant if their thoughts are not appropriate to contemporary affairs. We can know, for example, that when they prohibited "cruel and unusual punishment," they meant torture, because every Old World country—with the exception of England—permitted torture. Yet that phrase has been interpreted far more broadly than simply meaning the prohibition of torture.

We must not think we will solve problems by knowing precisely what an author meant. We must know what the author would have thought, meant, and done when confronted with the kinds of problems we face today.

Gunther: I do not think that the Constitution is a completely malleable, adaptable document, or that it is simply a judgment as to what current needs are.

I embrace the position of the Attorney General, in theory, with respect to using the text of the Constitution as a starting point, but I must say that he has sown some confusion. Mr. Markman said the Attorney General believes in interpretivism or original intent. But interpretivism is not limited to original intent. I am an interpretivist, and I battle the same law professors Mr. Markman referred to. But I do not think the Attorney General has clearly stated his position. If he embraces interpretivism, he has a large number of followers—including old-fashioned, card-carrying Democrats, such as me. But if he embraces original intent, he leaves himself open to being misunderstood or to justifiable attack.

I would be much more persuaded by the preaching of the Reagan Administration and the Attorney General about constitutional interpretation—whose substance I agree with in most respects—if their recent appointments to the bench, those praised by the Administration as judicial restrainers and as people who know that the job of a judge is not to remake the world, were in fact what the Administration claims they are. But these newly appointed judges do not take seriously the view of interpretivism as I think Mr. Markman understands it and as the Attorney General apparently means to express.

Many judicial activists want to read into the Constitution ideas for which I find no adequate basis in either the Framers' views or in the text of the Constitution itself. Some examples of bad judges are the late William O. Douglas and William J. Brennan, whose only major differences with the Reagan Administration's appointees are political in nature.

Jonathan D. Varat: In many cases we can know the intent of the Framers by looking at the text, history, and structure of the Constitution. But if the courts, after having exhausted those sources, were simply to say, "We have no guidance from those sources, therefore we have no grounds for holding any action unconstitutional," they would be abdicating their responsibility. I think Mr. Markman and Mr. Meese see that as the carrying-out of the courts' responsibility.

The Constitution was adopted as a political compromise. Deliberate ambiguities were put in the Constitution so that the differences of the Framers would not prevent the adopting of the Constitution. Those deliberate ambiguities also have something to say about how the Constitution shall be interpreted. The Framers were practical people: they understood that the deliberate ambiguities in the Constitution would eventually have to be applied to concrete cases.

Often we know little about how the Framers intended judges to interpret these ambiguities. Today some argue that, when faced with an ambiguity in the Constitution, the judges should throw up their hands and say: "We can't interpret that; someone else will have to do it." But, again, that is an abdication of the original intent of the Framers who wanted the Supreme Court to enforce the Constitution.

I question much of the reality and availability of the Framers' original intent as determining the answer to specific questions. Take natural law. History suggests that people feared that enumerating some rights would imply that other rights were not to be recognized. The Ninth Amendment was adopted to make sure that that was not the case. Is that a direction to the courts to seek those rights outside the document, since they were recognized but not listed? If so, why is natural law any less relevant a measure of Constitutional interpretation than what was contained in the records of the debates in the Constitutional Convention?

We can look to contemporary intellectual currents to judge what would be best for and acceptable to the people because there are such constraints as precedent of prior Supreme Court decisions; practical, political, and legal criticism of the Supreme Court when, in the view of many, it goes awry; and the Supreme Court's publicly stating the reasons for its decisions. To be sure, there is not complete restraint, and choices have to be made, but it is appropriate for the Supreme Court to make those choices. Someone must interpret the Constitution.

It is fine to say that we can use original intent as a guide to the meaning of the Constitution, but then we must accept a historian's, not a judge's, interpretation of what a group of people meant two hundred years ago. The debate would then be on whether a historical or a judicial interpretation of original intent is legitimate. We will never get away from the fact that when dealing with current problems, people will have to make some interpretation of the Constitution.

I am not saying that "anything goes" with respect to interpreting the Constitution, because parts of the Constitution are quite specific, while other parts are quite general. Take the equal protection clause and the clause that requires a member of the House of Representatives to be twenty-five years old. There is more room in the former than in the latter for interpretation. In *Brown* v. *The Board of Education*, even if it were true at the time of the adoption of the Fourteenth Amendment that the existing practice of segregated schools was thought to be consistent with the equal protection clause, the fact is they adopted a provision that contained language capable of growth: that no state shall deny any person the equal protection of the laws. Chief Justice Earl Warren was right when he said, "We must judge this in the light of today, not in the light of 1866."

Richard Flacks: In order for both our government and our Constitution to maintain stability, we need a Supreme Court to recognize certain rights not recognized in the Constitution. The Supreme Court has understood that certain rights should be recognized, not because it has looked into its own soul, but because it has looked at the political context of society in general, and at the emerging delegitimating pressures in society, in particular. A government that refuses to recognize the claims of its citizens to certain rights they feel they must have to lead a normal life cannot stand. The fundamental exigency is: How will a government preserve itself if it cannot adapt to the claims of its citizens to rights?

Thomas G. West: The authority of the Constitution comes from the people. It was the people who adopted, ratified, and amended the Constitution. Therefore, should the Supreme Court tell the people how they ought to live, or decide which rights the people should have? The Supreme Court may tell us what the definite meanings in the Constitution are, but if inferences must be drawn because of ambiguous language in the text, the Supreme Court then has no authority to tell citizens how they ought to live.

Paul L. Murphy: The Constitution has not always been changed and interpreted by the Supreme Court. Historically, when one branch of government consistently failed to interpret the Constitution and to apply it to the affairs of mankind, the other branches have done so. During the Civil War, Lincoln combined the Commander-in-Chief clause and the clause that charges the President with seeing to it that the laws are faithfully executed to make a body of Presidential war powers sufficient to blockade the South and raise Union troops. He even issued the Emancipation Proclamation based upon these war powers.

There have been times when Congress interpreted the Constitution. The Reconstruction period was one of the most dynamic, Constitutionally creative periods of American history. Radical Republican congressmen amended the Constitution three times, passed two civil rights acts and three enforcement laws, all of which radically changed the Constitutional structure. They did these things in good faith, as an agency of government responsible for seeing to it that the Constitution adapted to the changing circumstances and needs of the American people.

Edward J. Erler: In *The Federalist*, Hamilton said: "We are not just writing a constitution to meet the exigencies of the day, we are setting up a constitution that will be directed towards remote futurity as well." Hamilton meant they were establishing the principles of a self-governing polity. John Marshall said that the adoption of the Constitution was an exercise of the original right of the people, that the principles of the Constitution must be deemed to be the fundamental and permanent principles of a self-governing people. The Constitution, therefore, represents both the superior will of the people and the fundamental, legitimating agency of constitutional government.

We can know the intent of the Framers by looking at the constitutional debates and other sources. But we should look at these sources only after finding the language of the Constitution to be ambiguous. I can almost guarantee that no one at the Constitutional Convention said, "We are deliberately putting ambiguities into the Constitution." Also, every member of the Constitutional Convention knew he was engaged in an enterprise intended to apply the principles expressed in the Declaration of Independence.

The greatest compromise of the Constitution was slavery, which the Framers included to provide some limited protection for slavery. Chief Justice Taney believed he was explicating original intent when he made his decision in the Dred Scott case. He said that when you look at the Declaration of Independence and the Constitution you conclude that there is not one right that any black man enjoys that any white man is bound to respect. When Lincoln said that the principle of equality is the foundation of all our moral principles, he, too, believed he was explicating original intent. Lincoln showed that the Supreme Court was wrong in its interpretation of fundamental principles. In *Dred Scott*, Lincoln was right and Taney was wrong. That debate concerned original intention and the principles embodied in the Constitution. Of course, those principles must be applied differently as exigencies change, but the principles themselves do not change.

Mr. Varat mentioned that Chief Justice Warren correctly applied the Fourteenth Amendment in *Brown* v. *The Board of Education*. I think Warren's use of the Fourteenth Amendment was wrong. If we see the Fourteenth Amendment in terms of the principles of the Declaration of Independence—which the Framers believed they were implementing—we then see its adoption as the completion of the Declaration of Independence. Those who advocated the Fourteenth Amendment said that although the Framers found it necessary to postpone the implementation of the Declaration of Independence—by allowing the continued existence of slavery—it was time to bring the Constitution into harmony with the Declaration of Independence. Warren would not admit that the Constitution embodied any principles at all. He was saying, in effect, that because we do not know what those who opposed adoption of the Fourteenth Amendment meant, we therefore cannot use the Fourteenth Amendment as a reference point.

We know that the Framers intended separation of powers to be the central institution of the Constitution. They thought that if lawmakers could both execute the law and judge its execution, that would be tyranny. The question is not, was this what the Framers believed, but is that statement true of a constitutional government?

Also, the issue of activism and restraint is not about whether the Supreme Court is active or restrained, but about whether, if it is active, its activism supports Constitutional principles. The Supreme Court should be activist in order to vindicate Constitutional principles; it should be restrained in the pursuit of Constitutional principles when restraint is called for.

Murphy: But every Supreme Court says it is applying Constitutional principles.

Erler: Justice Brennan does not say he is applying Constitutional principles.

Gunther: He does say that.

Erler: He says we can infer from the Constitution that it stands for human dignity.

Gunther: I think Brennan is dead wrong on that, but you are equally wrong. How can you say that Lincoln was correct in the debate with Taney on *Dred Scott* on the ground of approaching some notion of basic principles of equality in the Constitution? That simply was not there.

Erler: It was there.

Gunther: Only by reading the Declaration of Independence into it.

Erler: Lincoln constantly referred to the Declaration of Independence.

Gunther: The document they were interpreting was the Constitution.

Erler: But both believed that the Constitution had to be read in the light of principles that had been enunciated in the Declaration of Independence.

Gunther: Then why did we need the Fourteenth Amendment?

Erler: Because the Constitution had compromised on the issue of slavery.

Gunther: The *Dred Scott* debate happened in 1857, before the adoption of the Fourteenth Amendment. Yet you praise Lincoln as an interpreter of fundamental principles for relying on the notions of the Declaration of Independence, which you say had not yet been incorporated in the Constitution.

Erler: You mistake both my meaning and Constitutional history. Lincoln had always said that the Declaration of Independence was the guiding principle of the regime. It simply had not been incorporated literally into the Constitution until the adoption of the Thirteenth and Fourteenth Amendments. How do we know whether what we are doing is right or wrong in Constitutional issues unless we have a standard maxim by which we can judge? Lincoln said the standard maxim principles are those of the Declaration of Independence that say that no one can be legitimately ruled without his consent.

George Anastaplo: It seems the argument in *Dred Scott* was ultimately between Congress and the Supreme Court as to who was reading the Constitution correctly. There are good reasons for believing that Congress read it correctly. In fact, in the great crises over the past two hundred years, when Congress and the Supreme Court have differed on major issues, Congress has been correct.

The question is, where does the ultimate authority rest among the branches of government? If one puts it where I believe it was intended to be, and for which the Constitution indicates it was intended to be, emphasis should be put not upon separation of powers, but upon the ultimate control of the government in the hands of the legislators. If that is true, the question of judiciary authority is of secondary importance.

In some ways the Attorney General is more correct than he realizes. If one understands that the government is not a limited government with respect to the powers given to it, and that Congress is the dominant controlling branch of the government, then one understands that Congress can legislate quite broadly with respect to many matters. The real debate is on how much and in what way the powers of Congress—not those of the courts—should be in these matters.

The Supreme Court has made too much of certain of its prerogatives and too little of its most important prerogative: the supervision of common law.

Allen: What in our politics and scholarship makes it difficult for educated men and women to discuss Constitutional principles, and to ascertain the strength and meaning of those principles as influencing the American character and providing for some sense of political choices to be made? One reason might be that we appeal to vague and ambiguous authorities because there has been a serious erosion of any genuine appreciation of this political order as being free. Almost instinctively people recur to implicitly despotic models of authority, rather than to principles of freedom, to assess the weight of Constitutional principles in our time.

Why do we wish to erect the Supreme Court into an ultimate authority? From listening to comments around the table here, I deduce that it is because there is an inherent distrust of the people, a belief that the people cannot preserve the rule of law or govern themselves, and that there must be someone who must say what the laws mean for them. I would like to hear the argument for that position.

Flacks: In addition to the four Constitutional principles Mr. Belz mentioned, I have always thought there was a fifth: the rights of minorities.

Belz: That principle is incorporated in the idea of the people as a constituent power.

Flacks: The people as a constituent power is pure fiction. There are many peoples in the United States, some of whom have not had the equal access to protections. That is why we have had social conflict in our society.

The honest answer to why the people cannot always be trusted to make the law is that the majority at any given time does not necessarily respect the rights of the minority.

Allen: Was there never a Constitution of the people?

Flacks: The Constitution of the people is worked out over time, as different constituent groups within the people struggle to gain equality.

Allen: So the Constitution is a result of the struggle of forces at any moment in time? It is an unwritten constitution?

Flacks: What I defend is the possibility that the constituted authority will be flexible enough to recognize, after such struggles, that rights that were not recognized previously by the majority do, in fact, exist.

Belz: Does the political process decide that?

Flacks: Clearly, the Supreme Court is necessary to protect those of the population whose rights are denied by majority rule or by the excessive abuse of power by some group.

Belz: Professor Commager's *Majority Rule and Minority Rights*, published in 1943, argues that the Supreme Court is not good at that.

Commager: It had not been good at that.

Belz: It is better now?

Allen: The argument certainly has evolved since that time.

Flacks: The argument has not evolved.

Allen: I don't see why.

Flacks: Because, if left to itself, Congress would apparently not have granted the rights that we not take for granted as necessary in a genuinely egalitarian society.

I am not saying that the United States Supreme Court is the sole and final arbiter of these matters. I am simply saying that that just happens to have been the case in recent history.

Erler: We have a separation of powers with checks and balances. You want to leave Congress out.

Flacks: Minority rights was not part of the basic principles of our Constitution, and that is why Attorney General Meese questions the right of the Supreme Court to rule on behalf of minority rights.

Erler: It was not minority rights, it was the rights of every individual that were embodied in the Constitution—that is, human rights.

West: Mr. Flacks, yours is a classic argument for hereditary monarchy. Your point is that this is a despotic model of government. You cannot trust the people; therefore, ultimate power must be independent of the majority.

Donald McDonald: Mr. Anastaplo said the legislature is the voice of the people who have agreed to delegate their power to their representatives, the legislators. But suppose legislators do not protect the rights of individual groups and minorities. Who but the Supreme Court, or a strong President, will stand up and speak for all the people? The Supreme Court has to do it. As to the kinds of rights that may need definition and protection, Amendment 9 of the Bill of Rights leaves open the enumerating of more rights.

Gunther: Clearly, a vast number of the new rights Mr. Flacks is talking about, which are a result of political and social pressure, are created by Congress. The 1964 Civil Rights Act and the 1965 Voting Rights Act are basic pieces of modern legislation. These are, of course, a legacy of the Civil Rights movement and of Martin Luther King, Jr., but they are not newly created Constitutional rights by a court.

Flacks: Why did the National Association for the Advancement of Colored People go to the Supreme Court to have school segregation abolished? Why did women's groups, or complainants in the abortion issue, go to the Supreme Court? Why has Congress not passed a law guaranteeing the right of women to have abortions under certain conditions? Is it because the majority of people, in fact, oppose abortion.

Gunther: The abortion movement—which I support politically, even though I am a vehement critic of *Roe* v. *Wade*—went to many state legislatures before the Supreme Court ruled in *Roe* v. *Wade* and succeeded in liberalizing state laws regarding abortion. That the Supreme Court took the abortion issue upon itself was a judicial abuse of power. *Roe* v. *Wade* is an abomination, an outrage, one of the worst Supreme Court decisions in terms of constitutionally mandating what ought to be legislatively mandated responses to political pressures.

Flacks: If a despised minority in our society seeks equality of rights, and if the American people, in their wisdom, keep denying equality to that minority, can that minority not petition the Supreme Court: "Please recognize our rights, even though the majority will not?"

Gunther: I am all for that minority group's access to the Supreme Court. But there are many claims the Supreme Court cannot legitimately grant.

Commager: Mr. Holmes said, "I do not think anything would happen to the Constitution if we should lose our authority to invalidate the law of Congress. But I do not believe the Union could survive if we should lose our authority to review the acts of states."

Markman: The question in the debate on original intent is this: Who in a free democratic society determines public policy? The Supreme Court on an average day determines more public policy in a greater variety of areas than does the Congress during an entire session. Most major social reforms in recent years have come from the Supreme Court: reforms in the areas of Civil Rights, criminal procedure, and social policy. Regardless of one's views on abortion, when the Supreme Court hands down a decision like *Roe* v. *Wade*, a decision that summarily overturns the considered legislative judgment of all fifty states, then that decision must be scrutinized. It is a decision that calls into question the appropriate role of the Supreme Court vis-à-vis the other branches of government.

If the authority of the Supreme Court comes from outside the Constitution, then it is entitled to no respect. If, on the other hand, its authority comes from the Constitution, then it is subject to the checks and balances and constraints in the Constitution. Of course, the Framers recognized that there would be evolving circumstances and new exigencies. That is why they put Article V in the Constitution: it allows the people to deal with changing circumstances.

I do not think there are any ulterior motives to the Attorney General's crusade for original intent. He is committed to ideas. For example, the Attorney General held a weekend conference on federalism with a dozen people from the Justice Department. I am hard-pressed to think of any other recent attorney generals who were that interested in federalism. He has also held conferences on the separation of powers and on original-intent jurisprudence.

Regarding the judicial selection process, that is not a perfect process. We make mistakes. We have selected people whom we possibly should not have selected. In his first year of office, the Attorney General made approximately seventy-five appointments to the bench. Since Ronald Reagan became President, we have made about 260 appointments to the bench. I don't think any other Administration has paid as much attention, or has been as thorough in making its judicial selection as has the Reagan Administration. Every individual who is considered for this judiciary undergoes seven or eight interviews, during which we ask them for their ideas of jurisprudence and their view of what the proper role of the judiciary is in our government. We do not ask candidates for their personal views on such issues as abortion or prayer in public schools.

Varat: The Supreme Court gets its authority to make antimajoritarian decision from the Constitution. One of the most crucial compromises essential to the ratification of the Constitution was that a Bill of Rights should be adopted before ratification. That a specification of antimajoritarian provisions ought to be included in the Constitution reflected the Founders' recognition that majoritarian policy would perhaps impinge on the rights of groups that were not in the majority at any particular time, and that it was important to have in the structure a body to protect from legislative and executive excesses those not in the majority.

The majority we are talking about—the "original will" of a group of people—would be looked at today as hardly pure democracy. It was a small elite that put the Constitution together. Times have changed. The will of the people has been broadened, in large part, by judicial decisions. This original will set up a structure, part of which was building a counterweight to majoritarian decisions while, at the same time, an equal part was the separation of powers. We gave that job to the Supreme Court, which ought to be given the opportunity to perform that job.

MR. MEESE, MEET MR. MADISON[5]

The Ambiguity of Intent

The Constitution turns two hundred next year, and Americans will be asked to celebrate the remarkable Convention that met in Philadelphia during that famous hot summer of 1787. Yet events may be conspiring to make the Constitution an object not just of celebration but also of controversy. For the past year, a flurry of op-ed pieces and other essays have debated the merits of Attorney General Edwin Meese's call for a return to "a jurisprudence of original intention." Now, however, with the retirement of Chief Justice Warren Burger, his replacement by Justice William Rehnquist, and the appointment of Antonin Scalia, the Supreme Court, which has often been narrowly divided on crucial questions, seems about to make the fundamental change in direction that Meese and many other conservatives have long demanded.

Whether such a change will in fact occur is another matter—especially since the same reorientation was supposed to result from the four appointments that Richard Nixon made during his first term. But whatever happens, the growing influence of conservative legal scholarship, coupled with real controversy over many of the Court's most significant decisions, guarantees that the issues Mr. Meese has raised will remain the subject of public debate for some time.

[5]Reprint of an article by Jack N. Rakove of the history department of Stanford University, as originally published in the December 1986 issue of *The Atlantic Monthly.* Copyright © 1986 by Jack N. Rakove.

What is this debate about? Taken at face value, the idea of a jurisprudence of original intention is simply that a judge interpreting the Constitution or a law should adhere as closely as possible to the expressed ideas and purposes of its framers. In this sense, original intent would explicitly tell judges how they should read the laws they apply and enforce: narrowly and with great restraint. But in a more fundamental sense, the question that conservatives are raising is not How do judges judge? but, rather, What role should the judiciary play within the constitutional system? For, conservatives argue, if judges can freely ignore the intentions both of the original framers of the Constitution and of legislators, they can substitute their own preferences or values for the decisions of popularly elected officials. As the branch of government least accountable to the public, the judiciary should hesitate before imposing its opinions on the political departments.

At another level, of course, conservative complaints spring from strong objections to key decisions of the past three decades—those controversial rulings involving abortion, mandatory busing, affirmative action, the rights of the criminally accused and convicted, school prayer, and aid to religious schools. In its rulings in these areas, conservatives argue, the Supreme Court has violated the original intent of the Constitution in three ways. First, the Court has often ignored or distorted the original meaning of the Bill of Rights and the Fourteenth Amendment, the textual sources that most clearly identify the rights the Constitution explicitly protects. Second, the Court has established new rights that the written Constitution does not even mention—most flagrantly in its rulings on abortion. Third, by creating new rights and by imposing radical remedies (like busing) for past wrongs, the Court has attacked the constitutional principle of the separation of powers. No longer content simply to decide individual cases, the federal judiciary has set itself the task of making broad social policy, a responsibility that properly belongs to the elective branches of government. A judge may properly strike down laws that promote segregation or administrative rules that confine prisoners in excessively vile conditions. But when he takes over the management of a school system (as Federal Judge W. Arthur Gerrity did in Boston) or mandates the expenditure of public funds to alleviate jail overcrowding, he acts as judge, lawmaker, and administrator together—and that concentration of power, James Madison wrote in *Federalist* 47, "may justly be pronounced the very definition of tyranny."

This attack on the undemocratic nature of the judiciary turns on its head the position that conservatives have traditionally favored. Conservatives once relied on the courts to protect the rights of property against regulation by progressive majorities in the state legislatures and Congress. Now they hope to restrain "the unfettered and inevitably arbitrary wills of an elite few"—which is how Terry Eastland, Meese's spokesman at the Justice Department, characterizes the Court—so that democratic majorities in the states can presumably restore prayer to the schools, restrict abortion, suppress pornography, and fill the jails to overflowing. And since these social issues would largely fall under the control of the states, the attack on activist judges also clothes itself in the garb of federalism.

This reversal has led many liberals to accuse Meese of opportunism. Anthony Lewis has argued that "what really interests the present Attorney General is not judicial philosophy but particular political results," while Arthur Schlesinger, Jr., suggests that the "shamelessly selective" way in which Meese applies his theory to actual cases proves that he is "the biggest chameleon of the lot." What respect does Meese show for original intent, some liberals have wondered, when he declares that the President need not faithfully execute a law whose constitutionality he questions? Meese's complaints about judicial activism would vanish, they suspect, if the Court were to strike down the War Powers Act, or if new appointments produced a reliable majority of conservative justices willing, say, to eliminate affirmative-action programs root and branch.

Lewis and Schlesinger are in effect interpreting Meese's remarks according to their view of his intentions. Ironically, in doing so they illustrate one of the key difficulties with the Attorney General's position. Establishing the intention behind any action is a tricky business—as Meese or any other attorney surely should know. It is difficult enough to gauge the intent even of a single person—whether it be Edwin Meese in his Bar Association address of 1985 or James Madison in 1787. The task grows geometrically more complex when we try to ascribe intent to groups of people—especially men who were acting two centuries ago, who left us incomplete records of their motives and concerns, and who reached their decisions through a process that fused principled debate with hard-driven bargains.

Justice William Brennan presented objections of this kind in an address last year at Georgetown University, in which he dismissed Meese's "doctrinaire" position as "arrogance cloaked as humility." In the first place, Brennan noted, our historical sources typically offer only "sparse or ambiguous evidence of the original intention" of the framers of the Constitution. (Here he echoed the late Justice Robert Jackson, who once wrote that the historical records were "almost as enigmatic as the dreams Joseph was called upon to interpret for Pharaoh.") Nor is it even clear, Brennan added, *whose* intent deserves the greatest weight. The Constitution and the Bill of Rights were the joint work of the fifty-five delegates to the 1787 Convention and the ninety-odd members of the First Congress. But they became supreme law only after being ratified by hundreds of convention delegates and legislators in the states—and arguably it is their understanding of what they were approving, not that of the framers, that we ought to respect.

Justice Brennan has a different idea of the role that history should play in jurisprudence. Rather than recover the "static meaning" that the Constitution had "in a world that is dead and gone," judges must trace the distance between the framers' time and our own, and then apply the great underlying principles of the Constitution to the modern problems that our litigious society asks the courts to resolve. And while judges should ordinarily defer to the expressed will of the legislature, they cannot make majority rule the only basis of decision. For within the larger scheme of our system the great duty of the judiciary is to protect individual and minority rights against improper actions by popular majorities.

How should an informed and reasonably impartial citizen respond to these claims? The great difficulty is that the Constitution does not tell us how to resolve disputes over its meaning. Nowhere does it explicitly endorse the idea of judicial review, the doctrine that gives the judiciary the special function of protecting the Constitution against violations by other branches of government—by Congress, the President, or the states. Nowhere does it say whether later interpreters should follow their best understanding of the original intentions of the framers and ratifiers of 1787–1791 (or 1865–1868, in the case of the critical Civil War amendments), as Attorney General Meese proposes, or whether they should seek to apply its general principles to new realities, as Justice Brennan argues in response. Nowhere does it tell us whether we should read what scholars call the "silences" of the Constitution as freeing us to interpret the document as we see fit or as withholding from the judiciary the broad power that its detractors insist the judiciary has usurped.

In all that has been written on this subject in recent months, little has been said about the historical Constitution itself. Yet one cannot talk about original intent without taking history far more seriously than the current disputants have so far done. That is precisely why the approach of the Constitution's bicentennial may serve an unexpectedly useful purpose. Because the debate between Meese and his critics may remain academic until we learn whether our aging justices will outlast our aging President, perhaps the bicentennial offers a convenient occasion to turn the discussion back to its eighteenth-century roots—to ask how and why the Constitution was made, and even how its framers thought it should be interpreted. And by the same token, the existence of serious controversy over the meaning of the Constitution may prevent next year's celebration from degenerating into the kind of pageant that the new patriotism otherwise promises it will become.

Founding Father

One proof of the dangers of allowing lawyers to meddle with history can be found in the efforts that both Attorney General Meese and Professor Laurence Tribe, a leading liberal scholar at Harvard Law School, have already made to enlist James Madison on their respective sides of the current controversy. In what are virtually textbook examples of "law-office history," Meese and Tribe both manage to get the point half right. The Attorney General rightly notes that Madison believed that judges should interpret the Constitution according "to the sense in which [it] was accepted and ratified by the nation," in 1788, while Professor Tribe correctly observes that Madison held that the intentions of the framers "could *never* be regarded as the oracular guide in expounding the Constitution." Neither cites, much less tries to resolve, the apparent contradiction in Madison's opinions.

Unlike his good friend Thomas Jefferson—who had the habit, Madison once wrote, of "expressing in strong and round terms, impressions of the moment"—Madison liked to savor his distinctions. The one he sought to develop here is among his most puzzling. And because that is the case, his attempt to explain how the Constitution should be interpreted offers a usefully ambiguous starting point for asking what an appeal to original intent means in practice.

Madison's distinction can be restated in this way: In trying to interpret the Constitution a judge should ignore whatever he may learn of the original intentions of its authors, the delegates to the 1787 Convention, but he should defer to the popular understanding of the Constitution that prevailed at the time of its ratification. The distinction has one great advantage. It is consistent with the idea that the Constitution derives its force from the consent of the governed. (One can ask, though, whether a consent given in 1788 expresses popular sovereignty more effectively than the "inevitably arbitrary wills of an elite few" justices can claim to do today.)

Yet if Madison's position has its logic, it creates as many problems as it solves. Why should we assume that those who merely ratified the Constitution grasped its meaning better than those who wrote it—or those who have since seen how it works in practice? The debates of 1787–1788 elicited a range of opinions about its likely effects. Some of these predictions were quite sensible, but others nicely illustrate what the late Richard Hofstadter called "the paranoid style in American politics." And how can we possibly discover what the anonymous voters and obscure local leaders who were passing judgment on the Constitution thought? Did they read *The Federalist* with the same insight that students of political theory now bring to it? And if we treat *The Federalist* as our best evidence of how the Constitution was understood—as so many commentators have done—do we not find ourselves again relying on the intentions of the framers, since Madison and Alexander Hamilton wrote all but a handful of its eighty-five essays?

Madison's objections to giving any weight to the framers' intentions present a more serious and perhaps fatal problem with a jurisprudence of original intention. Simply put, the appeal to original intent cannot be justified on its own terms. There is no reason to believe that the framers thought their intentions should guide later interpretations of the Constitution. They never considered publishing the journal of their deliberations, which would at least have provided a curious public with a skeletal history of the evolution of the text. Nor did Madison allow his notes of the debates at Philadelphia to appear in his lifetime—even though disputes over the meaning of the Constitution arose as soon as the new government was organized, in 1789.

There are many ways to set about examining the current controversy from the distant vantage point of the framers. But the one that perhaps best reveals the range of possibilities, difficulties, and ironies that the quest uncovers is to view the making of the Constitution from the perspective of Madison, the framer who is now regarded, as Michael Kammen has noted, "as the most profound, original, and far-seeing among all his peers." He is, in fact, the member of the Convention whose intentions we know best, and whose ideas now dominate our own understanding of the founding.

Madison the man hardly cut a commanding figure. He lacked the stern charisma of Washington, the restless ambition of John Adams, and the engaging charm of Jefferson. He was less cosmopolitan than Franklin, less bold than Hamilton. Thomas Paine was a far more pungent writer, and Patrick Henry a far more stirring orator. What set Madison apart and enabled him to exercise a special influence of his own was the relentlessly logical intellect that he brought to bear on all public questions. Once he was done examining an issue, even his opponents found it hard to avoid viewing it from the perspective he had fashioned.

Madison had just turned twenty-four when the Revolutionary War broke out, in April of 1775. Three years had passed since the completion of his studies at the College of New Jersey (now Princeton University), but Madison remained a directionless young man with little ambition. In our own time, he would have been a natural candidate for graduate school.

The Revolution changed all that. Slowly Madison found in public life the commitment and fulfillment that the management of a plantation or a legal practice could never have provided. From the moment of his election to the Orange County Committee of Safety, in late 1774, until the end of his presidency, in 1817, his active involvement in politics never flagged. And even in retirement, his concern with the Republic and *res publica*—public affairs—continued unabated, until his death in 1836 marked the passing of the last of the Revolutionary patriarchs.

For a number of reasons, virtually every attempt to explain the Constitution centers on Madison. To begin with, he played the most critical role throughout the course of events that led to the writing, adoption, and amendment of the Constitution. From the moment he entered the Continental Congress, in 1780, no one was more actively engaged in the efforts first to ratify and then to amend the Articles of Confederation, the country's original federal charter. When the delegates to the Federal Convention assembled in May of 1787, the ideas that Madison had incorporated in the fifteen-point Virginia Plan set their basic agenda. He quickly assumed a leading role during the debates that followed, forcing his colleagues to view the problems of republican government from the elevated heights he had scaled. And once the Constitution was ratified, Madison (now in Congress) took the lead in drafting the amendments that eventually formed the Bill of Rights.

Even more important, our understanding of what the framers intended is largely derived from Madison: from his speeches and writings as well as from the invaluable notes he kept of the debates at Philadelphia. The most profound statements of the theory of the Constitution, scholars agree, are found in his contributions to *The Federalist*, especially in papers 10 and 51, the seminal texts of American political science.

But most important, the issues that Madison struggled with were, finally, the same issues that we are being asked to consider today. Can the rights of individuals and minorities be safely trusted to the will of democratic majorities within the states, or will they be better protected by the presumably more enlightened officials of the national government? Can any constitution enumerate all the rights and liberties that deserve protection? How much latitude may judges exercise in interpreting the Constitution, and what weight are they obliged to give to the intentions and understandings of its adopters? Madison pondered the first two of these questions in great detail in 1787–1788, and the third in the years to follow, especially as he monitored the growth of judicial power that the great Chief Justice John Marshall did so much to foster— originally in the landmark 1803 decision *Marbury* v. *Madison* (the suit that most clearly established the principle of judicial review).

It is easy enough for both sides of the current controversy over constitutional interpretation to appeal to Madison's authority. Like today's liberals, Madison doubted that individual rights could be safely left to the judgment of democratic majorities. But like the conservatives, he had serious reservations about the political capacity of the judiciary. Indeed, when, in 1821, he criticized the Marshall Court for "mingling with their judgments pronounced, comments & reasonings of a scope beyond them," he might just as well have been attacking Professor Ronald Dworkin's argument that judges should decide cases not according to constitutionally sanctioned rights but rather in the light of broad principles of moral philosophy.

For the historian, however, the deeper challenges are to explain the complexity and nuance of Madison's thought, and—still deeper—to recapture what was experimental, and thus tentative and uncertain, in everything that he and his colleagues sought to accomplish. It is this self-consciously experimental nature of the Convention that, ultimately, makes the search for its definitive "original intention" so problematic.

"The Vices of the Political System"

Madison came to Philadelphia the best prepared of any of the delegates. He had spent the preceding months diagnosing what he recalled "the vices of the political system of the United States" and reviewing the history of the great republican confederacies, both ancient and modern. His readings, he recalled, had failed to satisfy his curiosity about "the process, the principles, the reasons, and the anticipations"—in a word, the intentions—"which had prevailed in the formation of . . . the most distinguished Confederacies," and this frustration led him to keep a detailed record of the debates. But what Madison set out to preserve, once a quorum appeared, on May 25, 1787—eleven days late—was the fate of his own intentions. For he approached the Convention in the grip of a great intellectual passion, with the same exultation that in 1776 had led John Adams to rejoice at being "sent into life at a time when the greatest lawgivers of antiquity would have wished to live."

Three sets of major issues that Madison knew the delegates would act on should be familiar to everyone who can recall school lessons on the Constitution. First, to free the union from its "imbecilic" dependence on the good will of the states, the new government required independent power to make and execute its own laws and to raise its own revenues. It proved far easier to forge agreement on these points than on a second set of issues, which involved balancing the conflicting interests that the delegates represented: small states and large, slave states and free, northern merchants and southern planters.

But the time and energy that the prolonged maneuvers over these claims commanded might better have been devoted to a third set of issues: how to divide power among the three independent branches of the new government. Here the delegates drew their major lessons from the new constitutions that most of the states had written at the time of independence. The central feature of these constitutions—as Gordon Wood has shown in his brilliant study *The Creation of the American Republic, 1776–1787*—was their concentration of power in the legislatures, and especially in the lower houses. How to prevent these sovereign bodies from running roughshod over both the state constitutions and the two weaker branches of government—the executive and the judiciary—had emerged as the great question of American constitutionalism.

Most of the framers shared Madison's concern about the failings of the state constitutions. What set Madison apart was the depth of his analysis of both the source of the problem and its potential solution. More than any of his colleagues, he believed that the time had come to rescue not only the union from the states but also the states from themselves. It was in his brilliant assessment of the problems of republican government within the states that Madison most directly challenged the position that conservatives affirm today—namely, that claims to individual and minority rights not explicitly protected in the text of the Constitution are better left to the judgment of democratic majorities within the states than to the arbitrary will of federal judges.

The simple truth, he thought, was that incompetent lawmakers were passing too many laws, and that these poorly drawn acts were in turn being revised or repealed before anyone knew how well they were working. More alarming still, the "injustice" of the laws that had been adopted since 1776 suggested that the will of the majority could not be regarded as "the safest guardian both of public good and private rights." Self-interested or "factious" majorities within the assemblies or among the people at large were giving free rein to their impulses, undeterred by any of the moral restraints that one might hope would check such "vicious" behavior—honor, or a sense of the public good, or even religion, whose effects on public policy Madison strongly distrusted.

What kinds of rights did Madison fear that these majorities would violate? Some of his concerns would warm the heart of the most ardent Republican. In 1787 Madison was particularly anxious to protect the rights of property against unjust laws arising from "the lower orders" of society. Alarmed by the passage of paper-money laws and by Shays' Rebellion (an uprising of debtor farmers in Massachusetts), he foresaw a day when "power will slide into the hands" of "those who will labour under all the hardships of life, and secretly sigh for a more equal distribution of its blessings"—when, for example, the number of Virginia tenant farmers, which was growing, would be sufficient to pass laws breaking up the great estates of Madison's own class.

Yet the rights of property hardly exhausted his fears. Madison was no less intent on protecting the rights of religious dissenters and nonbelievers against even the weak forms of established religion that still survived in six of the states. In 1785 he had led the opposition to a Virginia bill to levy taxes to support all "teachers of the Christian religion"—a measure that, in the context of the time, can be fairly equated with the kind of nondiscriminatory aid to religion in general which many conservatives now argue that the establishment clause of the First Amendment was *not* meant to prohibit. In his view, the private exercise of religion was to be entirely free from both regulation and support by the government.

Rights of property and conscience, as well as the body of civil liberties that had come to be recognized as part of the Anglo-American legal tradition, were thus among Madison's central concerns. But what is perhaps most striking about his thinking on this subject is that he strongly resisted the idea that any constitution or bill of rights could ever fully identify the entire range of liberties that deserved protection. Bills of rights had been part of many of the state constitutions of 1776; Madison's first notable action in public life had been to secure an amendment to the most famous of these, the Virginia Declaration of Rights. But by 1787 he and virtually every other framer of the Constitution believed that such statements, however carefully drawn, had little worth. Bills of rights were not self-enforcing; they were mere "parchment barriers" (he later wrote Jefferson) that "overbearing majorities in every state" had repeatedly violated, and that "an infinitude of legislative expedients" could always find ways to circumvent.

How to prevent majorities within the community or the legislature from violating individual and minority rights was thus Madison's overriding concern in 1787, and it was reflected in virtually every major facet of his constitutional thought.

The great discovery that Madison carried to Philadelphia was that laws destructive of private rights were far less likely to be enacted in an extended national republic than within the smaller spheres of the states. Because a national republic would embrace so many diverse and shifting interests, the danger of the wrong kinds of coalitions forming and enduring among the community at large would be greatly reduced. And the new Congress, he predicted, would consist of legislators far more enlightened and scrupulous than the petty demagogues who controlled the state assemblies. (This, of course, was the theory that took its mature form in *The Federalist* papers 10 and 51.)

But Madison was prepared to trust congressmen only so far. From his own experience of state government he had concluded that "the real source of danger to the American constitutions" was the "powerful tendency in the legislature to absorb all power into its vortex." What he accordingly feared in 1787 was that both the national executive branch and the judiciary would prove not too strong but too weak. Alone, neither could resist the legislature, which could claim to speak for the will of the community. To give the executive branch and the judiciary the influence and political strength they separately lacked, Madison proposed that they should be allied in a Council of Revision. This Council would "examine" every act of Congress before it took effect, and its "dissent" would "amount to a rejection" unless Congress overrode this veto.

This remedy would secure the national government against "the mischiefs of faction," Madison believed, but within the smaller spheres of the states, which would still conduct much of the ordinary business of government, majorities rooted in economic interests or religion or other passions would continue to violate private rights. To deal with this residual danger to liberty Madison formulated his most radical proposal: to give the national government a "negative" (or veto) over every state law, to be exercised in the first instance by the Council of Revision, with Congress (or perhaps just the Senate) retaining a right of final judgment. Of all the intentions that Madison voiced at the Convention, this was the most original and, to his mind, the crucial one. Armed with such a power, the union could protect itself against the interfering laws that the states might pass. But more important, the negative would further enable the national government to act as a "dispassionate and disinterested umpire in disputes" within each of the states, curbing "the aggressions of interested majorities on the rights of minorities and of individuals."

It is difficult to see how Attorney General Meese can invoke the true original intentions of the "Father of the Constitution" to confirm his opinion about the proper place of the judiciary. The idea that claims to individual rights could be safely left to the judgment of majorities—especially state majorities—runs directly contrary to everything that Madison thought at the time the Constitution was adopted. The Madison of 1787 would also have opposed the current conservative cry that judges should simply decide cases, not make policy. Far from isolating the judiciary from the political arena, the Council of Revision was intended to bring it into the lawmaking process itself as an advisory body to the legislature. Madison sought thereby to improve the quality of law at its source, so that American legal codes would gain "the perspicuity, the conciseness, and the systematic character" that they otherwise might lack. The judiciary would then actively protect "the community at large" against "those unwise and unjust measures which constituted so great a portion of our calamities." Thus Madison, who hoped that the judiciary would act "to restrain the legislature from encroaching on the other co-ordinate departments, or on the rights of the people at large; or from passing laws unwise in their principle, or incorrect in their form," was not an unqualified defender of legislative supremacy.

Nor, finally, can it be said that the principal author of the Bill of Rights believed that judges should protect only those rights that the text of the Constitution explicitly recognized. On the contrary, Madison, James Wilson, and other federalists took seriously the argument that the constitutional recognition of particular rights would imply "that those rights which were not singled out" would be rendered "insecure." Madison in particular feared that "a positive declaration of some of the most essential rights could not be obtained in the requisite latitude." Under political pressure and at the urging of Jefferson, Madison finally (but grudgingly) admitted that a bill of rights might help, over time, to instill in the people a greater respect for "the fundamental maxims of free government." But even as he was shepherding the first amendments through Congress, in 1789, he privately described them (amazingly enough) as a "nauseous project," required only for expedient reasons of politics.

Doubtless, Madison would look askance at many of the specific claims of "rights" asserted in recent litigation. It is difficult to imagine him using the First Amendment to protect pornography or invalidating state prohibitions of contraception on the grounds that (in the famous words of Justice William O. Douglas) "penumbras, formed by emanations" from the Bill of Rights established "zones of privacy" into which public authority could not intrude. Equally important, Madison and many of the framers might well have been staggered by the range of remedies that the courts have devised and imposed after finding that individual and minority rights have indeed been violated. It is, after all, one thing to say that judges should simply void laws that clearly infringe upon such rights. But when judges move further and provide practical remedies for the redress of past wrongs—by mandating schemes for hiring minority workers, say, or making teacher assignments to alleviate the effects of segregation—they may act in political and administrative capacities that outrun both the boundaries of judicial competence and the notions of separation of powers to which the framers were so deeply attached.

On balance, however, Madison's larger concerns lend greater support to Justice Brennan than to Attorney General Meese. His general theory did invite judges and legislators alike to be generous, not frugal, in defining and defending the range of personal rights. Moreover, one can readily project many of his eighteenth-century concerns to the civil-rights issues that lie at the core of the activist jurisprudence of the past three decades. What, after all, was the edifice of Jim Crow segregation that the Court struck down, if not a classic example of how self-interested majorities within the states could trample on the rights of minorities? One could easily argue, too, that Madison would support the "one man–one vote" decisions of the early 1960s: he endorsed the regular reapportionment of legislative seats as early as 1785. And almost certainly Madison would find "nauseous" the current conservative claim, backed only by the most tendentious and selective scholarship, that the First Amendment permits nondiscriminatory federal support of religion.

The fact that the critical modern steps in favor of desegregation, reapportionment, and separation of Church and State originated with the judiciary would probably have surprised Madison, but only because he expected that judges would command so little influence and respect. He would not, I think, be disappointed with the results. In each of these areas, expanded rights and liberties have had to be wrenched from the control of groups whose behavior arguably confirmed his prediction that "wherever there is an interest and power to do wrong, wrong will generally be done." And for better or worse, it is the difficulty of convincing "factious majorities" to do right that suggests why judges cannot confine themselves to invalidating wrongful laws and regulations but often must also go ahead to devise the further remedies that plaintiffs seek. Doubts about the political competence of the judiciary must be weighed, in other words, against doubts about the good faith of legislators and their constituents.

Judicial Review

Most of the framers at Philadelphia shared Madison's doubts about the value of a bill of rights, and his innovative proposals for a Council of Revision and a veto over state laws also enjoyed strong support in debate—notably from the Scottish-born James Wilson, who was the leading legal mind at the Convention. The fact remains that neither the Council nor the veto was adopted—and for that reason Madison left the Convention deeply disappointed with its results. Even before it adjourned, he wrote to Jefferson that the Constitution would fail to "prevent the local mischiefs which everywhere excite disgusts against the state governments." In a second letter, written in late October, he provided an elaborate justification for the veto on state laws, and again predicted that the Constitution would prove "materially defective," because without that veto power the new government could not protect private rights. Only four weeks later, however, Madison published *Federalist* 10, which explained why the national government would be free of all those vices that its author privately felt (but did not say) would continue to plague the states.

For the serious student of "original intent," Madison's early disillusionment with the results of the Convention raises awkward questions. To begin with, consider how it affects our reading of *Federalist* 10. One could argue that this essay still deserves greater weight than Madison's earlier ideas, since *The Federalist* describes what was actually adopted, not simply proposed. But then one has to ask whether a public essay written largely to answer objections to the Constitution merits more attention than its author's private and presumably more honest assessment of the Constitution's failings.

Other problems remain even after a status has been assigned to *Federalist* 10. What weight can we assign to Madison's ideas when his colleagues rejected the conclusions to which he thought they led? Can we even ask whether Madison has been overrated, if not as a thinker, then at least in terms of his final influence on the Constitution?

Yet in fact even in defeat Madison's intentions are highly relevant to the current controversy over judicial power. For it was in rejecting the Council of Revision and the veto on state laws that the framers most clearly delineated the role of the judiciary in the constitutional system.

Until very recently the hoary question of whether the framers intended the judiciary to exercise the power of judicial review had ceased to be a subject of active scholarly interest. But at some point controversy over the *scope* of judicial review and the specific uses to which it has been put naturally raises questions about its *legitimacy*, and these in turn prove difficult to address without considering the evolution of judicial power since 1787. This is not a new concern, provoked only by the oratory of Attorney General Meese. In fact, it was Alexander Bickel, a leading scholar at Yale Law School, who raised most of the critical issues in his seminal book of 1962, *The Least Dangerous Branch* (whose title was taken from Alexander Hamilton's classic definition of judicial review in *Federalist* 78).

Judicial review, one should also note, is a power with multiple uses. At the narrowest, it may simply be the means by which the judiciary defends itself against efforts by the other branches to interfere with its own particular functions. More broadly, judicial review works to protect the Constitution against improper acts by Congress or the President, and the entire federal government against interference by the states. Finally—and what has been the true source of controversy over the past three decades—judicial review has enabled the judiciary to recognize and advance claims of individual rights against the actions of both the federal government and the states.

Madison's original notion of judicial power had rested on three fundamental assumptions. First, the judiciary by itself would lack the political strength to resist the improper acts of either Congress or the state legislatures. Second, even if the courts did overturn wrongful laws, their rulings would often come too late to undo or remedy the injuries to private rights that would already have been committed. That was why the Council of Revision was to act before a law took effect. But, third, Madison also believed that the final right to judge whether a national or state law was constitutional should belong not to the judges but to Congress. He may have hoped that Congress would rarely override the Council of Revision, but he was too much a republican to allow the least accountable branch of the government to have the final say on the Constitution.

Here at last conservatives can find in Madison's original position support for their attacks on judicial supremacy. But, ironically, it was precisely on this point that the majority of the Convention turned Madison's logic and his reservations about judicial power upside down. They believed that the influence and independence of the judiciary would be reduced, not enhanced, if it acquired the advisory functions he proposed. The fatal defect in the Council of Revision was that it would impair the ability of the judiciary to check the other branches. "Judges ought to be able to expound the law as it should come before them," Rufus King argued, "free from the bias of having participated in its formation." They argued against the veto over state laws on the grounds that neither Congress nor the Council could possibly review the enormous volume of legislation that the states would submit. In its place—and without debate—they put the supremacy clause, which bound the state judiciaries to enforce the federal Constitution and laws over conflicting state statutes.

By rejecting Madison's proposals, then, the delegates expressed their confidence in the capacity of the national and state judiciaries alike. But more than that, they revealed that they expected judges to exercise the power of judicial review. "As to the constitutionality of laws, that point will come before the judges in their proper official character," Luther Martin flatly stated. "In this character they have a negative on the laws." Martin, the original author of the supremacy clause, may have hoped that only state courts would review state laws; but his colleagues expected that appeals involving federal questions would fall to the national judiciary.

Such statements leave one wondering how anyone could ever have doubted whether judicial review was part of the original constitutional design. True, in 1787 the idea that courts could overturn laws was still a novelty, realized in only a handful of state cases to which little attention had yet been paid. Elbridge Gerry was not announcing a self-evident fact when he informed the Convention that "in some states the judges [have] actually set aside laws as being against the constitution." Even so, the delegates repeatedly spoke as if they simply presumed that the federal judiciary would be able to overturn both state and national laws.

Yet, remarkably, the framers never discussed judicial review systematically or even directly. Virtually all of their comments on the subject were uttered during the debate over the Council of Revision—in other words, over a proposal that was defeated, not the one that was adopted. They defined neither the scope of judicial review nor the basis on which judges would test whether laws were constitutional—the issues that lie at the crux of the current controversy. Resisting the idea that the Constitution should include a comprehensive list of private rights, they never considered whether the federal courts were restricted to protecting only the handful of rights that the Constitution explicitly mentioned. The best we can say is that the delegates considered the various uses of judicial review—ranging from simple self-protection to the judicial function to the voiding of state and federal laws—without definitively determining how or when it might be exercised.

One final point deserves emphasis. Where Madison would have explicitly given Congress the final word on constitutionality, the majority implicitly allowed Congress to override only presidential vetoes, not judicial decisions. Madison conceded as much in October of 1788. By failing to state how disputes over "expounding" the Constitution would be resolved, he noted, the Convention by default left that judgment to the courts, simply because they were the last to act and thus to determine whether a law would be executed. This result, Madison complained, "was never intended, and can never be proper"—but inadvertently or otherwise, it seemed to be part of the Constitution.

This revealing comment again reminds us that the relation between the meaning of the Constitution and the intentions of its authors can never be taken for granted. But more than that, it encourages us to ask how the framers could have treated so vital a matter as judicial review in so seemingly careless a fashion. And this in turn can lead to a more realistic, balanced, and even critical appraisal of the great work of 1787—to a view that still celebrates "the miracle at Philadelphia" but restores the framers, with all their wisdom and political skill, to the imperfect historical context in which they acted.

In theory, the need to balance the legislature should have led the delegates to focus their greatest intellectual efforts on designing the two weaker departments. It should have led them to explore, for example, how the Supreme Court was to exercise its novel and potentially momentous power of judicial review, and to define the nature of the "executive power" that Article II vested in the President. But here, where they had to be most inventive, the delegates also proved most tentative. In practice they shied away from sustained discussions of the substance of executive and judicial power, perhaps because they felt so much more comfortable with the familiar subject of legislative power. And even when they could no longer avoid the subject of the other two branches, much of their discussion centered on issues of election, appointment, and tenure. We can plot in excruciating detail "the tedious and reiterated discussions" (as Madison described them) that led to the establishment of the electoral college, but when it comes to explaining why the Convention finally allowed the President to share the power of treaty-making with the Senate, we have to rely on scraps of debate and circumstantial evidence to account for one of the most historic decisions the framers took.

Some scholars try to close such gaps in what the framers said by attributing to them ideas derived from what it is believed they read in the writings of the Enlightenment, or by tracing their concerns to precedents in the British Constitution. Obviously, the framers did not act in an intellectual vacuum. Yet what is most apparent in their deliberations is not how much they learned from Old World sources but how little they depended on outside authorities once they had set about designing the new government. (Madison once dismissed appeals to such luminaries as Locke and Montesquieu as "a field of research which is more likely to perplex than to decide.") Only in the crudest sense did the Convention model the branches of the new government on their British counterparts. The Senate was not a House of Lords, and the President was to be neither a constitutional monarch nor a prime minister. And the idea of an independent judiciary took a distinct form in America precisely because our Constitution was to be a concise written charter, not a complex and fluid mass of statutory law, common-law precedent, royal prerogative, and custom such as together made up the British Constitution.

This intense self-awareness of the originality of their achievement stands out strongly in the writings of the framers and their contemporaries, and remains compelling after two centuries. Originality is not perfection, however. Because fears of disunion and domestic turbulence did exert a powerful influence in the late 1780s, the framers and their supporters were eager to describe the Constitution as a document designed to last "for ages to come." Yet having learned so much from the experience of a mere decade of self-government, and having celebrated their ability to do so, they would, I believe, find it incredible that later generations would not improve upon their discoveries, would not indeed understand the meaning of the Constitution and the liberties they designed it to protect better than they had.

Amid all the platitudes and heroic accolades to which we will be subjected during the celebrations ahead, an awareness of the imperfections and ambiguities of the Constitution or of the limits of the framers' vision will not be easy to maintain. We can better understand what the framers accomplished by grasping the problems that they failed to resolve than by attributing to them a perfect knowledge and foresight that they never pretended to possess.

BIBLIOGRAPHY

An asterisk (*) preceding a reference indicates that the article or part of it has been reprinted in this book.

BOOKS AND PAMPHLETS

Adler, Mortimer Jerome. We hold these truths: understanding the ideas and ideals of the constitution. Collier Books, Collier Macmillan. '87.

The American public's knowledge of the U.S. Constitution: a national survey of public awareness and personal opinion. Hearst Corp. '87.

Barbash, Fred. The founding: a dramatic account of the writing of the Constitution. Linden Press/Simon and Schuster. '87.

Berns, Walter. Taking the constitution seriously. Simon and Schuster. '87.

Berry, Mary Frances. Why ERA failed: politics, women's rights, and the amending process of the constitution. Indiana University Press. '86.

Browne, Ray Broadus and Browne, Glenn J. Laws of our fathers: popular culture and the U.S. Constitution. Bowling Green State University. '86.

Chemerinsky, Erwin. Interpreting the Constitution. Praeger. '87.

Cox, Archibald. The Court and the Constitution. Houghton Mifflin. '87.

Currie, David P. The Constitution of the United States: a primer for the people. University of Chicago Press. '88.

Curtis, Michael Kent. No state shall abridge: the fourteenth amendment and the Bill of Rights. Duke Univ. Press. '86.

Dorsen, Norman. The evolving Constitution: essays on the Bill of Rights and the U.S. Supreme Court. Wesleyan University Press. '87.

Feinberg, Barbara Silberdick. The Constitution: yesterday, today & tomorrow. Scholastic. '87.

Fisher, Louis. Constitutional conflicts between Congress and the President. Princeton University Press. '85.

Grimes, Alan Pendleton. Democracy and the amendments to the constitution. University Press of America. '87.

Hall, Kermit. The formation and ratification of the Constitution: major historical interpretations. Garland. '87.

Hall, Kermit. Women, the law, and the constitution: major historical interpretations. Garland. '87.

Hauptly, Denis J. A convention of delegates: the creation of the Constitution. Atheneum. '87.

Holder, Angela Roddey, Lewis, John W. (John Walter), and Lewis, Polly Philbrook. The meaning of the Constitution. 2nd ed. Barron's Educational Series. '87.

Hyman, Harold Melvin. Quiet past and stormy present?: war powers in American history. American Historical Association. '86.

Kammen, Michael G. A machine that would go of itself: the Constitution in American culture. Vintage Books. '87.

Kurland, Philip B. and Lerner, Ralph. The Founders' Constitution. University of Chicago Press. '87.

Levy, Leonard Williams, Karst, Kenneth L., and Mahoney, Dennis J. Encyclopedia of the American Constitution. Macmillan, Collier Macmillan. '86.

Levy, Leonard William and Mahoney, Dennis J. The framing and ratification of the Constitution. Macmillan, Collier Macmillan. '87.

Lieberman, Jethro Koller. The enduring constitution: an exploration of the first two hundred years. Harper & Row. '87.

Lurio, Eric. The cartoon guide to the Constitution of the United States. Barnes & Noble Books. '87.

McConnell, Michael W., Tribe, Laurence H., and Gewirtz, Paul D. The Senate, the courts, and the Constitution: a debate. Center for National Policy. '86.

Mead, Walter B. The United States Constitution: personalities, principles, and issues. University of South Carolina Press. '87.

Morris, Richard Brandon. The forging of the Union, 1781–1789. Harper & Row. '87.

Morris, Richard Brandon. Witnesses at the creation: Hamilton, Madison, Jay and the American Constitution. Holt, Rinehart & Winston. '85.

Murphy, Paul L. The Constitution in the twentieth century. American Historical Association. '86.

O'Brien, David M. Storm center: the Supreme Court in American politics. Norton. '86.

Schreibman, Vigdor. Essays on the impact of the Constitution and legal system on American life and government. Amicas Publications. '87.

Sgroi, Peter P. The living Constitution: landmark Supreme Court decisions. J. Messner. '87.

Siegan, Bernard H. The Supreme Court's Constitution. Transaction, Inc. '86.

Smith, David G. The convention and the Constitution: the political ideas of the Founding Fathers. University Press of America. '87.

Spier, Peter. We the people: the story of the U.S. Constitution. Doubleday. '87.

Tribe, Laurence H. Constitutional choices. Harvard Univ. Press. '85.

Whicker, Marcia Lynn, Strickland, Ruth Ann, and Moore, Raymond A. The constitution under pressure: a time for change. Praeger. '87.

Wolfe, Christopher. The rise of modern judicial review: from constitutional interpretation to judge-made law. Basic Bks. '86.

PERIODICALS

THE BICENTENNIAL CELEBRATION

Celebrating the real Constitution. America. 157:3-4. Jl. 4-11, '87.

The Constitution 1787-1987. American Heritage. 38:7, 30-51+. My./Je. '87.

The Constitution across the nation. Long, James. American Heritage. 38:132+. My./Je. '87.

Philadelphia, 1987. American History Illustrated. 22:26-33. My. '87.

Celebrating the Constitution. Goldsborough, Reid. Americana. 15:70+. My./Je. '87.

The Constitution at 200. Christianity Today. 31:18-30. Jl. 10, '87.

The Constitution chronicles. Nevins, Jane. The New York Times Magazine. 106+. S. 22, '85.

The great voyage: two hundred years of the Constitution; a special issue. The New York Times Magazine. S. 13, '87.

A republic, if you can keep it. Newsweek. 109:44-52+. My. 25, '87.

Celebrating the Constitution. Deigh, Robb. The Saturday Evening Post. 259:54-6+. My./Je. '87.

Making the Constitution work today. Scholastic Update (Teachers' edition). 116:1-8+. O. 28, '83.

The Constitution: how it shapes your world. Scholastic Update (Teachers' edition). 119:1-21. S. 8, '86.

* . . . by the unanimous consent of the states. Bowen, Ezra. Smithsonian. 18:32-43. Jl. '87.

200 years of the American Constitution. Society. 24:5-62. N./D. '86.

The Constitution at 200. Time. 130:20-30+. Jl. 6, '87.

*The ark of America. Morrow, Lance. Time. 130:22+. Jl. 6, '87.

There's a big party on. Clarke, Gerald. Time. 130:62-4. Jl. 6, '87.

It is a rising sun, Dr. Franklin. Snyder, Richard A. Vital Speeches of the Day. 52:140-4. D. 15, '85.

CHANGING THE CONSTITUTION

*Should the U.S. Constitution be amended to permit school prayer?— pro. Thurmond, Strom. Congressional Digest. 63:138+. My. '84.

*Should the U.S. Constitution be amended to permit school prayer?—con. Hatfield, Mark O. Congressional Digest. 63:139+. My. '84.

If you think it can't happen here, think again. Waldman, Michael. The Nation. 239:233-5. S. 22, '84.

Calling for a constitutional convention. Noonan, John Thomas, Jr. National Review. 37:25-8. Jl. 26, '85.

Saving the Constitution. National Review. 39:30-7+. Jl. 17, '87.

Let's get representative. Hertzberg, Hendrik. The New Republic. 196:15-18. Je. 29, '87.

*Move over, James Madison. The New Republic. 196:19-21. Je. 29, '87.

*How hard it is to change. Berry, Mary Frances. The New York Times Magazine. p. 93+. S. 13, '87.

Is it broke? Should we fix it? Changing the Constitution is not easy, but plenty of people keep trying. Lacayo, Richard. Time. 130:54-5. Jl. 6, '87.

JUDICIAL ACTIVISM VERSUS JUDICIAL RESTRAINT

*Mr. Meese, meet Mr. Madison. Rakove, Jack N. The Atlantic. 258:77-82+. D. '86.

*The Constitution and original intent. Commager, Henry Steele. The Center Magazine. 19:4-17. N./D. '86.

Reasons and arguments in the Constitution. Noll, Mark A. The Christian Century. 104:499-500+. My. 20-27, '87.

*How the Constitution disappeared. Graglia, Lino A. Commentary. 81:19-27. F. '86.

Government by lawyers & judges. Berns, Walter. Commentary. 83:17-24. Je. '87.

The Court and the Constitution: Meese v. Brennan. Taylor, Stuart, Jr. Current. 285:30-5. S. '86.

The Constitution and the Court: could Meese be right? Levinson, Sanford. Current. 292:32-5. My. '87.

Ronald Reagan and the Supremes. Navasky, Victor S. Esquire. 107:77-80+. Ap. '87.

Morality and the judge. Bork, Robert H. Harper's. 270:28-9. My. '85.

A constitutional shell game. Schwartz, Herman. The Nation. 241:607-10. D. 7, '85.

Was the Constitution a good idea? Graglia, Lino A. National Review. 36:34-9. Jl. 13, '84.

The Brennan doctrine. National Review. 37:20-1. N. 15, '85.

Reagan's Constitution. Tribe, Laurence H. The New Republic. 193:10-11. S. 30, '85.

Meese v. Brennan. Taylor, Stuart, Jr. The New Republic. 194:17-21. Ja. 6-13, '86.

Court jester. The New Republic. 195:4+. N. 17, '86.

Reagan's Justice. Dworkin, Ronald Myles. The New York Review of Books. 31:27-31. N. 8, '84.

What did the Founding Fathers intend? Kaufman, Irving R. The New York Times Magazine. 42+. F. 23, '86.

Intent of the framers. Press, Aric. Newsweek. 106:97-8. O. 28, '85.

*Interpreting the Constitution. Meese, Edwin, III. USA Today. 115:36-9. S. '86.

The Supreme Court's dilemma and defense. Polin, Raymond. USA Today. 115:43-5. S. '86.

What Ed Meese and Thomas Jefferson have in common. Cutler, Lloyd. The Washington Monthly. 18:45-6+. D. '86.

THE CONSTITUTION IN ACTION

The crèche and the Constitution. Drinan, Robert F. America. 149:265-8. N. 5, '83.

To form a more perfect union. Black Enterprise. 17:11, 51+. Jl. '87.

*The quest for liberty. Camper, Diane. Black Enterprise. 17:53-56. Jl. '87.

Four views of the Constitution. Black Enterprise. 17:59-60+. Jl. '87.

The republican roots of our constitutional order. Appleby, Joyce. The Center Magazine. 19:3-19. My./Je. '86.

The Constitution: an application of natural law. Jaffa, Harry V. The Center Magazine. 19:40-9. Jl./Ag. '86.

The Constitution and modern social science. Mansfield, Harvey C., Jr. The Center Magazine. 19:42-59. S./O. '86.

*The Constitution and the 14th Amendment. Murphy, Walter F. The Center Magazine. 20:9-30. Jl./Ag. '87.

The Constitution and the congregation: time to celebrate. Marty, Martin E. The Christian Century. 104:523-5. Je. 3-10, '87.

*Why blacks, women & Jews are not mentioned in the Constitution. Goldwin, Robert A. Commentary. 83:28-33. My. '87.

Our secular Constitution. Doerr, Edd. The Humanist. 47:43-4. Mr./Ap. '87.

Our flawed and glorious Constitution. Kocol, Cleo. The Humanist. 47:37-8. My./Je. '87.

*A citizen reads the Constitution. Doctorow, E. L. The Nation. 244:208-9+. F. 21, '87.

Constitutional questions. The New Republic. 188:4+. Mr. 28, '83.

Too clever by half. Farber, Daniel A. The New Republic. 195:11–13. S. 1, '86.

*The Constitution and American diversity. Glazer, Nathan. Public Interest. pp. 10–22. Winter '87.

Unraveling the Constitution. Pollack, Sheldon D. Society. 24:56–9. Ja./F. '87.

Mixing politics with prayer. Church, George J. Time. 123:12–15. Mr. 19, '84.

*The Constitution of the United States: contemporary ratification. Brennan, William J., Jr. University of California, Davis, Law Review. 19:2–14. '85.